"Finally, a truly comprehensive guide to specialty coffee retailing! Written by a host of industry professionals, *Achieving Success in Specialty Coffee* provides the start-up or established specialty coffee retailer insight into all aspects of the business, from coffee knowledge to employees, customers to financing, equipment to marketing, and more."

—*Edward Loeb, Publisher,* The Gourmet Retailer

"Finally, an easy-to-understand book that assists existing specialty coffee retailers in improving their businesses, and, ultimately, their bottom line. Like all of the other high-quality and extremely well-made materials offered by Bellissimo, this book is a must for coffee retailers new and old. Once again, Bellissimo has shown its foresight and commitment to our industry. Don't wait another day ... order this book!"

—*David Heilbrunn, Show Manager, Coffee Fest Trade Shows and Seminars*

"Designed to help keep your business as strong as a short shot of espresso, this book is a must-have resource for the specialty coffee retailer. It's full of priceless advice from practically every industry expert. Each chapter brings another dimension and voice to the rich collage of knowledge and know-how."

—*Elizabeth Pollock, Senior Editor,* Fancy Food Magazine

"Imagine a three-day coffee seminar and conference captured in the pages of a book! Finally, a thought-provoking and mind-expanding reference for the experienced coffee retailer who really wants to be better."

—*David B. Dallis, President, Dallis Bros. Inc.; Past President, SCAA*

"*Achieving Success in Specialty Coffee* is an excellent follow-up to the myriad 'How to get started' books available in our industry. The segment on employee training is particularly important. I strongly endorse any body of information aimed at raising the bar of quality in all facets of the specialty coffee industry, and this book does just that."

—*Heidi Brown, Wholesale Accounts, Caffe Vita Coffee Roasting Co.*

"Crammed with information on how to be successful, this book should pay for itself in one day's profits or less!"

—*Penny Usher, Owner, Grumpy's Coffee Company, Ashland, Ohio*

"A consuming passion for the world's best coffee and up-to-the-minute information are hallmarks of success in the specialty coffee industry. Bellissimo brings us another great publication filled with valuable insider knowledge and written by many of today's top experts. *Achieving Success in Specialty Coffee* contributes a personalized view of the facets of coffee that stir our passions. Bravo, Bellissimo!"

—*Bell Herne, Director of Coffee Quality and Education, Timothy's World Coffee, Canada*

"Whether you think you know everything there is to know about coffee or you don't know anything at all, this is the absolute best coffee-oriented book anyone could own. In the words of Eldridge Cleaver, if you can't afford it, 'Steal this book!'"

—*Donald Harrell, V.P. National Accounts, Monin Inc.*

"Finally, a guide for the specialty coffee retailer that goes beyond finding a location and buying equipment. Concise and informative; a primer to success that we will be sure to recommend to our espresso equipment customers."

—*Michael Myers, President, Michaelo Espresso Inc.*

"*Achieving Success in Specialty Coffee* is the only book that can advise retailers on how to stay ahead of the game in a very competitive retail market!"
—*Michael Girgis, National Sales Manager, Rosito Bisani Imports*

"Written by a virtual Who's Who in the coffee business, this book should never stray far from the desk of owners and managers of any coffee establishment focused on quality and success. I know it will never leave mine."
—*Arne Holt, Founder/Co-Owner, Caffé Calabria Coffee Roasters, San Diego, Calif.*

"In the specialty coffee market, where competitors are always nipping at your heels, you need information to help you sustain. *Achieving Success in Specialty Coffee* will help you keep ahead of the rest. The contributors have seen businesses come and go, and have witnessed the growth of the specialty coffee market firsthand. They live in this most challenging market on a day-to-day basis. This book is a must-read for any retailer that needs to stay ahead."
—*Mark Spini, V.P. of Industrial Sales, Guittard Chocolate*

"Bellissimo has found the most knowledgeable leaders in retail coffee to write about their areas of expertise. The reader gets over 500 years of experience in one book!"
—*Saira Beig, President, Canadian Coffee Expo and* Coffee Culture Magazine

"Not a book about how to get into the coffee business, but a book on how to be successful once you've opened your doors! You must own this book if you are in retail coffee!"
—*Lisa Dahl, Owner, Mia Coupa Espresso, Colorado Springs, Colo.*

"Bellissimo has put together another creative reference that is a must-have for all those who are serious about succeeding as specialty coffee retailers. This book is dedicated to providing the tools needed to not only survive, but to thrive in the coffee business. This book will raise the bar for excellence and success within the industry."
—*Matt Brandenburger, Vice President of Sales, Torani Specialty Italian Flavoring Syrups*

"*Achieving Success in Specialty Coffee* covers every aspect of operating a successful coffee establishment. From marketing to product quality, this book is packed with pertinent information from the industry's leading experts. A must-read!"
—*Michael F. Baccellieri, President/CEO, Longbottom Coffee and Tea Inc.*

"Never before could so much retail coffee business information be found in one place written by so many of the top experts."
—*Scott Tucker, Manager, Islands Kona Coffee, Orange, Calif.*

"Over two decades ago when several dozen entrepreneurs began the specialty coffee revolution, everything had to be learned by the seat of the pants. While trial and error can be invigorating—especially when a success is discovered—it takes a lot of time combined with costly mistakes. *Achieving Success in Specialty Coffee* is a road map given to the new members of the specialty coffee movement by its pioneers. Drink hardy of its passages. Welcome to the movement!"
—*Phil Jones, President, Barnie's Coffee & Tea Company; Past President, SCAA*

Dedicated to my mother, my sweet son Matthew,
& Whitney, my little bean

acknowledgments

Last summer when I looked through the dozens of books on specialty coffee in my library, I found multiple titles on the history of coffee, roasting and numerous books instructing individuals on how to get started in the coffee business. What was missing—and to my knowledge hadn't been written—was a book advising those already operating how to remain in business, achieve maximum profitability, and juggle the many balls of retailing without dropping a few each day.

I decided to write such a book. The subjects in which I had limited expertise I would research. I soon realized this endeavor could take a few years at best, but I believed the specialty coffee industry needed this information now. I spoke to a number of friends and colleagues in the business and explored the possibility of taping some key individuals discussing their particular areas of expertise. The results were astounding. Everyone I spoke with saw the same need and was more than happy to contribute his or her expertise immediately.

The project fits perfectly into the mission statement of my company, Bellissimo Coffee InfoGroup: "To enhance, nurture and expand the quality of specialty coffee worldwide." In my mind, this mission has never been better served by a product than it has by this book.

It becomes obvious when one scans the list of contributors and reviewers of this book that many others share the desire for quality. I have never witnessed an industry more open to sharing its knowledge than specialty coffee. This book would still only be a dream were it not for the names that appear in the table of contents. I say "thank you" to each and every person who made this collaboration a reality.

In addition to the authors and reviewers, above all I want to thank Kris Larson, Bellissimo's jack-of-all-trades, who rode herd on this endeavor from its inception. Other noteworthy contributors include editor Rivers Janssen and design and layout artist Jerrod Philipps. The wonderful black and white watercolors found in these pages were painstakingly drawn and painted by artist and friend James Cloutier. Julia Schnabel and Kate LaPoint were also of immense help, and Charlie Magee, our computer artist, worked his Photoshop magic yet again.

It's my hope this book will inspire everyone associated with specialty coffee to reach a little higher, never allow complacency to creep in, and to always pay the ultimate respect to our industry and the little brown bean we call coffee.

Ciao,
Bruce Milletto, publisher

Published in the United States by Bellissimo Inc.
260 East 15th Avenue, Suite D, Eugene, Oregon, USA, 97401
Tel: 541-683-5373 Fax: 541-683-1010

Grateful acknowledgment is made to the following for permission to
reprint previously published material:

The American Premium Tea Institute (APTI): "Marketing Tea to New
Heights in your Operation" by Wendy Rasmussen. Reprinted from
APTI's Advanced Training Seminars.

ISBN 1-893344-02-9

Library of Congress Catalog Card Number: 99-60665

Editor: Rivers Janssen
Managing Editor: Kris Larson
Cover design: Charlie Magee
Interior design: Jerrod Philipps
Illustrations: James Cloutier

Bellissimo Inc. Website addresses:
www.espresso101.com
www.coffeeuniverse.com
www.virtualcoffee.com

ACHIEVING SUCCESS
IN SPECIALTY COFFEE

A BELLISSIMO COFFEE INFOGROUP PUBLICATION

index

foreword

When I first started in the coffee business some 30 years ago, there were few, if any, educational resources like the one offered in this new book from Bellissimo. When seeking start-up help and advice from the "industry experts" I knew at the time, I received words of wisdom that ranged from "pray for divine intervention" to "follow your nose for inspirational development." Both were correct. Without proper training, divine intervention will become necessary for you to succeed in coffee. Without some connection to the product—most often through its wonderful aromas—no amount of growth or prosperity will provide the inspiration needed for you to remain in business.

If you are new to coffee and picked out this book as your first primer, you have much to look forward to. You are about to begin the most incredible voyage of discovery you ever imagined. It is hard to conceive finding a more qualified "set of guides" than the ones trekking through these pages. Coffee is an incredible beverage, a "movable feast" in its own right. Few products in the world have the mystery, magic and domination that coffee has enjoyed since its inception. Without question, it is the world's leading hot beverage. There is a strong possibility it may become a leading cold beverage as well.

If you are in the middle of your coffee career and selected this work to broaden your knowledge of your favorite product, you are also in for a rare treat. Our peers have shared with us their "pearls and gems." This book is a treasure trove of information mined from hundreds of years of experience in investigating, studying, reviewing, reporting, and profiting from coffee. While none of us would agree on all the concepts or positions presented in these pages, I do believe all of us would applaud the magnificent voyages of discovery that make all our journeys into higher learning memorable.

If you are in the twilight of your coffee career, this book will become a great stepping stone in your transition from "risking to reflecting": what might have been ... if only ... what I know now ... what I knew then. There is a place and space between these pages for all of us to remember, rekindle and relive our great love affair with coffee.

If you are now the proud owner of this book, take the time to read it. What good is owning a diamond mine of a coffee business if you never take the time to learn how to mine the diamonds? Unless divine intervention is your thing, learn what it means to follow your nose. It seldom leads you down the wrong path, particularly in coffee.

Ted R. Lingle
Executive Director, Specialty Coffee Association of America

Kenneth Davids

Kenneth Davids' formal involvement with coffee began in the early 1970s when he opened a coffee business in Berkeley, Calif. His first book, *Coffee: A Guide to Buying, Brewing and Enjoying,* initially appeared in 1975. It has since sold over 250,000 copies in four editions, and has cumulatively helped shape the specialty coffee movement in the United States. A British edition under the title *The Coffee Book* was published in 1980.

Davids' book on espresso, *Espresso: Ultimate Coffee,* appeared in 1994 and was nominated for a James Beard award. His third book, *Home Coffee Roasting: Romance and Revival,* was released by St. Martin's Press in May of 1996, the same month he was awarded a "Special Achievement Award for Outstanding Contributions to Coffee Literature" by the Specialty Coffee Association of America.

Davids contributes regularly to consumer and industry coffee periodicals. He also works as a coffee consultant and presents seminars on various coffee subjects. His writing appears monthly on the award-winning World Wide Web publication *Coffee Review.* Reviews and other notices of his work have appeared in the *Los Angeles Times,* the *Wall Street Journal,* the *Manchester Guardian,* and the *New York Times,* on CBS News and CNN Headline News, and in many smaller publications.

17

Chapter 1

45 Points About Properly Tasting Your Coffee

19

1. The importance of sensory evaluation or tasting of coffee. Integrating a regular tasting program into any coffee business is crucial to its long-term success. The palate and nose together are the subtlest, most acute and ultimately most reliable instrument for measuring the quality and distinction of coffee in every phase of production—from growing through buying to roasting through brewing. *There is no substitute for it.* Not only is the human palate far more subtle and complete in its ability to read coffees than any instrument, but it also automatically builds the kind of nuanced cultural information that a business can use to market coffees to consumers.

2. Sensory evaluation in itself is not difficult. Most people have no problem registering fundamental sensory differences between coffees set out side by side. What is difficult is obtaining proper training, developing confidence in your own tasting judgments, and (above all) actually doing it—tasting coffee on a regular, systematic basis.

3. Tasting for what? Your place on the coffee chain determines what you're tasting for and how to organize the tasting. Typically, those who do business on the consumer end of the coffee industry taste for one or more of the following purposes:
- To select and approve green coffee for purchase.
- For roast development and profiling, or to determine the optimum degree and handling of roast for a given coffee.
- To control the quality and consistency of production roast batches.
- Blending.

Each of these purposes requires somewhat different attitudes and variations in procedure.

4. Tasting for whom? We need to balance our preferences with "expert" preferences and our customers' preferences. We taste only within ourselves, but not *for* ourselves. This means we need to taste coffee in the company of others as often as possible, taste our successful competitors' coffees as often as possible, and listen to our customers when they talk about favorites. But, ultimately, we need to incorporate all that information into our own palates and the palates of our key employees, and learn to act on it with confidence.

5. Two suggestions for facilitating regular tasting. The key to regular tasting is to approach it as habitual routine rather than occasional adventure.
- Set up dedicated space and equipment for tasting. A basic cupping facility need not be expensive. Assuming you have a counter and a sink, you can put together a simple but very efficient facility—including a functional sample roaster—for as little as $400. On the other hand, equipping a state-of-the-art tasting and cupping facility with such tools as a commercial espresso machine and sophisticated instruments for precision roast-profiling experiments can cost as much as $20,000. Most installations fall somewhere between the two estimates.
- Establish a regular tasting routine that is consistent, familiar and easily supported by the space and equipment you have installed.

6. There are two fundamental approaches to tasting coffee.
- Formal and systematic.
- Informal—or living with the coffee.

7. Introduction to formal, systematic tasting. The coffee profession has evolved a standard procedure for "cupping," also known as a systematic sensory evaluation of coffee. The cupping procedure is suitable for most coffee evaluation purposes with the exception of espresso evaluation, which requires a specialized procedure (see points 13-15).

By following the standard cupping procedure, you assure consistency, you facilitate communications with others in the coffee business, and you sharpen your tasting abilities by framing the tasting experience in a consistent structure that minimizes the distractions of outside factors.

8. Introduction to informal evaluation. Although most coffee decisions are made through formal, systematic tasting or cupping, it's also useful to confirm important judgments simply by drinking the coffee as you normally take your coffee and sharing it with others in the same informal manner. For example, coffee professionals often follow up on a formal cupping by brewing a pot of the best or most interesting coffee on the table and sharing it around the office. Summer blends that are intended for use in cold coffee drinks obviously need to be tested in a variety of iced contexts. If you are introducing a new blend or single-origin coffee that you intend to keep on your menu for some time, you should certainly work it through as many different contexts as possible, including running it through some informal test marketing.

9. Equipment for formal, systematic evaluation, or cupping. Here is a brief overview of the equipment needed for formal cupping. See point 40 (page 34) for equipment sources.
- *Sample-roasting equipment.* Coffee samples offered for sale by dealers and brokers arrive in an unroasted "green" state, and obviously must be roasted before they can be evaluated. Equipment suitable for roasting small samples of green coffee range from $6000 machines with sophisticated electronic controls to modified hot-air popcorn poppers that cost $25. The most common sample-roasting installation is a battery of two to four small, open-ended drum roasters. Such roasters were manufactured for years by Jabez Burns (now a division of Buffalo Technologies

Corporation) and then imitated by other manufacturers. Although I'm sure many industry experts will disagree, my experience indicates that for simple, consistent roasting of small samples of green coffee, a Proctor-Silex corn popper (particularly when modified to accept a deep-fry thermometer or other improvised heat probe) works as well or even better than the traditional, open-front drum sample roaster.

But for roast-profiling experiments (in other words, to experiment with the best temperature to roast a given coffee), a more expensive sample roaster that approximates the design and control system of your batch roaster is best.

- *Identical 6- to 7-ounce cups, glasses or bowls with open, flared tops.* You will need 50 to 100 of these identical receptacles. If in doubt, purchase more rather than fewer.
- *Display trays for beans.* It's standard practice to place a sample tray of beans from each coffee behind the cups for visual inspection, or two trays (one containing roasted beans and one containing green) if you are evaluating green samples. Coffee equipment supply companies sell special "photographic blue" colored trays, but for cuppers on a budget, any uniform, shallow set of receptacles—small plastic dessert bowls, for example—will do.
- *Cupping spoons.* Any soup spoon with a round (not oval) bowl will work, but silverplate spoons specifically designed for cupping are best. You will need one spoon per cupper.
- *Gram scale (optional).* Many cuppers measure coffee by volume rather than weight when preparing for a cupping. Others use an electronic gram scale. Whichever method you use, use it consistently.
- *Burr mill or grinder.* It's most convenient to use a grinder that permits you to place the cup directly under the outlet to catch ground coffee.
- *Something to spit into.* Any largish mug or receptacle you can carry as you cup works fine. Large floor spittoons look impressive, but are cumbersome and useful only if your cupping table is of the round, rotating variety.
- *A counter or table at a height you and your colleagues can bend over comfortably.* Remember that you need to virtually plant your nose in each cup when sampling aroma. If you prefer sitting on a rolling stool or task chair while cupping, then the counter obviously should be lower than if you prefer to cup while standing and walking. You will need about 18 inches of counter length per coffee you intend to cup, or 12 inches for fast-and-dirty screening of samples. A counter placed in island fashion in the middle of the room obviously doubles the length available for lining up cupping samples. Specialized round cupping tables that spin like lazy Susans look romantic, but from a practical point of view, they're overpriced frills.

10. Budget approaches to equipping a cupping room. Don't let a tight budget prevent you from setting up a cupping facility. Here are a few corners you can cut if you are short on cash.
- *Sample roaster.* See the roaster suggestions in point 9.
- *Cups.* Any set of identical, flare-topped, 6- to 7-ounce cups or heat-proof glasses.
- *Grinder.* Although a laboratory or commercial grinder that deposits the ground coffee directly into the cup is best, you can cup effectively using *any* feed-through, burr-type grinder, including home models that retail for around $50. Do *not* use a blade grinder, however, because the grind is far too inconsistent.
- *Scale.* Many of the world's most experienced cuppers measure coffee into the cup by volume rather than weight, which means you don't need a gram scale. But if you do wish to use a scale, the Specialty Coffee Association of America (SCAA) sells a pocket-sized digital electronic version for under $100.
- *Spoon.* Any round soup spoon works.

21

Coffee Review Espresso Tasting Form

Taster _____ Date _____

Sample Number [ ]   Coffee Name _____   Coffee Source _____

Roast and Whole-Bean Appearance

Agtron: _____ / _____

Surface:
Shiny
Light sheen
Patches
Dry

Blend Notes _____

Brewing Notes and Cup Appearance

Length Shot: _____ oz.

Crema
(Circle one item each column)

Color	Texture	Persistence
Reddish-brown	Dense & fine	Persistent
Golden brown	Loose & coarse	Very persistent
Streaked brown & gold	Open button hole	Moderately persistent
Dark brown		Evanescent
Yellowish		
Whitish		
Blackish		

Fragrance/Aroma
Score should reflect a judgment that considers both intensity and quality from 1 (low) to 10 (high).

0 ———————— 5 ———————— 10

Fine	Rich	Floral	Weak
Elegant	Complex	Fruity	Carbony
Clean	Deep	Chocolaty	Burned
Delicate	Resonant	Vanilla-like	Banal
	Sweet	Nutty	Coarse
	Pungent	Spicy	
		Herbal	
		Tobacco-like	
		Toasty	
		Acidy	

Flavor
Score should reflect a judgment that includes both balance of fundamental tastes (sweet, acidic, bitter) plus olfactory sensations from 1 (low) to 10 (high).

0 ———————— 5 ———————— 10

Sweet	Floral	Complex	Ordinary
Acidy	Fruity	Deep	Simple
Pungent	Winy	Resonant	Rough
	Berry-like	Balanced	Unbalanced
	Prune-like	Complete	Thin
	Chocolaty	Fine	Carbony
	Caramelly	Elegant	Burned
	Licorice-like	Soft	Bitter
	Spicy	Lively	Harsh
	Smoky		Sharp
			Sour

Aftertaste (Persistence)
Score should reflect a judgment that includes quality, intensity and persistence from 1 (low) to 10 (high).

0 ———————— 5 ———————— 10

Long	Floral	Thin	**Defective**
Resonant	Fruity	Negligible	Fermented
Round	Winy	Fast-fading	Baggy
Fresh	Berry-like	Bitter	Musty
	Prune-like	Carbony	Moldy
	Spicy	Sharp	Grassy
		Astringent	Woody
			Medicinal
			Rioy

Remember, state-of-the-art equipment is best, but don't shy away from cupping just because you don't have fancy equipment. *The most important principle in cupping is consistency in procedure; the most important equipment is your own nose, palate and nervous system.*

11. Cupping procedure: General considerations.

- *Degree of roast.* When roasting green samples for potential purchase, you should terminate the roast relatively early, before the second crack. The resulting light-to-medium "cupping roast" permits you to easily detect taints in the sample while also clearly revealing distinctive nuances. In the second round of cupping, however, most roasters roast samples to a somewhat darker degree that resembles their signature roast style so as to cup the coffee closer to the way their customers will taste it. In both cases, every effort should be made to maintain a consistent degree of roast among the samples.

- *Ratio of ground coffee to water.* SCAA standards stipulate 7.25 grams (1/4 ounces) of finely ground coffee measured by weight—usually by digital gram scale—to 150 milliliters (5 ounces) of water. In practice, most experienced American cuppers measure by volume: One standard coffee measure of whole beans to however much water it takes to fill the cup, which is typically somewhere between

Body (Tactile Sensation)
Score should reflect a judgment that includes the relative weight of the sensations constituting body as well as their balance and quality from 1 (low) to 10 (high).

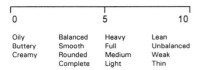

0		5	10
Oily	Balanced	Heavy	Lean
Buttery	Smooth	Full	Unbalanced
Creamy	Rounded	Medium	Weak
	Complete	Light	Thin

Persistence/Flavor in Milk
Score should reflect a judgment including intensity and quality when a 1 1/4 oz. shot is combined with 1 1/4 oz. of whole milk heated to approximately 150 degrees F but not frothed.

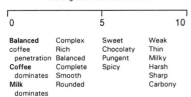

0		5	10
Balanced	Complex	Sweet	Weak
coffee	Rich	Chocolaty	Thin
penetration	Balanced	Pungent	Milky
Coffee	Complete	Spicy	Harsh
dominates	Smooth		Sharp
Milk	Rounded		Carbony
dominates			

Overall Score
Summary evaluation of overall quality taking into account the categories on left (including any defects) from 50 (lowest) to 100 (highest)

95–100 ..Truly exceptional
90–94 ....Outstanding
80–89 ....Good to excellent
70–79 ....Fair to good
>70........Poor to below average

23

5 and 6 ounces. Whether you pursue the precise SCAA standard or take the looser general industry approach, be absolutely certain to do it the same way every time.

- *Number of cups per sample.* Typically cuppers prepare multiple cups per sample, always grinding the coffee for each cup separately. The reason is simple: Taste defects usually are not consistent throughout a lot or sample of coffee. One cup can be clean of defects and the next defective. Even with meticulously prepared coffees, a sequence of cups will reveal slight differences in character.
- *The number of cups you prepare depends on your purpose.* When you are performing an initial, quick-and-dirty screening of green coffee samples for purchase, three cups per sample is probably enough to weed out the losers. However, before finally agreeing to buy a given lot of coffee, you should prepare at least 10 cups of that sample to thoroughly interrogate the coffee for defects. If there is a shadow defect in the coffee, sampling multiple cups will permit you to gauge its extent and intensity. When determining whether to accept delivery of a coffee shipment, the rule of thumb is to extract samples at random from at least 10 percent of the total number of bags that make up the lot, mix the beans from these samples, and brew either five or 10 cups. If one cup in 10 is defective, for example, 10 percent of the coffee may contain defects; if one in five, it may have a 20 percent rate, etc.

If you are cupping production roasts, your main goal is to taste for consistency and quality of the day's roast batches, not for defects in green coffee. Therefore three or even two cups per batch may be enough. Remember, if you are pushed for time at the end of the roasting day, it is better to sample even one cup per batch than no cups at all.

- *Water quality.* As in all coffee brewing, you *must* use clean, chlorine-free water. Avoid using distilled water, but bottled "drinking waters" sold in retail stores are taint-free and contain about the right amount of dissolved solids for good brewing. Whatever water you use, use it consistently from session to session.
- *Freedom from distraction and preconception.* Distractions come in many forms: taste distractions (chilies with breakfast, garlic for lunch); sound distractions (the phone, the receptionist, the sales manager); odor distractions (Christmas cologne, birthday aftershave, enchiladas in the microwave); and conceptual distractions ("I know this is a Brazil and Brazils are always bland"). Cupping in the same place at the same time every day using the same procedure tends to reduce material distractions. You can minimize preconceptions by cupping coffees blind before identifying them.

12. Steps in cupping procedure.

- *For each cup,* measure one coffee measure of whole beans (if measuring by volume) or 1/4 ounces (7.25 grams) if measuring by weight. Always use the same method of measurement. Always grind the coffee for each cup separately to dramatize any inconsistencies present in the sample. Use a fine-to-medium grind. Deposit the ground coffee in a 6- to 7-ounce flared cup or glass.
- *Fragrance* (scent of the dry, freshly ground coffee) is sampled by sniffing the ground coffee before adding water.
- *Pour approximately 5 ounces* (150 milliliters) of water at brewing temperature (just short of boiling) over the grounds, saturating them. The saturated ground coffee forms a crust on the surface of the cup. Technically inclined cuppers carefully measure 5 ounces of water in a beaker before pouring over the coffee. The more common procedure is to use a 6-ounce cup and pour water until the puffy crust of saturated grounds reaches the top of the cup, resulting in five-plus ounces of liquid.
- *Aroma* is sampled by "breaking the crust" of the saturated grounds with the cupping spoon while attentively sniffing the released aroma. Allow about three minutes for the coffee to steep before breaking the crust.
- *After the crust is broken,* most of the ground coffee will sink to the bottom of the cup. A ring of froth and suspended grounds will remain on the surface of the coffee, however, and you must scoop them off using the cupping spoon. You can ignore fragments of ground coffee clinging to the sides of the cup, but it is very important—particularly with darker roasted coffees—that no floating coffee grounds contaminate the cupped coffee. Even one small fragment can imbalance the perception of flavor.
- *After the coffee has cooled to sipping temperature,* the cupper tastes it. Standard cupping ritual is to take up about a half-spoonful of coffee and suck it explosively from the spoon. In effect, you are literally inhaling it by drawing in a sharp breath simultaneously through your nose and mouth. The goal is to simultaneously expose the tongue and nasal passages to the coffee so you will experience a comprehensive taste sensation. Then roll the coffee around in the mouth and hold it for a moment. This gauges body and helps you study how flavor develops toward finish. To gauge tactile sensations and body, you may want to literally rub the liquid against the roof of your mouth. Now spit the mouthful out and register the aftertaste. (Note that the explosive sucking part of the procedure is helpful but not essential. The main thing is to taste the coffee attentively, not to impress people with your professional slurping technique.)

• *As the coffee cools*, sample it repeatedly. Certain defects and positive characteristics will display themselves most clearly when the coffee has cooled to room temperature. If you are interrogating a coffee in depth, do *not* omit this step, as it is one of the most informative steps of the procedure.

The extent and depth of your interrogation of a coffee depends on your purpose. If you are screening a large number of new green samples, you may dismiss many of them almost immediately because clear defects show up in fragrance and aroma. If, however, you are considering buying a coffee or evaluating blend formulas, you will want to carry out every part of the procedure attentively, from sampling fragrance to observing aftertaste when the coffee is cold.

13. Formal procedure for tasting espresso. You can taste coffees intended for espresso using standard cupping procedure, but ultimately the only way to determine how a coffee will taste as espresso is to brew it as espresso. There is no standard procedure for espresso tasting, but here is a procedure that I find works well. Keep in mind that, as always with sensory evaluation, *consistency in procedure from cup to cup and session to session* is crucial.

14. Espresso tasting procedure in detail. For special notes on cupping categories and characteristics as they specifically apply to espresso, see point 37 (page 33).
  • Pull test shots using the double portafilter. Either weigh approximately 6.5 grams per dose (or 13 grams per double dose) or use the leveling technique (loosely fill portafilter to top with ground coffee, sweep hand across top of filter to level, then tamp). Again, whichever measurement procedure you use, *use it consistently.* Adjust the grind after each test shot until you produce a shot that fulfills consistent, predetermined criteria—either your own or those proposed by the SCAA.
  • Using the double portafilter, pull four 1 1/4-ounce shots into preheated shot glasses (the coffee, including crema, should fill the glass to a point slightly above the 1-ounce line). Place two shots directly on the tasting table; combine one shot with 1 1/4 ounces of hot water and one shot with 1 1/4 ounces of hot (but not frothed) milk.
  • Sample the aroma of one of the straight shots, then taste it. Observe the color and persistence of the crema in the second straight shot. Take notes on both. Then taste the water-diluted shot and the milk-diluted shot. Leave both water- and milk-diluted shots on the tasting table for follow-up sampling at room temperature.
  • After all coffees have been sampled, go back around the table and taste the water- and milk-diluted cups as often as you need to confirm and refine the impressions you noted when smelling and tasting the coffee when it was hot.

15. Additional important points in regard to tasting espresso.
  • Because producing a good espresso shot requires attention, espresso coffees must be tasted one at a time, in sequence, rather than in sets of several coffees at a time. Pull test shots and adjust the grinder for *each* coffee you are evaluating to make certain you are tasting that coffee at its best.
  • Take notes after sampling every coffee, but reprise the tasting at the end of the session by resampling the water- and milk-diluted shots you have left on the cupping table.
  • Taste straight shots sparingly to avoid clouding or fatiguing the palate, and clear the palate regularly with unsalted soda crackers and water.

16. Making sense of sensations: Introduction to understanding and describing what we taste. Many coffee decisions do not require descriptions or verbal translations of what we experience. We only need to make simple decisions: yes/no, buy/reject.

25

Coffee Review Cupping Form

Cupping: _____   Cupper: _____

General Information

Origin: _____

Defects	**Aroma/Fragrance**	**Acidity**
Indicate the number of cups exhibiting a defect, as well as the intensity of the defect(s) from 1 (minor) to 3 (intense).	Score should reflect a judgment that considers both intensity and quality from 1 (low) to 10 (high).	Score should reflect a judgment that considers both intensity and quality from 1 (low) to 10 (high).

Sample

#	#Cups	Intensity

Green moisture (%): _____

Green density: _____

Agtron: _____ / _____
            Whole   Ground

Aroma/Fragrance: 1 2 3 4 5 6 7 8 9 10

Acidity: 1 2 3 4 5 6 7 8 9 10

Defects Notes:
Fermented Moldy Grassy Pulpy
Medicinal Musty Woody Earthy
           Baggy   Groundy

Aroma/Fragrance Notes:
Floral Nutty   Spicy   Acidy
Fruity Caramelly   Herbal
Winy   Chocolaty   Smoky
        Vanilla-like Turpeny

Acidity Notes:
Bright Floral   Sour   Soft
Brisk   Fruity   Bitter   Sweet
        Winy   Harsh
                 Sharp

Sample

#	#Cups	Intensity

Green moisture (%): _____

Green density: _____

Agtron: _____ / _____
            Whole   Ground

Aroma/Fragrance: 1 2 3 4 5 6 7 8 9 10

Acidity: 1 2 3 4 5 6 7 8 9 10

Defects Notes:
Fermented Moldy Grassy Pulpy
Medicinal Musty Woody Earthy
           Baggy   Groundy

Aroma/Fragrance Notes:
Floral Nutty   Spicy   Acidy
Fruity Caramelly   Herbal
Winy   Chocolaty   Smoky
        Vanilla-like Turpeny

Acidity Notes:
Bright Floral   Sour   Soft
Brisk   Fruity   Bitter   Sweet
        Winy   Harsh
                 Sharp

26

Other situations, however, require a more complex response. For example, when formulating a new blend—or when attempting to maintain consistency in a single-origin coffee from crop year to crop year—you may want to take notes and communicate your response to colleagues who are collaborating with you.

Also try attaching words to sensations; it will facilitate learning about taste. In other words, using familiar words and concepts can help unlock sensations and make them available to your palate. That's why it's good to develop a thorough cupping vocabulary.

17. Cupping categories vs. flavor notes and characteristics. It is useful to distinguish between words that define tasting *categories*—or primary characteristics—and those that describe more specific flavor characteristics. Cupping categories are defined as general sensations from which to interrogate or experience coffees. Characteristics, on the other hand, are words that attempt to describe what we experience when we interrogate a coffee in one or more of these categories. For example: *Aroma,* or the fragrance of freshly brewed coffee, is a category. *Fruity, nutty, vanilla-like,* and *bright* are all characteristics or flavor notes that one might experience in the aroma category.

18. Quantitative vs. qualitative assessments. Care should also be taken to distinguish between quantity and quality within a category. *Acidity,* for example, can taste intense in a pleasurable way, and exhibit positive characteristics like brightness or briskness. It can also taste intense in a negative way, and exhibit an unpleasant astringency or sourness.

19. Traditional cupping categories and related characteristics. Following are some traditional cupping categories. They are close to universal and are invoked in cupping forms and discussions across the world of coffee. Within each category, I have listed just a few of the many descriptive terms cuppers tend to use when responding to coffees.

Date: _____ Cups/Sample _____

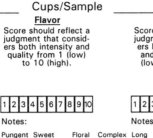

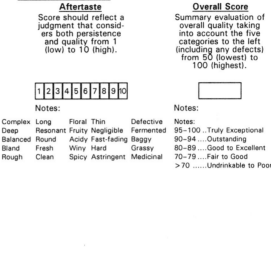

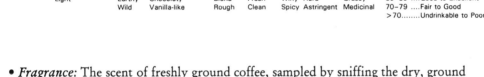

Body	Flavor	Aftertaste	Overall Score
Score should reflect a judgment that considers both weight and quality from 1 (low) to 10 (high).	Score should reflect a judgment that considers both intensity and quality from 1 (low) to 10 (high).	Score should reflect a judgment that considers both persistence and quality from 1 (low) to 10 (high).	Summary evaluation of overall quality taking into account the five categories to the left (including any defects) from 50 (lowest) to 100 (highest).

1 2 3 4 5 6 7 8 9 10 1 2 3 4 5 6 7 8 9 10 1 2 3 4 5 6 7 8 9 10

Notes: Notes: Notes: Notes:

Oily	Thick	Heavy	Thin	Pungent	Sweet	Floral	Complex	Long	Floral	Thin	Defective	Notes:
Buttery	Viscose	Full		Spicy	Nutty	Fruity	Deep	Resonant	Fruity	Negligible	Fermented	95–100 ..Truly Exceptional
Creamy		Medium		Herbal	Caramelly		Balanced	Round	Acidy	Fast-fading	Baggy	90–94 ....Outstanding
		Light		Earthy	Chocolaty		Bland	Fresh	Winy	Hard	Grassy	80–89 ....Good to Excellent
				Wild	Vanilla-like		Rough	Clean	Spicy	Astringent	Medicinal	70–79 ....Fair to Good
												>70 ......Undrinkable to Poor

1 2 3 4 5 6 7 8 9 10 1 2 3 4 5 6 7 8 9 10 1 2 3 4 5 6 7 8 9 10

Notes: Notes: Notes: Notes:

Oily	Thick	Heavy	Thin	Pungent	Sweet	Floral	Complex	Long	Floral	Thin	Defective	Notes:
Buttery	Viscose	Full		Spicy	Nutty	Fruity	Deep	Resonant	Fruity	Negligible	Fermented	95–100 ..Truly Exceptional
Creamy		Medium		Herbal	Caramelly		Balanced	Round	Acidy	Fast-fading	Baggy	90–94 ....Outstanding
		Light		Earthy	Chocolaty		Bland	Fresh	Winy	Hard	Grassy	80–89 ....Good to Excellent
				Wild	Vanilla-like		Rough	Clean	Spicy	Astringent	Medicinal	70–79 ....Fair to Good
												>70 ....Undrinkable to Poor

- *Fragrance:* The scent of freshly ground coffee, sampled by sniffing the dry, ground coffee in the cup before adding water. For typical fragrance characteristics, see *Aroma* below.
- *Aroma:* The scent of freshly brewed coffee. Aroma can range from intense to negligible, depending partly on how soon the coffee is cupped after roasting. Typical positive characteristics displayed by aroma include floral tones, fruit tones, and vanilla, nut, and vanilla-nut tones. Aromatic notes can tend toward sweetness, toward dry and acidy, or toward a complex balance between the two. For processing-related flavor characteristics, taints or defects displayed in Aroma, see points 21-27.
- *Acidity:* The dry, bright sensation of relatively high-grown, high-quality, medium-roasted arabica coffees. Acidity as a cupping category is related to the objective laboratory measurement of pH, but the sensations associated with acidity are so complexly influenced by other elements of coffee taste that the cupping category of acidity and literal measurements of pH should not be confused. Generally, acidity as a cup sensation can tend toward the sweetly fruity (some Costa Rica Dotas); the dryly fruity or wine-like (many Kenyas); the dryly berry-like (some Kenyas); the dry, pungently prune-like (many dry-processed coffees); and so on. Some positive terms applied to acidity include brisk, bright, clear, and pungent; frequently used negative terms include sharp, sour and muddy.
- *Body:* The tactile sensation of a coffee. Characteristics of body include sensations of weight (heavy, medium, light) and texture (thin, smooth, buttery, oily, rough). As noted earlier, you can often clarify sensations of texture by literally rubbing the liquid coffee against the roof of your mouth with your tongue.
- *Flavor:* A very broad category that, in practice, includes all flavor sensations not included in the other categories. Terms describing positive flavor tones or notes: floral, fruity, vanilla-like, nutty, vanilla-nut-like, chocolaty, caramel, spicy, herby, tobaccoish, and pungent. General evaluative terms that describe flavor include

27

complex, balanced, deep, ordinary, bland, inert, imbalanced, and rough. The primary tastes (sweet, salt, sour, bitter) also come into play. Sweetness in particular modifies other categories and nuances. Natural sweetness is almost always a sign of quality in coffee. It indicates that the coffee fruit was picked when ripe and processed with care. For processing-related flavor characteristics, taints and defects displayed in Flavor, see points 21-27.
- *Aftertaste:* The sensations that linger after the coffee is spit out or swallowed. Positive attributes of aftertaste can include long, resonant or round. Negative characterizations include thin, negligible or fast-fading. Shadow versions of aroma, acidity and flavor may resurface in aftertaste, sometimes intriguingly transformed. Because defects are displayed in aftertaste with particular clarity, cuppers frequently use positive characterizations like clean and fresh. People often detect astringency in aftertaste. Mild astringency may be tolerated, but intense astringency is always considered a weakness.

20. Another useful set of cupping categories. The standard cupping categories described in the preceding paragraphs are fundamental and useful, but somewhat limiting. I use the following three categories in conjunction with the standard set.
- *Development.* For me, this describes the way a coffee changes (or doesn't change) from aroma through cup to finish and aftertaste. Some coffees progressively reveal new sensations, others make their statement at the onset and stand pat.
- *Range.* Describes the range of sensation displayed by the coffee in categories such as aroma, flavor and aftertaste. At the top of the range are evanescent, barely detectable aromatic nuances (often floral or vanilla-like). A bit lower in range are high notes (often related to acidity), then mid-tones, and, finally, body-related bottom sensations (usually varieties of pungency). Some coffees concentrate sensation in one sector of the range rather than another. The best coffees display a wide range of attractive sensations.
- *Dimension.* Describes the sense of echoing space or resonance *behind* sensations. Some of the world's greatest coffees—La Minita Costa Rica Tarrazu, for example, or the best Kenyas—are remarkably deep dimensioned.

21. Processing-related characteristics, taints and defects. Although processing-related characteristics, taints and defects can surface in any cupping category, in practice, cuppers tend to treat them as a category unto themselves. You can most easily detect processing-related characteristics, taints and defects in two contexts: after the coffee has cooled to room temperature and in aftertaste. All are caused by flaws or variations in picking the coffee fruit or in the procedures (together called *processing*) that transform coffee from the delicate seed of a fresh fruit to a cured and stable "bean," ready to be transported and roasted. In other words, defects and taints are not inherent in the coffee, but are created by the impact of the picking and processing procedures.

22. Taint as flavor defect vs. taint as flavor characteristic. Purist cuppers may reject a coffee if it shows any sign of taint whatsoever. These cuppers want the impact of the steps that transform the coffee from seed to bean to be transparent, invisible and without influence on taste. Their ideal is the classic *washed* or *wet method* of processing, which, impeccably performed and accompanied by rigorous selection of sound beans, achieves such processing transparency.

Other cuppers tolerate or even celebrate certain processing "taints" as positive characteristics, analogous, for example, to the celebrated taste imparted French Sauternes and certain other wines by the "noble rot," or botrytis mold. For these cuppers, the rich variety of flavor nuances imparted by traditional regional variations in processing is part of the exotic diversity of the world of coffee.

23. Deliberate influencing of taste through processing variations. In some cases, coffees are deliberately subjected to controlled deviations in processing so as to create planned taste variations that many coffee drinkers admire. Some Indian coffees are *monsooned*—systematically exposed to moisture-laden winds in open-sided sheds—which creates a heavyish body and sharp pungency. Indonesian coffees are sometimes deliberately *aged*, a process wherein coffees are (I'm told) periodically removed from bags, exposed and raked, then rebagged.

24. Specific taints, characteristics and defects. There are many names for taints and many of these names overlap. Rather than offering a long, mind-numbing list, I have concentrated here on taints that are particularly common, grouping them under general flavor tendencies.

25. Coffee-pulp-related characteristics and taints (ferment, fruit). The length of time the coffee fruit or fruit residue remains in contact with the seed or bean during processing and how skillfully that contact is managed profoundly affects coffee taste, both positively and negatively. On the upside are coffees that display sweet, fresh-tasting fruit tones or clean dry-wine tones. On the downside are varieties of fermented-fruit and rotten-fruit tastes.

Following are some specific terms for coffee-pulp-related characteristics and taints.

- *Ferment:* The taste of fruit gone rotten, which is exactly what causes the problem. When the sugars in the coffee fruit begin to ferment before the fruit has been stripped from the seeds/beans, the ferment taste lingers in the coffee. Full-on ferment is not a pleasant sensation; imagine drinking coffee that tastes like fruit rotting in the compost.
- *Fruity-flirting-with-ferment: Fruity* describes a positive characteristic for most cuppers, a defect for others. The fruity sensation can be sweet and fresh-tasting, in which case most cuppers consider it a positive characteristic. On the other hand, the sensation can teeter on the edge of ferment—over-ripe and disturbingly lush but not quite rotten, in which case it's your call.
- *Stinkers:* These are beans inadvertently recycled during the confusingly named wet-processing stage called fermentation (not to be confused with "ferment" as a term for flavor defect). Fermented a second time, these beans turn overwhelmingly foul.
- *Dry process flirt-with-ferment:* For years I've wrestled with the right term for this edgy aftertaste common to many otherwise fine dry-process coffees, like Yemens and Ethiopia Harrars. Recall that dry-process (also called natural-process and unwashed) coffees are spread on patios or roofs to dry with the fruit still clinging to the seeds/beans. If some of the fruit ferments as it dries, it imparts a now-you-taste-it, now-you-don't edge of ferment to the otherwise pleasant fruitiness of the coffee. Cuppers who admire the distinctive fruitiness of Yemens and Harrars are willing to overlook this taste. Purists are not. Skillful dark-roasting tends to eliminate this taste while preserving the attractive fruity character of the coffee.

26. Mold-related defects and taints. These hard, flavor-flattening taints are caused by various problems with drying and storage. Again, *in very mild forms* these taints can be attractive to some coffee drinkers. Personally, I am considerably more tolerant of flirt-with-ferment faults, which tend to supplement rather than drown positive taste nuances, than I am with the often deadening, harsh taints associated with mustiness and mold.

- *Sharp, hard:* A very general set of terms for a harsh sensation that drowns out sweetness and nuance. It usually originates when coffees are rained on or remoistened while drying, or are not properly cured or rested before shipment. Cuppers with coffee production experience can often identify these drying/storage problems based on variations in the hard taste.

29

- *Rioy, phenolic:* A medicinal, iodine-like taste. This taint is peculiar to some dry-processed coffees—especially those from certain parts of Brazil—but it can turn up in other origins as well. I am told this taste is caused by a particular mold that invades the coffee fruit as it dries, especially when rain or dampness interrupts the drying. Some coffee drinkers in Eastern Europe and the Middle East admire this taste, but coffee drinkers in the North American tradition find it unpleasant.
- *Baggy:* A hard, rope-like sensation. Literally, it tastes like the coffee bag or sack. This taint originates from a common variation of storage-related hardness.
- *Faded:* Another variation of storage-related hardness that is very faint, accompanied by a weakening of the coffee's positive characteristics.
- *Earthy:* With a clear dirt taste, this taint is attractive to many coffee drinkers. It is said to derive from literal contact with earth during drying.

  Note that the earthy taste is imparted to the coffee *while the beans/seeds are still fresh,* thus integrating into the structure of the coffee. In other words, the dirt itself is long gone by the time someone roasts and brews the coffee, allowing you to enjoy this taste without fearing you are literally drinking residue from someone's backyard. To me, the earthy taint is attractive only if it is sweet-toned and soft rather than harsh or hard.
- *Pondy, mushroomy:* A taste that can turn pleasantly toffee-like under the impact of dark roasting. It's apparently caused by certain molds that make contact with the coffee during drying. It is common in some Indonesian coffees, especially Sulawesis.
- *Pungent:* My word, not the coffee industry's word, for a blunted, rounded, often herb-tinted hardness or mustiness that some coffee drinkers find quite pleasant. It arises inadvertently during moisture-inhibited drying, and deliberately in the case of monsooned coffees from India and some aged coffees.

30

27. Astringency, greenness. Coffees that are processed with too many green or unripe beans lack sweetness, leaving an unpleasantly brassy, astringent aftertaste. Coffees that *are* properly acidy, on the other hand, display a natural sweetness that enriches and complicates the dry, acidy tones.

28. Tasting for "varietal distinction," or specific characteristics related to origin. One of the pleasures for the coffee professional and aficionado is savoring the various distinctive flavor profiles related to coffee origin: the intense, wine- or berry-toned acidity of Kenyas, for example; the floral perfumes of Ethiopia Yirgacheffes; the ambiguously smoky or spicy notes of Guatemalas; and so on.

Some origins are simply more distinctive than others. A professional may praise a quality coffee that is clearly different from the standard Latin American high-grown norm as *distinctive.* But a professional often compares coffee from a specific origin to an *ideal of distinctiveness* typically associated with that origin. A Kenya that displays certain dry berry tones may be more admired (and more in demand) than an equally good Kenya with less distinctive and more generic flavor characteristics, for example. An Ethiopia Yirgacheffe without the unique floral bouquet associated with that origin probably won't be sold to the American specialty market except as a neutral coffee for blending. On the other hand, some origins, like Costa Rica and Colombia, are not associated with specific or dramatic flavor characteristics, and hence tend to sell on the basis of general quality alone.

Unfortunately, professional cuppers are still the only ones who really match specific flavor profiles to countries of origin. The worldwide specialty coffee trade is beginning to make some progress on the very complex task of formally defining origins and associated cup characteristics, but coffee appellation systems—ideally modeled after the French wine-growing systems that guarantee a Bordeaux is really grown in Bordeaux—are still many years, if not decades, away.

29. Learning about "varietal distinction," or specific characteristics related to origin. The best way to cultivate an awareness of cupping characteristics is to cup with more experienced colleagues. One approach is to take cupping seminars offered by the SCAA. Another is to visit your coffee suppliers or brokers and ask them to set up a cupping of the origin coffees that most interest you. Mail cupping clubs also are useful (see point 43, page 34). Books can help, but they're usually too general for anything more than an introductory overview. You can supplement these books, however, by reading reviews in publications like the World Wide Web newsletter *Coffee Review* (coffeereview.com) and industry print magazines like *Tea and Coffee Trade Journal*.

30. Cupping for specific flavor characteristics related to roast. So far, this chapter has covered the flavors of green coffee without regard to how those coffees are roasted. Yet roast is one of the most important influences on coffee taste. Two of the most significant uses of sensory evaluation are related to roast:
  • Defining the optimum degree of roast and roast profile for individual coffees.
  • Monitoring production roast batches for quality and consistency of roast.

31. Distinguishing between the flavor impact of the degree of roast and the roast profile. It's useful to distinguish between the flavor impact of the *degree of roast* (how "dark" a coffee is roasted) and the *roast profile* (encompassing the various strategies for modulating temperature and air velocity inside the roasting chamber during the roast).

A roaster can measure the degree of roast by two methods. First, he or she can measure the temperature in the roasting bed at the moment the roast is terminated. Or second, the roaster can use a specialized spectrophotometer, or roast analyzer, commonly called an "Agtron" (See point 41, page 34).

On the other hand, one can only assess the flavor impact of temperature and air velocity variations through sensory evaluation. One of the most pervasive errors that novice roasters commit is to assume that degree, or "color," of roast as measured by eye or Agtron is the only determiner of roast taste. *How* the roast is achieved or profiled can be every bit as important as the degree of roast when determining the flavor. For further information on roast profiling, see point 41, page 34.

31

32. Roasting faults. Most outright faults in roasting are relatively easy to identify in the cup. Here are some common terms for these faults.
  • *Baked:* Flat, dull and aroma-less. This occurs when a roaster holds the coffee too long at too low roasting temperatures.
  • *Bready:* A common term for underroasted coffee, or coffee that a roaster stopped roasting before the full onset of the transformation signaled by the "first crack." This isn't a common fault among American specialty roasters, who, if anything, tend to overroast.
  • *Tipped:* A flat, cereal-like taste that occurs when a roaster chars the bean tips during the onset of the roasting cycle.
  • *Carbony, burned:* The fault of preference among many novice American specialty roasters, given their tendency to attempt to imitate the darker roast styles popularized by Starbucks and Peets Coffee & Tea. Starbucks and Peets do *not* burn their coffees, but many of their less-experienced imitators do. These roasters burn the sugars in the bean rather than caramelize them, causing the coffee to taste thin and carbonized rather than round and richly pungent. At worst, carbony coffees taste like watery creosote. Roasters typically achieve carbony flavors by escalating temperatures in the roast chamber near the end of the roast cycle.

33. Positive roast-related characteristics. This depends on your company's signature roast style(s) and your customers' tastes. Some roasters want the roast to simply highlight the positive characteristics of the coffee. Given contemporary tastes, this optimum point typically ranges from just before the second crack to soon after. If your company's signature roast style is a very aggressive, dark style, then obviously you need to work within a range defined by that style. You'll need to choose coffees that will sustain a dark style without completely losing their character to the "taste of the roast"—the combination of sweetness and bitter pungency that are so attractive to lovers of dark-roast styles.

34. Developing the roast profile for single-origin coffees. The most common way to develop an origin roast profile is simple, if time-consuming—sample roast the coffee to several slightly different degrees of roast. You might terminate one sample just before the second crack, another at the very beginning of the second crack, another ever so slightly into the second crack, etc. Then you cup each one of them and decide when to terminate the roast.

Next you do a rough profiling on the sample roaster, always terminating the roast at roughly the same degree, until you have a general profiling strategy. Along the way, you may change your termination point slightly as the results of your profiling become apparent in the cup. (If you are a technical roaster who roasts by formula, *a la* Agtron and Agtron innovator Carl Staub, you will already have a general profiling strategy.)

Then you refine the strategy on the batch roaster, cupping as you go, aiming to maximize the coffee's distinctiveness and unique qualities within the parameters of your signature roast style.

35. Sensory evaluation in developing special-purpose blends. Blends typically fulfill a role within a product line. Sometimes the niche is distinguished by brewing method (iced coffee blend, brisk breakfast blend for drip brewing, straight-shot espresso blend, or caffè latté espresso blend, for example).

- *First steps in blending.* Some roasters design blend formulas on paper based on their knowledge of the cup characteristics of coffees they carry and know well. Then they'll test and modify the blends on the cupping table. Others start on the cupping table, assuming an empirical approach that takes little for granted about the influence of one coffee on another. When designing an espresso blend for straight shots, for example, they might start by simply cupping a large range of available coffees, looking for those that display sweetness, roundness and body. One or more of these coffees will eventually supply the foundation of the blend. Then they may cup coffees that add brightness or some other valued nuance to the blend, proceeding in the same open-ended, empirical fashion.

  Whether you pre-design blends based on your knowledge of certain coffees or you take a more open, experimental approach, you will eventually end up with a short list of candidate coffees for your blend.

- *Cup blending.* At this point you will need to combine the candidate coffees in various combinations and proportions on the cupping table. In other words, each set of cups will represent a slightly different variation of the proposed blend. With patience and some weeks or months of sporadic cupping, you will arrive at a set (or three or four sets) of coffees and proportions that seem promising.

- *Blending varying degrees of roast.* Some roasters deliberately blend coffees brought to dramatically different degrees of roast. For example, they may introduce 10 or 20 percent of a dark-roasted *blend* into a blend of standard-roasted single-origin coffees, aiming to achieve a slightly bittersweet character.

- *Batch testing blends.* Now you test the promising blend formulation(s) by batch-roasting the components and sampling the blend with everyone you know. Meticulous roasters always roast each green coffee separately to best maximize its individual contribution to a profile. In the case of volume blends, however, some roasters blend before roasting, providing the component coffees are relatively closely matched in bean density and size.

36. Sensory evaluation for control of roast quality and consistency. You should ideally cup all batches at the end of the roasting day to check consistency and quality. Set aside a portion of each batch, then prepare two or three cups of each. If something is off with one or more of the batches, brew additional cups to better focus on the fault raised in the first round of cupping. Such a routine is particularly crucial when more than one person is roasting, when you're breaking in new machinery or new personnel, or when you're introducing new origins or blends.

37. Taste characteristics of espresso blends. The acidy notes and distinctive flavor characteristics associated with single-origin coffees are generally unimportant when tasting espressos. Rather, tactile sensations (body and texture), sweetness, pungency, balance between sweet and dry tones, and overall qualities like development, range, and dimension (see point 20, page 28) are more important than specific, recognizable flavor nuances. The exception may be the very desirable chocolate (and sometimes vanilla) tones some roasters develop by dark roasting the coffee.

What are you looking for in an espresso blend? That's partially determined by its function: Is the espresso blend intended for straight shots and short milk-based drinks, or for mammoth caffè lattés and flavored drinks? Maybe it's intended for somewhere in-between?

For lattés and similar beverages, it's important to design a blend with a substantial body and a distinct pungency bordering on sharpness to keep the coffee flavor from disappearing in the milk and syrups. Sweetness, roundness, complexity, and nuance are more important for straight-shot and short milk-drink blends.

Given Americans' taste for milk-based beverages, it's essential that roasters taste their espresso in milk as well as straight (as proposed by the espresso tasting procedure described in points 13-15).

38. Forms and record-keeping. For some sensory evaluation purposes, it may suffice to keep simple lists of coffees or blends marked with occasional notations ("buy," "taste again," "close but not sweet enough," etc.). It's often more helpful, however, to use a formal cupping or tasting form.

- *Forms provided with this chapter.* A form for coffee cupping and a form for the evaluation of espresso coffee (not espresso brewing) are provided with this chapter (pages 22-23 and 26-27). They were developed for the Web publication *Coffee Review* (coffeereview.com). Readers are welcome to reproduce them for their own use, but republication or resale of the forms is prohibited without written permission from Kenneth Davids, *Coffee Review* and Bellissimo Coffee InfoGroup.
- *Other forms.* The SCAA has developed a Universal Cupping Form (point 42). This form uses an ingenious formula to determine numerical ratings for each coffee, but fails to provide a vocabulary to assist in description and thus may be a bit too ingenious for many cuppers. SCAA Executive Director Ted Lingle's booklet *The Basics of Cupping Coffee* (point 42) contains an excellent form. The small handbook *Espresso Tasting (L'Assaggio dell'Espresso)* (point 42) includes a useful form for evaluating espresso blends and espresso brewing.

39. Further resources and where to find them. Except as specifically noted, all resources mentioned here are available from the SCAA Resource Center (800-647-8292).

40. Cupping and tasting equipment. Comprehensive sources include Roastery Development Group (650-343-1333; stuff@coffeebiz.com) and Equip for Coffee (650-259-7801; info@equipforcoffee.com).

41. Roasting information and seminars.
- *Home Coffee Roasting: Romance & Revival* by Kenneth Davids ($14.95/$13.95 for SCAA members). Despite the "home" in its title, this book offers the most complete introductory overview of small-batch coffee roasting currently available in print. The book includes directions for outfitting corn poppers with *ad hoc* heat probes (for use as sample roasters) and a general introduction to origins and blending.
- *Agtron* (775-850-4600; agtron@aol.com) offers seminars on technical roast profiling ($600 first attendee, $200 each additional attendee). Technical roasting is based on using a formula to fine-tune your control of roast temperature and other parameters. Although such formula roasting may appear to sap the romance from the act, the Agtron seminar and system are an excellent way for a novice roaster to learn about roasting principles. The best way to *truly* learn about roasting is apprentice with a master roaster, but most people entering the specialty business today are far too impatient for that route. Agtron also manufactures and sells specialized roast analyzers, popularly called "Agtrons" ($7000 to $12,000), that assign an objectively determined, standardized number to the degree of roast.
- *Agtron/SCAA Roast Classification Color Disk System* ($290/$190 for SCAA members). This is a poor man's method to analyze the degree of roast the Agtron way.

42. Print materials on cupping and tasting.
- See point 38 for information on cupping and tasting forms. *Coffee Review* forms are reproduced with this chapter. The SCAA Universal Cupping Form is available from the SCAA ($5 per pad of 50).
- *The Basics of Cupping Coffee* by Ted Lingle ($15/$10 for SCAA members) is a short introduction to cupping that will enrich beginners without confusing them. The glossary is particularly useful.
- *Coffee Cupper's Handbook* by Ted Lingle ($42/$27 for SCAA members) is a detailed, technically precise overview of cupping issues and terminology. At this writing, it is being revised and is currently unavailable. This book is probably most useful for intermediate cuppers.
- *Espresso Tasting (L'Assaggio dell'Espresso),* released by the International Institute of Coffee Tasters ($15/$14 for SCAA members), provides a useful overview of espresso evaluation from an Italian perspective. It includes a tasting form.

43. By-mail cupping and tasting clubs.
- The SCAA recently opened a *Coffee Sampling Club*. Membership provides 10 green coffees per year complete with SCAA Arbitration Panel reports ($100 annually).
- *Coffee Review* (coffeereview.com; 877-478-5282) offers an *Associate Cupper's Club* ($12.95 per month) through which you receive a roasted coffee each month along with an in-depth description and rating as it appeared in the publication's monthly review of coffees.

44. Cupping and tasting seminars.
- Through its *"University of Specialty Coffee,"* the SCAA holds cupping seminars several times a year for both beginning and intermediate cuppers at various locations across the country.
- *Guided Coffee Discoveries* (800-729-8114) offers concentrated, four-day

instructional programs on a coffee farm in the classic Antigua growing region of Guatemala. A regular feature of the programs are twice-daily cupping sessions led by experienced cuppers that expose participants to a wide variety of coffee origins, types and processing methods. Recommended.

45. Cupping and tasting kits. Again, the best way to learn to cup and taste is to do it with other, more experienced or similarly experienced coffee professionals. The following two resources help, but are no substitute for cupping in company.

• *Le Nez du Café (The Nose of Coffee)*, designed by Jean Lenoir ($325/$225 for SCAA members), is an impressive piece of work that isolates 36 aromas present in certain coffees and presents their essences in vials accompanied by information cards. When you detect an aroma or aromatic flavor tone that seems related to one of the 36, you sniff the relevant vial and observe how the aroma in the cup relates. Le Nez du Café is extremely useful as a single component in a comprehensive cupping program, but it's quite limited in scope. For one thing, the kit isolates only 36 aromas, some of which are quite common while others strike me as rare and arbitrary. The kit also "murders to dissect," as Wordsworth put it, by isolating singular aromatic elements from among the hundreds present in freshly brewed coffee. Again, it's a fine achievement, but it should not be used as a crutch or replacement for comprehensive evaluative tasting.

• *The Specialty Coffee Association of America Taste Training Kit* (around $200) includes 15 vials of taste/flavor essences plus an instruction book. You add several drops of a flavor essence to a cup of brewed coffee to learn to recognize or pick out that particular flavor in the cup. In other words, the flavor essence acts to accentuate or intensify characteristics already present in the coffee, making the characteristic recognizable and memorable. The kit is more contextual than Le Nez du Café but less wide-ranging. Like Le Nez, it's useful but not definitive. ● *35*

Dr. Ernesto Illy

Ernesto Illy has served as chairman of illycaffé S.p.A. of Trieste, Italy, since 1963. His wife, Anna, is a member of the board, and their four children—Francesco, Riccardo, Anna, and Andrea—all hold positions in the company. Dr. Illy obtained a degree in chemistry from the University of Bologna in 1947, and, in 1956, became co-owner of illycaffé and the manager responsible for sales development.

Dr. Illy is a well-known figure in the coffee industry, both for his expertise and for the positions he has held in many international organizations. On June 2, 1994, he was granted the title of Cavaliere del Lavoro (Knight of Industry) by Italian President Oscar Luigi Scalfaro. In April 1997, he was awarded a "Lifetime Achievement Award" by the Specialty Coffee Association of America.

Dr. Illy is former president and founder of ASIC (Association Scientifique International du Café, Paris)—the international body that studies the biological, chemical and physical aspects of coffee—and today serves as senior vice president of the organization. In 1981, he served as president of Physiological Effects of Coffee (PEC), an organization that studies the physiological effects that coffee has on the body. He is also past president of Institute for Scientific Information of Coffee (ISIC), an organization that studies the scientific aspects of coffee and its preparation as well as promoting discussion on the subject of coffee and health.

Chapter 2

Espresso: The Future Generation's Way to Enjoy Coffee

Espresso was always meant to be fast. Legend endures that espresso originated when an impatient Neapolitan friend of a Milanese engineer asked, "Why can't you add some pressure to this damned coffee pot to prepare a fast cup?" (Ironically, the "Neapolitan" is a slow-working drip pot.) The engineer accepted the challenge and the first espresso machine, the Bezzera, was born.

But at odds with a drink defined literally as "fast coffee," this early espresso machine required a great deal of sensitivity and skill to operate. It has never been as simple as pushing a button.

The Bezzera had a large basket, the ground coffee bed was very thin, and the valve had three positions: steam, water and discharge. To access the water, you had to first pass the steam position, and the resulting burst of steam would disrupt the bed of coffee.

Even worse was the machine's tendency to overheat—understandable given that the boiler generating the steam and hot water was set at a pressure between 1.4 and 1.8 bars. The water temperatures at these pressures was much higher (230 to 248 degrees F, or 110 to 118 degrees C) than the 195 to 205 degrees F (92 to 94 degrees C) that experts later adopted as the best value. As a result, the machine drifted steadily from lower to higher temperatures. Sometimes the first cup of espresso was good, but the following cups were increasingly bitter and woody tasting due to the excessive water temperature and the burning action of the steam.

Nonetheless, the primitive machines were a hit. The time to prepare a cup of espresso was now drastically shorter than with alternative brewing methods. Espresso also offered the presence of a foam crowning the surface and trapping the aroma, in addition to a concentrated taste. On top of that, the machine supplied dry steam from the nozzle to heat and foam milk.

In 1935, my father, Francesco Illy, the founder of illycaffé, patented a revolutionary espresso machine boasting many novelties—it was fully automatic; it was mechanical; it controlled the water and steam and compressed air dosage; and it contained a water treat-

39

ment system that prevented lime build-up in the boiler. This machine was far ahead of its time, generating large crowds of enthusiastic consumers in Italy. Its biggest installation was in the Italian Ministry of Aeronautics, where four machines—each with four group heads—served the pilots and personnel. The four machines could make 16 espressos in 40 seconds for a total of around 5000 cups per hour.

The machine's most important novelty was its use of alternative energy sources for hot water and pressure. In a boiler, pressure and temperature are tied together; if you increase the pressure, you increase the temperature. The acceptable pressure limit to produce water at a temperature of 242 degrees F (117 degrees C) is 1.2 bars. But a pressure of 1.2 bars is too low if you want a concentrated espresso.

Then manufacturers discovered that good espresso would result from keeping the pressure at 6 to 9 bars and the water below boiling temperature. Thus the modern espresso machine was created. Further developments didn't occur until the 1950s, when Achille Gaggia developed a mechanical device that, like a vine press, produced the right pressure and temperature for the espresso without using an expensive and noisy air compressor. This was the first piston-driven espresso machine.

The piston-driven machine operated on the principle of the separation of the heat boiler, which generated the hot water and steam for the cappuccino, from the source of pressure—the piston.

In 1961, Faema added an external hydraulic pump, which raised the pressure on the water that traveled through the heat exchanger in the boiler. Later, La Marzocco developed a thermally stable unit that used two boilers—one for steam and hot water, the other for espresso. Many companies have introduced electronically controlled heat exchangers that have shown a very high thermal stability—even in small household machines. The importance of the higher pressure of modern machines is reflected in the small diameter of the portafilter basket and the consequent thicker bed of ground coffee. This allows baristas to prepare the concentrated brew in small volumes with a strong extraction rate, which is the way Italians like their ristretto.

Perhaps a further look at the history of the espresso machine will help clarify the long struggle that accompanied the development of the modern machine. A new model takes 25 to 30 seconds to extract—from a bed of 13 to 14 grams of ground espresso—25 percent of its components in 60 milliliters of water. This is a very powerful extracting tool compared to a drip filter machine, which will extract some 17 percent of the coffee in six to eight minutes. And the drip machine uses some 100 milliliters of water for 10 grams of coffee.

As a consequence of this power, users of modern espresso machines make frequent errors. Some use coarse ground coffee to speed up the preparation time. A cup prepared in 10 seconds, however, will not contain the same components as an espresso prepared in 25 to 30 seconds. It will taste acidic and flat, produce a foam with large bubbles and short persistence, and will leave a poor aftertaste and after-flavor.

Now it's time to differentiate between espresso and regular filter coffee.

The latter is a transparent solution with a concentration of some 10 to 15 milligrams of coffee per milliliter of water. Light will pass through filter coffee without any scatter.

The former is a polyphasic system (it has more than one step) formed by a solution, an emulsion, a suspension, and a foam. Light does not pass through an espresso; rather it is scattered. The liquid is turbid, which means it contains some particles similar to light waves. These particles can be any of three things—very small fragments of ground coffee, little drops of emulsified oil, or microscopic bubbles of gas.

The bubbles are often smaller than 5 microns (thousandths of a millimeter). This size gives them a special character. They belong to the world of dispersed matter called colloidal dispersion. Because the surface of the particles is very big if volume is very small, they will show a special behavior and interaction with the surrounding water molecules.

While looking through a microscope at a drop of espresso magnified 1000 times, one would be surprised by the continuous motion of these colloidal parts. They show the famous Brownian motion, caused by the thermal agitation of the water molecules that hit the dispersed matter in a perpetual dance—the dance of life. This strong interaction produces the important changes that characterize an espresso: the density and viscosity (a measure of the internal friction of a liquid) are bigger, and the surface tension (the force that keeps together a drop) is different from that of drip coffee.

The high surface tension manifests big drops, much like mercury. Low surface tension, on the other hand, produces small drops, like a soap or a detergent solution. This infiltrates the taste buds on the tongue, which causes the long aftertaste and after-flavor that espresso fans appreciate. All this is possible only if the concentration of the liquid is in the range of 40 to 60 milligrams per milliliter, and this is only achieved in a cup of 30 to 40 milliliters prepared from 6.5 to 7 grams of coffee.

Let's review what we've learned so far. Espresso is a polyphasic colloidal solution prepared with 30 to 40 milliliters of water at a temperature of 195 to 205 degrees F (92 to 94 degrees C) in 25 to 30 seconds. The concentration is 40 to 60 milligrams per milliliter and extracts 22 to 25 percent of the ground coffee used.

This definition tells us that espresso is very complex, and that the quality of flavor will depend upon several initial conditions. These conditions are as follows: The pressure and the temperature of the water, the resistance of ground particles in the filter basket, the particle size distribution, and the thickness and compactness of the bed.

Ground coffee must be compacted to a threshold of 36 percent for a perfect extraction. Lower thresholds show, in computer models, that parasitic water channels will arise and will move with a speed eight to 10 times the speed of working water. This dilutes the liquid and doesn't contribute to the extraction process.

Espresso extraction is a chaotic process; its evolution is dependent upon its initial conditions. Any change or alteration of those conditions produces a completely different cup. To prepare an espresso is to tame chaos—not an easy feat, and one that explains why consistency is so rare.

It also explains why Italian espresso is different from espresso in other regions—simply because of the way it is served, its small volume, its purity, and the amount of sugar used. U.S. espresso consumers, on the other hand, like a full cup of espresso, which dilutes and over-extracts the coffee. As a result, the quality suffers.

In order to reduce inconsistencies when making espresso, roasters often over-roast their blends, thereby obtaining consistency through bitterness. The darker the coffee is roasted, the more bitter it becomes. Dark roasting also sometimes masks flavor faults in a specific coffee.

Because consumers don't like bitterness, they try to buffer bitter espresso by adding milk. The bitterer the coffee, the more milk they add. Over-roasted coffee loses all its aroma in the smoke, and consumers compensate for this insufficient aroma with artificial flavors or sweet and rich syrups, all of which totally cover the coffee's smell and flavor. This creates a kind of chain reaction that, if not understood, jeopardizes the potential of consumers in a new market to truly enjoy good espresso and all its benefits. If consumers believe that bitter espresso is the best that espresso has to offer, they aren't likely to make it a permanent part of their lives. Some believe espresso and cappuccino represent a kind of meteor, a lot of light that lasts for very short time. I hope it will become a permanent star—maybe not shining with a blinding light but lasting for future generations.

Let me explain why bitterness represents such a big risk for the further growth of the coffee market in the U.S. If you let a newborn boy taste something sweet, he will smile. If you let him taste something bitter, he will make a face or even weep. Why? He does not have any experience—he is just a few hours old—and all he knows is that bitterness is dangerous. This knowledge is written in his DNA, the genetic code that contains the survival instructions for every living being.

The danger of bitterness can be explained in the long story of our ancestors, who were permanently hungry and looking for nutrient rich berries, a basic staple of primitive humans. Some very beautiful colored berries contain glycosides, which are poisonous and very bitter chemicals. Those who did not perceive the bitterness of the berries died.

Contemporary humans carry in their DNA the information that bitterness can be dangerous. Therefore, few among us intrinsically enjoy bitter flavors; we have to learn to appreciate bitterness. In the Mediterranean, people enjoy bitter liquors and frequently use them as digestives, but they have to learn to use these liquors. In the U.S., consumers are very sensitive to bitterness and generally don't like it. No bitter liquor is available in the U.S. Importers had to reduce even the slight bitterness of Israeli grapefruits to meet the taste of American consumers.

In my estimation, the excessive bitterness that characterizes American espresso is counter productive, and can only be explained by some roasters' decisions to achieve consistency the easy way by over-roasting their coffees. Green coffees are very different in their taste and aromas, reflecting the influence of their genetic structures, the species, the environment in which the coffee was grown, and in their processing. It's very difficult and time-consuming to blend coffees that achieve a consistently good taste and aroma. It takes a great deal of experience, patience and love to reach this target. Over-roasting is not the answer because the only consistency one can achieve is taste consistency. Aroma disappears in dark roasts because it is roasted into the air. It produces a fine-smelling smoke during the roast, but it doesn't stay in the cup. And espresso is all about what's in the cup.

The pleasurable flavor of coffee is achieved through the presence of emulsified oil drops—the flavor carriers—and a foam that traps the volatiles and concentrates them. It is important these qualities are not lost during the roasting only to be replaced by the burnt smell of over-roasted coffee.

The espresso and cappuccino culture is based on a shift from the use of coffee for its caffeine content to its use for physiological activity. In addition, people have begun to appreciate the unique fusion of a very intense and long-lasting taste with a powerful aroma concentrated in the foam.

Espresso is a kind of organoleptic amplifier. Taste and flavor are both magnified through the complexity of this very unique brew. Coffee drinkers love espresso because of the strong sensation it delivers without the excitement of the caffeine.

Espresso delivers less caffeine because of its short percolation time. The caffeine in an espresso represents 60 to 75 percent of the caffeine available in a bed of ground coffee. For instance, 7 grams of arabica coffee with a 1.3 percent caffeine ratio will contain 91 milligrams of caffeine. Therefore, an espresso with a 65 percent extraction will have some 60 milligrams of caffeine. This explains why Italians can drink some five or more espressos per day. It also explains why when they visit the U.S. and find the coffee so weak, they get shaky with the same number of cups.

I must stress the physiological activity present in coffee. The relationship between the caffeine concentration in the body and physiological activity is characterized by an inverted "U" curve. This means small quantities of caffeine produce an important effect, but if we increase this quantity the phenomenon flattens. If we increase the quantity still more, our bodies will start to revert and we'll experience contrary effects.

Dr. Harris Lieberman of MIT showed that 30 milligrams of caffeine (half a cup of espresso) increases our environmental "alertness" by 30 percent. This alertness will not increase proportionally the more caffeine we consume. At a level of 120 milligrams, both our alertness and our ability to relax are heightened. If we continue to increase our caffeine intake, we will stop relaxing and instead become anxious and distracted. At very high levels of caffeine, we'll even turn lethargic!

This tells us some interesting things. Scientists try to find absolute solutions in their experiments and tend to use high dosages to show the negative side effects of caffeine. Only recently have scientists performed studies using dosages that correspond to the average coffee consumer's intake. This also explains why coffee consumers keep the same consumption pattern for all their lives: Too much caffeine produces unpleasant side effects, such as dry eyes, extra stool or anxiety. Coffee consumers tend to have a quota for coffee cups, i.e. the three-cup guy, the seven-cup guy or the two-cup guy. Each person's consumption corresponds to their optimum feeling.

Two populations that show a maximum enjoyment of coffee are Italians and Brazilians. And it's true that the consumption pattern of coffee plays a role in the two cultures. Both tend to drink frequent small cups of coffee—espresso in Italy and espresso and *cafesinho* in Brazil. People in both countries are relaxed and efficient, and the cultures promote the idea that they really know how to enjoy life.

Recent research at the University of Cagliari by Professor de Chiara associates caffeine intake with the activation of the "Prefrontal Cortex," the area of the brain that stores short-term memory. If this discovery is confirmed, it will explain why young students so frequently drink espresso and cappuccino to improve their learning activity.

Thus from the above examples, we can see how the new culture of coffee enjoyment—based on low caffeine intake and big flavor and taste—can help increase our intellectual performances and our joy of life. We also can witness the creation of a new environment, one in which coffee, which stimulates the yin and the yang of our brain, attracts the younger generation around the brightness and clarity produced by an espresso. Alcohol was once the big attraction, but the blunting affect of alcohol on the brain seems out of line with a culture where abstract thought, brilliant ideas, novel correlations, and creativity are the sources of our future success.

One last consideration on the ratio of elegance and ambiance within the espresso culture. In recent years, the U.S. has seen an incredible proliferation of cafés and gourmet shops trying to attract consumers with a maximum of visibility, splendor, colors, and elegance. We have also seen some very unforeseen failures. Why? Because many of these businesses place too much attention and capital on appearance and not enough on the quality of the products.

Consumers are growing more sophisticated every day. They're learning the language of the old chemical senses—taste and the smell—and are becoming competent critics. A gorgeous ambiance is like a big light in the dark. It will attract many people by virtue of their curiosity. But what transforms a curious man in his habitué? A consumer who returns day after day to visit a business is no longer curious. Rather, he returns because he appreciates the quality of the offerings.

To attract a crowd of espresso and cappuccino lovers, one must supply the best raw materials, the best possible coffee, the best equipment, the best people behind the machine, and the nicest waiters. Only if these conditions are respected will one's investment generate the expected results.

And to meet these conditions, one must transform one kilogram of roasted coffee into 140 cups of unforgettable quality espresso. This will generate 140 smiling consumers who have but one wish—to return as soon as possible to your place of business and experience again the deep aesthetic appreciation that a great cup of perfection brings. ●

Ted R. Lingle

Ted R. Lingle is one of the founding co-chairmen of the Specialty Coffee Association of America and is currently its executive director.

During his 20-year coffee career, Lingle was vice president of marketing for Lingle Bros. Coffee Inc., a roastery in operation since 1920. He directed the company's sales programs for the foodservice, office coffee service and specialty coffee market segments from 1970 to 1990.

In 1975, Lingle pioneered the development of the Coffee Conductivity Meter, an electronic instrument used for the measurement of soluble solids. In 1985, he wrote the *Coffee Cupper's Handbook* to promote the discussion of more meaningful and accurate coffee flavor terminology. The book was written to assist new specialty coffee retailer-roasters and combines the traditions of the cupping table with the science of flavor chemistry to help teach the art and science of sensory analysis that coffee roasters employ in their craft.

In 1995, Lingle wrote the *Coffee Brewing Handbook* to promote excellence in beverage preparation. The handbook pulls together the past 50 years of research on coffee brewing to help new specialty coffee café operators understand how to maximize the potential of the high quality coffee beans they buy.

Lingle is a graduate of the U.S. Military Academy, and holds an MBA from Woodbury University in Los Angeles.

Chapter 3

Brewing Good Coffee

Success as a specialty coffee retailer requires you to possess the skill and knowledge to brew good coffee. Although you sell coffee in its whole-bean or ground form, most retailers make their money from the sales of coffee beverages. And the quality of the coffee beverage relates directly to your ability to transform it into an enjoyable form. To make the beverage flavorful, you must observe the essential elements of good brewing.

Coffee begins this transformation as a green bean. The beans come from many growing regions around the world, each with its own distinctive flavor characteristics. Roasters often blend these green beans. The types of beans and the proportion in which they are blended largely determine the flavor of the beverage. The roasting technique—including the rate and length of heating—also plays a critical role in determining the ultimate flavor of the brew.

Before you can brew the beans, however, you have to grind them into small particles that range in size from slightly coarse to extremely fine. You then immerse a specified portion of these coffee particles in a predetermined portion of water. The size of the particles, the specific ratio of coffee to water, the duration the coffee is in contact with the water, and the quality of the water all affect the flavor.

The Flavor of Coffee

Coffee gets some of its flavor from the great variety of chemical compounds released during the brewing cycle. Under preferred circumstances, the water extracts about 70 percent of the available water-soluble flavoring compounds that constitute the beverage's aroma, taste, body, and color. Together, these compounds create the sensory aspects of coffee's flavor.

Flavors differ among coffees not only because of variances in blend and roast, but also because the water removes each flavoring compound at a different rate. For example, water readily extracts the aromatic compound. Although small and hardly measurable in relation to the total extract, aromatic compounds contribute significantly to flavor perception. The compounds responsible for taste (which dissolve in the water) and for body (which don't dissolve) extract at a slower rate. Both sets of aromatic and taste compounds contain many different chemical components that combine to produce different beverage flavors.

During brewing, the total amount of flavoring material in the beverage changes, as does the proportion of each compound. In other words, the flavor changes continuously the longer the coffee brews. As a general rule, water extracts the most flavorful compounds first. As the coffee particles remain in contact with the water for longer periods, the less-flavorful compounds begin to release. Prolonged extraction results in an unacceptable flavor. The most desirable mixture of flavor elements occurs before you extract all the compounds. Consequently, for optimum results, you must stop the brewing process before reaching the point of maximum extraction.

Six Essential Elements

Here are the six elements necessary to transform roasted beans into a great-tasting cup of coffee:

1. Correct coffee-to-water ratio. The finished brew is a balance between strength (solubles concentration) and extraction (solubles yield). Shifting the balance either way greatly affects the final product. For example, coffee has an extremely concentrated flavor, meaning you must dilute it with water. The best proportions fall between one percent and 1.5 percent coffee and between 98.5 percent and 99 percent water. Coffee strength of less than one percent is too weak, and coffee strength above 1.5 percent is too strong.

The most acceptable yield lies between 18 percent and 22 percent. Underdeveloped yields (below 16 percent) create flavors that are grassy to peanut-like. Over-extracted yields (above 24 percent) result in bitter and astringent flavors.

It's also possible to extract a large amount of flavoring material into a small amount of water, or, conversely, extract a small amount of material into a large volume of water. The brewing formula becomes your guide for controlling both the solubles concentration and yield.

2. A coffee grind that matches the brewing time. Once you've established a coffee brewing formula, the brewing method and equipment come into play. To prevent underdevelopment or over-extraction of the flavoring compounds, you must match the correct particle size (grind) of the coffee to the brewing method and type of equipment used. As a general rule, pair longer brewing times with larger (coarser) particles and shorter brewing times with smaller (finer) particles.

3. Proper operation of brewing equipment. Brewing equipment normally controls three variables:

- Time of contact between the coffee grounds and water. It takes time for the coffee particles to absorb the water, for the water to dissolve and extract the soluble material in the particles, and for the dissolved material to migrate into the beverage. Because the water extracts different chemical compounds at different rates, the mixture of soluble materials in the beverage changes continuously. Therefore, controlling the brewing time contributes to optimal extraction and produces uniform results.

- Water temperature. Cold water doesn't extract coffee as completely or as rapidly as hot water. Water that ranges in temperature from 195 degrees F to 205 degrees F (92 degrees C to 96 degrees C) liberates the aromatic materials faster and properly extracts the other solubles within a reasonable time. As a general rule, water temperature should remain constant throughout the brewing cycle.

- Turbulence. The dynamics of the water passing through and over the coffee grounds creates a mixing action. Sufficient turbulence is necessary to first wet the coffee particles and then to cause the water to flow uniformly through them. Wetting allows the water to penetrate the particle fibers, and a uniform flow allows the soluble material to dissolve. In addition, adequate turbulence prevents the fluid that is in immediate contact with the coffee from becoming so saturated with dissolved material that it can no longer remove additional flavoring compounds.

4. Optimum brewing method. Using the same type of coffee in different brewing equipment will create coffee beverages with different taste and body characteristics. All coffee equipment uses one of six basic methods to extract the flavoring materials from the ground coffee:

- Steeping. In this method, the user mixes coffee grounds in a container with hot water, leaves them in contact with the water for an arbitrary length of time, and then separates them from the extract or brew. The steeping time depends on the particle size, the water temperature, how much the grounds are agitated, and how quickly you separate the grounds from the beverage.
- Decoction. The user mixes loose coffee grounds in a container with water that continues to boil for an arbitrary length of time. You usually achieve complete extraction during this preparation method, due to the elevated water temperature—as high as 212 degrees F (100 degrees C)—and the extreme turbulence created by the boiling water.
- Percolation. The user places the ground coffee in a container that serves both as a brewing chamber and a means to separate the grounds from the beverage. A pump moves the hot water to and through the coffee again and again. First the water and then the beverage extract recirculate through the grounds. The time of contact depends upon grind size, water or extract temperature, and recirculation rate.
- Drip filtration. As with percolation, the user places the grounds in a container that serves both as a brewing chamber and a means of separating the grounds from the beverage. In this method, however, the hot water flows only once through the coffee. The extract drips from the brewing chamber into a pot or other beverage receiver. The time of contact depends principally upon the rate the water flows into the brewing chamber and the particle size of the grind. Other important factors include the water temperature, the chamber's shape, and the filter type.
- Vacuum filtration. This method, which uses a two-chamber device, is a variation on the steeping method. Steam pressure forces hot water from the lower chamber up through a filtering unit into the upper chamber, which contains coffee. Escaping vapor and stirring serve to agitate the coffee and water. When the brewer turns off the heat, steam eventually condenses in the lower chamber and creates a vacuum. The vacuum pulls the beverage down through the filter but leaves the grounds behind. The time of contact depends on how quickly a vacuum forms, the properties of the filter unit, and the particle size of the ground coffee.
- Pressurized infusion. The brewer forces highly pressurized water (as much as 9 to 10 atmospheres) through the coffee grounds, which are compacted into a small cake in the brewing chamber. The combined heat and force of the water extracts soluble flavoring materials, emulsifies insoluble oils, and suspends both ultra-fine bean particles and gas bubbles. This creates a beverage with an extremely high solubles concentration. To produce a uniform beverage with this method, it's essential to use rapid brewing times and extremely fine particle sizes. The brewing temperature—190 to 195 degrees F (88 to 92 degrees C)—is slightly lower than in other methods. This method is usually referred to as espresso extraction.

The majority of these brewing methods will produce a quality coffee beverage. The exceptions are decoction and percolation, which over-extract the coffee and lead to undesirable tastes.

5. Good-quality water. When preparing a coffee beverage, water is as important as the coffee. In fact, water represents more than 98 percent of the beverage. Water with a mineral content of 50 to 100 parts per million (3 to 6 grains) will typically produce the best-tasting beverage. The water should taste like fresh, good-quality drinking water, have no odor, and contain no visible impurities.

Water that is very soft or very hard doesn't yield a good beverage. Treat such water before using it for coffee brewing. Water filters can remove insoluble materials and sediments, while demineralization can remove excessive dissolved solids. Activated charcoal—or preliminary chlorinating followed by an activated charcoal treatment—can remove odors. In many instances, polyphosphate treatment of the water will prevent scaling and corrosion of brewing equipment without affecting beverage flavor.

It's not recommended to soften water by substituting sodium ions for dissolved minerals, especially for water containing high concentrations of bicarbonate solids. This treatment often increases alkalinity, which has an undesirable physical effect on the taste of coffee. In addition, this method of treatment will increase the contact time with the water, causing over-extraction of the grounds and objectionable bitterness in the coffee beverage.

6. An appropriate filtering medium. Unless something separates the extract from the coffee grounds, the resulting beverage will be murky and difficult to drink. Filters, to varying degrees, clarify the beverage by separating the insoluble material from the brew. As a result, the filtering method directly affects the body of the beverage—and indirectly affects the flavor of the beverage.

Body, which contributes to flavor, is created in part by the insoluble materials the water carries into the finished brew. These insoluble materials (principally oils and small particles of bean fiber) create brew colloids, which trap soluble material and gases that are later released on the palate. This time-delayed release of flavoring materials adds to the overall enjoyment of the beverage.

Filters fall into four general categories:

- Perforated metal plates. These plates have holes that allow extract to escape the brewing chamber, yet hold back some of the fine particles in the coffee grounds. The size and number of holes vary but must relate to the level of grind used in the brewing equipment. Perforated plates provide virtually no clarification of the beverage, and most fine and very fine particles are able to pass through.

- Woven wire screens. Compared to metal plates, wire screens have smaller holes in the filter barrier. The screens can be woven to hold back different amounts of the fine particles, but, like perforated plates, woven wire screens offer only slightly better clarification of the beverage.

- Cloth. Either sewn into bags or shaped to cover various forms, cloth can serve as a filtering medium. The type of cloth and weave used determine its retentive capabilities. You can achieve very good beverage clarity with material that has, at most, a weave of 64 x 60 threads per inch and a weight of 5.75 square yards per pound. Before the first use, cloth filters require soaking and rinsing in hot water. With ongoing use, you'll need to implement special procedures to prevent the filter from absorbing oils that later decompose and alter beverage flavor. Store cloth filters in cold water after each use.

- Paper. Of the four types of filters, paper yields the clearest beverage. With paper, however, it's difficult to establish ideal brewing conditions. Paper is weak. Without adequate support, it often resists the flow of the beverage to such an extent that over-extraction occurs. Paper filters should be strong enough to permit the use of wire supports that don't impede the extraction flow. In addition, paper shouldn't transfer any tastes to the brew or by itself impede the extract.

A Successful Transformation of Beans to Beverage

Ultimately, the coffee's quality depends on your ability to follow the steps outlined above. Even if you start with one of the world's finest coffees you may end up with a less-than-ideal beverage if you use an inappropriate brewing method or poor quality water. A successful transformation from beans to beverage requires understanding of and adherence to these six essential elements of good brewing.

The Brewing Process
Brewing good coffee is a craft. The key lies in finding the optimum balance between the strength of the brew and the degree of extraction.

Strength refers to the brew's intensity—how concentrated it is—and needs to be adjusted for consumers' individual tastes, just as you'd adjust the volume on a stereo. Strength can be quantified as the percentage of solubles concentration in the brew. Extraction refers to the brew's quality—the amount of flavoring materials released from the grounds. You must control extraction to optimize taste, just as you'd adjust the mix of treble and bass coming from the stereo's speakers. You can quantify extraction as the percentage of solubles yield from the amount of coffee grounds used in preparing the brew.

Aroma + Taste = Flavor
The strength of coffee comes from the chemical compounds in the roasted, ground beans. Some of these solubles evaporate easily and are responsible for the brew's aroma; others aren't so volatile and are the source of the brew's taste (See Table 1). Aroma and taste combine to produce a coffee's flavor. The insoluble compounds that do not dissolve become the coffee's body.

Table 1

Chemical Compositions of Soluble and Insoluble Portions of Roasted Coffee (Approximate, Dry Basis)

Nonvolatiles	% Solubles	% Insolubles
Carbohydrates (53%)		
Reducing Sugars	1 - 2	-
Caramelized Sugars	10 - 17	0 - 7
Hemi-cellulose (hydrolyzable)	1	14
Fiber (not hydrolyzable)	-	22
Oils	-	15
Proteins (N x 6.25); Soluble Amino Acids	1 - 2	11
Ash (oxide)	3	1
Acids (nonvolatile)		
Chlorogenic	4.5	-
Calleic	0.5	-
Quinic	0.5	-
Oxalic, Malic, Citric, Tarlaric	1	-
Volatile Acids	0.35	-
Trigonelline	1	-
Caffeine (Arabicas 1%; Robustas 2%)	1.2	-
Phenolics (estimated)	2	-
Volatiles		
Carbon Dioxide	trace	2
Essence of Aroma and Flavor	0.04	-
Total	27 - 35%	73 - 65%

* Source: Sivetz and Desrosier (1979)

Coffees roasted differently can contain vastly different amounts of aroma and taste materials. Coffee gets its taste from extractable nonvolatile materials in the beans. These materials potentially amount to about 30 pounds of each 100 pounds of coffee. The extractable *volatile* materials, however, amount to less than 1/2 ounce in each 100 pounds of coffee. In other words, the ratio of taste-to-aroma components is about 1000-to-1. Consequently, the perception of beverage strength relates directly to the perception of taste.

Taste is also tied to the brew's chemical composition, which changes continuously during the brewing cycle. The changes occur because each flavoring compound dissolves at a different rate.

Three Phases of the Brewing Process

To achieve the optimum balance between strength and extraction, it's essential to control the brewing process. The brewing process itself proceeds in three stages:

Wetting. As the bean fiber absorbs hot water, gas is driven from the coffee particles and interstitial voids (the small spaces between the particles). This phase prepares the particles for extraction.

Extraction. During this second phase, the water-soluble flavoring compounds rapidly move from the bean fibers and enter the water.

Hydrolysis. At this point, large molecules of water-insoluble carbohydrates break down into smaller molecules that are water soluble. These are mostly reducing sugars but also include some proteins.

24 Variables of Coffee Brewing

Because the brewing process proceeds in three distinct phases—wetting, extraction and hydrolysis—the design and operation of the brewing equipment has a direct bearing on the composition of the brew. Therefore, controlling the brewing process means controlling the multiple variables related to the coffee as well as the variables related to the brewing equipment.

In total, 24 variables interact during the brewing process. Controlling all these variables to achieve the optimum balance between strength and extraction is a true craft. You can categorize the variables as follows:

Table 2

Variables Affecting Strength and Extraction

Coffee Product
Blend Components:
    1. Ratio of blend components
    2. Bulk density of beans
    3. Chemical composition of beans
Roast Development:
    4. Methodology of roasting
    5. Rate of roasting
    6. Degree of roast
    7. Rate of degassing
Grind:
    8. Average size of particles
    9. Size distribution of particles
    10. Particle shape

Brewing Equipment

Time of Brewing:
    11. Time of water contact

Temperature:
    12. Contact temperature
    13. Gradient temperature during brewing

Turbulence:
    14. Complete wetting
    15. Uniform flow
    16. Particle movement

Filtering Method:
    17. Method of separation
    18. Degree of clarification

Holding Conditions:
    19: Length of time and method of holding
    20. Holding temperature

Ingredients

Brewing Ratio:
    21. Coffee (by weight)
    22. Water (by volume)

Water:
    23. Water composition
    24. Water treatment

Coffee Product

The coffee roaster is usually responsible for controlling the 10 variables related to the coffee product.

- *Blend components.* The ratio of different coffees (1) used in the blend can range from a single-origin coffee on one extreme to a mix of arabica and robusta coffees on the other. Also affecting the blend is the beans' bulk density (2)—a measure of a bean's weight in relation to its physical volume. Finally, the chemical composition (3) of the beans themselves affects the brew's resulting flavor and intensity. Chemical composition varies by the type of coffee plant that produced the coffee and the microclimate in which it grew.
- *Roast development.* The methodology of roasting (4), particularly the efficiency of heat transfer within the beans, determines if the beans are uniformly roasted from the outside to the center of the bean. The rate of roasting (5) controls both the structural expansion of the bean fibers (which affects extraction rates) and the chemical composition of the roasted beans (which affects the flavor of the extract). Other variables include the degree of roast (6)—usually evaluated by the beans' color—and the rate of degassing (7), which generally relates to the storage method or the length of time that elapses before brewing.
- *Grind.* Relative to brewing, a critical aspect of the coffee product is the grind, or particle size. Within certain limits, the amount of soluble material extracted from the coffee varies inversely with the particle size—the smaller the particles, the greater the extraction (See Table 3). In controlling the particle size, you must take into account both the average size of the particles (8) and the size distribution of the particles (9) (See Table 4). In addition, the particle shape (10) will impact the rate at which soluble material will extract from the coffee.

Table 3

Effect of Particle Size of Coffee Grounds on Extraction of Soluble Solids

Particle Size (Tyler Screen #)	Contact Time (in seconds)	Soluble Solids (as percent)	Extraction (oz./lb.)
on #10	142	0.63	1.67
on #14	143	0.73	1.93
on #20	136	0.93	2.45
on #28	156	1.28	3.40
on #40	292	1.46	3.87

- Water to coffee ratio at 2 1/4 gallons per pound
- Water temperature at 200 degrees F
- Results averaged from five trials with each size fraction

Source: Coffee Brewing Center, Publication #40

Table 4

Particle Size and Distribution for Typical Grinds

	Regular	Drip	Fine
Percent on			
#10 mesh	13%	0%	0%
#14 mesh	20%	7%	0%
#20 mesh	25%	33%	10%
#28 mesh	30%	40%	60%
Percent thru			
#28 mesh	12%	20%	30%

Source: Coffee Brewing Center, Publication #118

54

Brewing Equipment

Ten of the variables balancing strength and extraction relate to the brewing equipment. Of these, the equipment manufacturer usually controls six, all involving time, temperature and turbulence.

- *Time of brewing.* The contact time (11)—how long the coffee remains in contact with the water—determines the percentage of solubles yield. The longer the contact time, the greater the extraction of soluble materials. Generally speaking, rapid extraction occurs during the first third of the brewing cycle, yielding as much as 70 percent of the available soluble material.
- *Temperature.* For proper extraction to occur, water must reach the coffee at contact temperatures (12) near 200 degrees F (94 degrees C) and must remain at a constant temperature gradient (13) throughout the entire brewing cycle (See Table 5).
- *Turbulence.* The way the brewer distributes water over the bed of grounds, leading to complete wetting of the coffee (14); the velocity of the water flowing through the coffee bed, creating a uniform flow rate (15); and the bed's size, depth, configuration, and degree of containment, limiting the particle movement (16)—all affect turbulence. The design of the brewer's spray head and brew basket controls turbulence. A successful design results in complete wetting of all the coffee particles in the brew basket, a uniform flow of water through the entire bed of coffee, and a separation of the particles while they are in contact with the water.

Table 5

Effect of Change in Water Temperature on
Beverage Solids and Extraction from Grounds

Temperature (degrees F)	Beverage Solids (as percent)	Grounds Extraction (oz./lb.)
205	1.22	2.85
195	1.30	3.00
185	1.24	2.87
165	1.11	2.58
125	0.98	2.08
85	0.63	1.48

- Urn grind coffee
- Water to coffee ratio at 2.00 gallons per pound
- Time of contact at 3 minutes

Source: Coffee Brewing Center, Publication #40

Control of the four remaining variables related to brewing equipment often falls into the hands of the person preparing the beverage.

- *Filtering method.* The type of filter determines how the finished brew (17) separates from the coffee grounds and the degree of clarification (18)—the extent the brewer removes non-soluble materials as they pass into the holding container. Often, the type of filter establishes the configuration of the brew basket, while the degree of clarification relates directly to the amount and size of brew colloids suspended in the beverage.
- *Holding conditions.* The length of time and method of holding (19) are critical to preserving the coffee's flavor. For best results, serve coffee immediately after brewing or hold it in a sealed thermal container. Coffee stored in a heated open vessel grows stronger as the water evaporates from the brew; it also changes in flavor because the applied heat causes the chemical compounds to change. A holding temperature (20) between 175 and 185 degrees F (80 to 85 degrees C) should be maintained over the holding period for optimum flavor and serving requirements. Important chemical compounds in the coffee are at their most stable in this temperature range. At no time should the temperature drop below 175 degrees F (80 degrees C).

Ingredients

Once the coffee product and brewing equipment are selected, the person preparing the beverage directly controls the final four variables.

- *Brewing formula.* The most important variable related to ingredients is the ratio of coffee (by weight) (21) to water (by volume) (22). The coffee-to-water ratio must be within the range of preferred strength and desired extraction (See Table 6). Too much coffee—or too little water—will result in beverages that have an underdeveloped flavor if brewed at the preferred strength, or too strong a taste if brewed at the desired degree of extraction. Too little coffee—or too much water—will result in beverages that have an over-extracted and often bitter flavor if served at the preferred strength, or too weak a taste if brewed at the desired degree of extraction.

55

Table 6

Effect of Water to Coffee Ratio on Beverage Solids and Extraction From Grounds

Water to Coffee Ratio (gallons per lb.)	Beverage Solids (as percent)	Grounds Extraction (oz./lb. and %)
1.62	1.76	3.35 - 20.9%
2.00	1.22	2.85 - 17.8%
2.35	1.13	3.15 - 19.6%
2.67	1.00	3.20 - 20.0%
3.33	0.79	3.25 - 20.3%
4.00	0.67	3.30 - 20.6%

- Urn grind coffee
- Water temperature at 205 degrees F
- Time of contact at 3 minutes

Source: Coffee Brewing Center, Publication #40

- *Water.* Water contains dissolved minerals that give it taste. These minerals contribute to coffee taste as well. If present in too great an amount, these dissolved inorganic substances will interfere with the brewing process by either restricting the flow of the water through the coffee particles or by preventing soluble material in the coffee from entering the extract. Water may also contain excess concentrations of hydrogen ions or excess concentrations of hydroxide ions that unfavorably alter its chemical properties. Water may also contain organic compounds that give it an unpleasant odor. Water composition (23) is a critical aspect of coffee brewing.

  Water treatment (24) can improve the flavor of coffee by removing unwanted chemicals, such as chlorine. Certain methods of water treatment, however, may also detract from the brew by adding unwanted compounds—such as sodium—that interfere with the brewing process or affect the beverage acidity.

Maintaining Control

To master the craft of coffee brewing, you must control the many variables that contribute to both the strength (intensity) and extraction (acceptability) of coffee's flavor. The skill lies in learning how to control all the variables so that the solubles concentration is balanced with the solubles yield, resulting in the "perfect cup" of coffee that exceeds the consumers' expectations.

Although the possible combinations of the 24 variables are virtually limitless, you can reasonably control the process by adhering to the key principles of good brewing: quality blends, excellent equipment, clean water, and a proper brewing ratio. ●

Mauro Cipolla

Mauro Cipolla is the owner of Caffé D'arte, an award-winning, Seattle-based roaster with an international reputation. Cipolla's apprenticeship in artisan roasting took place in Naples, Italy, under the demanding eye of traditional third-generation Master Artisan roasters. His insight into the art and science of espresso has gained him international recognition and placed him in demand as a speaker at specialty coffee conventions and as a writer for trade magazines worldwide. Caffé D'arte® academy presentations have been recognized by such programs as CBS News, NBC News, the Today Show, and The Charles Kuralt News Show.

59

Caffé D'arte has made a powerful statement in the marketplace regarding the value of traditional knowledge. Although the company is founded on traditional values, Caffé D'arte has recognized the need to incorporate current market trends into its training programs. Art, science and innovation have always been the cornerstones of the company, and, as a result, Caffé D'arte will remain a leader and trendsetter into the year 2000 and beyond.

1-800-999-5334

Chapter 4

**Evaluating Espresso
Extraction:
A Troubleshooting Guide**

Is the specialty coffee industry sacrificing its quality standards? Has the consumer been exposed to a quality dilution in his or her total coffee experience? Are we really as good as we should be at extracting the best and most consistent coffee flavors from our espresso machines and our roasted espresso blends? Can we deliver an ongoing supply of satisfied and loyal customers?

If you can read this chapter without thinking, even once, that these writings are merely theoretical concepts applicable to researchers and authors and not to the barista behind your retail counter, then together as industry professionals we may have a chance to continue building this industry.

Why do we need to place so much focus on the extraction process? Because consumers are becoming more educated, and now we have "qualified demand and supply" (not the reverse, the well-known supply and demand). Our customers understand more about quality coffee delivery. They expect us to improve what we do. They expect baristas to deliver not just an espresso drink, but an extraction process artistically performed, using all the barista's senses in a knowledgeable, detailed and passionate manner.

The first point to understand is that real physical and chemical changes occur in coffees after the extraction process. The good news is that baristas can control these changes. The control parameters can bring either extremely negative or positive results in taste and consistency.

We are all familiar with the cliché that espresso extraction at its best is a combination of art and science. But do we really appreciate and understand what this means? This terminology refers to a balance that suggests while there are scientific realities in the extraction process, we must approach the process with artistic, culinary skills. Our culinary skill should compensate for all the variables in an effort to create a consistent and superior product. It is in this environment that a seemingly simple process of tasting and self-evaluation will go a long way in raising quality standards. We must learn to respect history. We must further learn from espresso traditions that have stood the test of time.

Finally, we are obligated to invest our knowledge as professional specialty coffee retailers and baristas in our fellow workers for a better future for our industry.

You may be successful in the espresso business and believe your extraction methods do not need improving. However, an espresso business that has remained "successful" over a period of years indicates, in all likelihood, that the business uses standard boiler-plate methods that stand in the way of progress. We must avoid following the adage, "if it works, why fix it?" A system can work well enough to survive, and, at the same time, lose competitive advantage in a mature industry.

If you are ready to accept that no matter how many years of experience you have as a specialty coffee retailer or barista, you too can and should still care to improve, start by understanding and accepting the following rules:

1) You must question every element, in detail, through the entire extraction process to prevent or determine the problem(s). *Details grow your skills.*

2) When in the grip of a daily routine, even the best barista can be stumped by seemingly simple challenges. *No one is beyond learning.*

3) Advanced knowledge through continued research will allow us to detect equipment and operator extraction errors. It is important to find the real problems of taste before placing the blame where it may not belong. *Have a plan to keep on researching espresso extraction.*

For proper extraction to occur, the barista must consistently control many variables. This is easier said than done. The variables are many, and, taken singularly, each presents itself as an extremely simple task "that anyone can perform with 'little effort.'"

As we study these variables, we learn how and when to control them. Before we know it, we are immersed in a world full of details that in their singular simplicity can be understood by some and appreciated by most, but in their total delivery can be appreciated and consistently mastered by few.

Controlling Your Tasting Environment

Obviously the environment surrounding each espresso extraction is constantly changing. To achieve consistent delivery of quality beverages, the professional barista should thus "alter" his or her extraction methods to meet the changing demands of this environment.

While the altered variables of a dynamic environment are many, we will focus only on the variables that most often affect espresso extraction. These are: ambient temperature, ambient moisture, direct sunlight, direct and indirect drafts, air reaching the coffee beans, light, and nearby auxiliary equipment.

• *Ambient temperature*

The best time of day to taste coffees for most people is mid-afternoon. It is very important that the environment is not too cold or too hot. A cold environment will have negative effects on the coffee. It tends to diminish the water absorption capabilities of the coffee grounds. This in turn will increase the speed of the water flow, resulting in underextraction. A hot environment makes coffee sweat coffee oils and delivers pungent flavors if not controlled properly. As ambient temperature increases, the roasted coffee beans will respond differently to the espresso extraction process.

The tasting room should be free of strong odors, as they may impart a negative taste and aroma on the coffees and will also affect the olfactory sensations of the tasters.

For best results, people should perform all testing using a preheated portafilter with a double basket and a double pouring spout. The sensitive barista will grind coffee immediately prior to extracting espresso. He or she will run the grinder as little as possible. During warmer ambient temperatures, the barista will set the grind just a touch coarser. The barista should also pack the ground coffee in the portafilter a little firmer and should "cycle" the group head for the proper water temperature a little longer than usual to obtain a lower water temperature for espresso extraction.

(Please remember that the properties of many espresso machines will vary, and the amount of water volume you need to cycle for proper temperatures will also vary. Please refer to the "Becoming One With Your Machine" section of this chapter, page 73).

Finally, the barista should decrease the water volume passing through the coffee grounds during espresso extraction in warmer ambient temperatures.

• Ambient moisture
If not controlled, ambient moisture will greatly affect the quality of the coffee beans. In extreme cases mold could appear, which would change the reaction of the ground coffee beans to the extraction process. When roasted beans have been exposed to excessive ambient moisture, baristas should set the grind coarser and not tamp as firm as usual.

• Direct sunlight
Direct sunlight can be extremely harmful to espresso extraction because it directly affects the temperatures of the roasted beans prior to the extraction process, allowing more oils to sweat out of the beans' cell structure. The beans may also be damaged due to accelerated oxidation and aging processes.

In most cases, roasted beans left exposed to such conditions will deliver irregular and inconsistent extraction, little body, a flat flavor profile, and a more pungent aftertaste.

The best way to prevent this scenario is for professional baristas to act immediately and prevent any such exposure of roasted beans to direct sunlight. This may require the barista to reposition grinders and/or install shade protectors.

• Direct and indirect drafts
The first concern here is the temperatures of the ceramic mugs and espresso and cappuccino cups. The second concern is with the pour of the espresso into the cups.

I have personally tasted immense differences in the flavor profile, body, texture, and aftertaste of espresso beverages prepared by the same operator in the same group head, with an identical source of ground coffee within the same basket, extracted at the same rate, but poured into two different cups stored in two different areas of the room. I've found as much as 10 to 15 degrees F difference in the temperature of ceramic cups due to storage near draft areas.

Drafts can also influence the body and texture of extracted espresso drinks by affecting the pour of the crema just before it drops into the serving cup. When there is enough of a draft to make the pouring crema move laterally, you will experience a direct loss of beverage quality.

The solution here is to pay particular attention to the storage of glass and ceramic cups, and to position equipment in a way that it will be affected as little as possible by direct and indirect drafts.

• Air
Air that reaches roasted coffee initiates oxidation and leads to an old, flat, stale taste and smell. Proper storage will delay the effects of oxidation. Store roasted coffees in an airtight, sealed container for best results.

• Light
Light helps speed up the oxidation process because it forms certain free radicals in roasted coffee. Keep roasted coffee in a dark container that cannot be penetrated by light.

At Caffé D'arte, we simply take the coffee bags (which are made with dark foil film) and open them on the very bottom so the beans will flow directly into the grinder hopper. The foil bag still fully covers the roasted coffee on the inside of the hopper, making sure no light reaches the beans.

Obviously, clear plastic bags that allow light to penetrate are not acceptable.

63

• *Auxiliary equipment*
Are there nearby refrigerators, freezers and the like in your store? Have you asked your-self what this equipment does to the immediate espresso environment as it runs? Does it affect temperature differently at different times of the day? What about ceiling fans?

You may be laughing at this idea by now, but I know a very good barista who after months of detailed research could not understand why his espresso drinks where thin and flat only in the afternoon hours of hot summer days.

In fact, this Seattle barista is used to receiving immaculate extractions from cup to cup, starting from the first cup he makes every morning at 4:30 a.m. when he opens his store. An extraction expert, this detail-oriented barista suddenly started pulling thin, weak and flat espresso shots. He looked, searched and trouble-shot every possible detail that could affect extraction.

Eventually he realized his extraction problem occurred only in the afternoon hours when it was very hot and he was forced to turn on his newly installed ceiling fans. One day he forgot to turn on the ceiling fans, and while he was pouring some fantastic shots, some of his customers reminded him that the shop was getting a bit warm. He turned the ceiling fans on, and within a few minutes he saw a dramatic difference in the pour of his espresso shots. The fans were the problem—not the equipment, not the water, and not the coffee! The fans drastically changed ambient temperature, ambient moisture and drafts within the premises.

Organizing Your Troubleshooting Tools

Now that you have given attention to your espresso environment, we need to make sure you are armed with the proper tools to evaluate and taste your espresso extraction. The proper preliminary tools are of course a clean and properly maintained espresso machine and an espresso grinder. In addition, it's important to purchase espresso machines with basket inserts that are of proper design and detail. This is an important detail because the size, depth and overall circumference of the portafilter baskets will make an immense impact in the extraction process.

The basket height to diameter ratio is of most concern, because a very high basket will require a higher water pressure and a much coarser grind setting. The opposite is true for a height to diameter ratio shorter than proper specifications

The correct size of the double baskets for optimum extraction is 11 to 13 millimeters in height and 59 to 61 millimeters in width.

Should your basket have widely different dimensions, ask your equipment support company about replacing the baskets with other sizes.

Aside from the preliminary tools described above, here are a few "primary" tools: proper lighting, a digital thermometer with a wire probe, a digital scale, a Total Dissolved Solids/Soluble Solids tester, an extraction graph for the aforementioned tester, a neutral palate cleansing element, properly fine-tuned senses, a personal tasting record book, and undisturbed time. Let's look at each and every one of these important troubleshooting tools.

• *Proper lighting*
The tasting room should have good natural light, as this condition will help you reach a more objective conclusion about extraction qualities. This will also favor our predisposi-tion to "taste" foods first with our eyesight and then our taste buds. Light is an essential tool for the evaluation process that people often don't take into account.

For example, proper lighting directed on the espresso can reveal important clues about the crema. Proper lighting directed on the crema extraction point and the top of the serv-ing cup helps analyze the color, shades of colors, texture, density, viscosity, microscopic air and gas content of the crema, and the dissipation rate or persistence of the same. All these elements will tell the expert barista something about the just-performed extraction.

A proper espresso extraction will yield a thick crema (a minimum of 4 to 6 millimeters in depth), showing a very fine and tight molecular structure typified by thousands of fine and well-textured bubbles. Perfect crema will last for quite some time without dissipating or breaking up at the center of the shot. This thick consistency should easily hold up to a couple of teaspoons of sugar.

A pale, light beige crema color is indicative of an under-extracted espresso. And, generally speaking, a dark crema indicates an over-extracted espresso. There are several reasons over-extraction occurs. Perhaps the water temperature is set too high, the water pressure is too strong, the grind is too fine, the barista is running the extraction too long, or the barista is packing too much coffee too tightly into the portafilter.

However, one must remember there are different types of "dark cremas" that occur for very different reasons. For instance, a dark crema with a lighter crema in the center of the cup indicates the barista put a little more coffee into the basket than necessary. A dark crema with a thin, watery, white-looking liquid in the sides or middle of the cup indicates the extraction was too long. A very dark crema with large bubbles reveals the water temperature was too hot. A marble-like crema means the barista tamped with uneven pressure or the grinder disks are becoming dull. Crema that dissipates very fast could indicate pour coffee quality, too fast of a pour, or excessive air in the water delivery. A modestly thick crema that's very dark in color could mean the grind is set too fine and the barista packed the coffee too hard, creating a slow pour.

A thin crema with white highlights and big bubbles means the water temperature is too high. No crema at all could indict the quality of the coffee, the poor working condition of the equipment, the age of the coffee, an over-stuffed portafilter, or improper grinding disks installed in your espresso grinder.

• *Digital thermometer*

Espresso extraction allows for the extraction of water soluble substances and the emulsification of insoluble oils. The extraction of these two elements is directly related to proper water temperature and the equilibrium or consistence of these temperature ranges under different load and demand conditions. These loads are dictated by the varied levels of customer demand in your store.

It is therefore imperative to understand how to set, test and fine-tune your water temperature in three steps:

First, you must set the water temperature with your espresso machine "at rest."

Second, the barista must spend time testing and simulating different levels of customer demand to understand how the particular brand and model of machine will react to different situations. All espresso machine brands and models will differ in their delivery of water temperature, thermic stability and temperature consistency. Most importantly, the barista needs to understand how to operate the machine properly to reach the equilibrium of temperature ranges under different demand cycles.

Observing and recording the data of this simulated test will give the barista enough knowledge to learn how to "cycle" the water through each group head ("cycling" the water means running a certain amount of water freely through the group head). This will help the machine achieve the proper water temperature equilibrium during the extraction process. A barista can also learn how to alternate between different group heads to achieve the same goal.

All retailers should perform this simulated test because some machines deliver a more stable water temperature in demanding environments. Other brands respond just the opposite. If the water is too hot, for instance, some machines will require the barista to cycle 1 or 2 ounces of water through the group head prior to the extraction. Other brands or models may require the barista to cycle as many as 12 ounces of water.

Once the first two steps are completed, the barista needs to implement the third operating step.

The barista must reset and fine-tune the water temperature "at rest" at least once a month. This step is very important because thermostats are vulnerable to normal wear and tear. The professional barista must use the correct thermometer to properly perform the temperature test in the three modes.

The best thermometers are sensitive electronic digital devices that can be calibrated with the highest degree of accuracy. They offer a temperature probe flexible enough to be inserted inside portafilter blind baskets (where operators should record water temperature readings), but strong enough to withstand the pressure of the blind basket as it tightens on the group head gasket. Make sure the temperature probe is easily replaceable, as the need will arise from time to time.

• *Digital scale*
You must consistently apply learned theory to become a master barista. Practice, practice, practice.

A good digital scale is a fundamental tool in evaluating extraction and taste. This is true for both people performing exacting evaluation tests and baristas in the middle of a shift. Make it one of your practiced personal rules to use a scale to check how much coffee you're dosing into the portafilter baskets. Are you accurate and consistent? What can you do to become even more accurate? Try different hand movements to sweep the coffee grounds into the baskets. Change the angle at which you keep your sweeping finger(s). Test the coordination of your eye to your hand's mechanical movements over the coffee grounds. Discover the difference the coffee grind (fine or coarse) makes in your dosage techniques.

A good digital gram scale is a must for the evaluation process and for the evolution of every professional barista.

66

• *The Total Dissolved Solids/Soluble Solids tester*
This readily available instrument is another tool to which every professional barista should have access. It measures both the Total Dissolved Solids in parts per million in the water used for espresso extraction and the percentage of Soluble Solids in the brewed beverage itself.

These two measurements are vital to evaluating the extraction process and taste. The first measurement reveals the levels of specific elements ($NaCl$, $CaCO3$) that contribute to whether your water is hard or soft. The second measurement can be used to calculate the actual percentage of extraction (low, medium or high) of the final brewed beverage.

To calculate the extraction percentage, take the instrument's probe, dip it into the finished espresso beverage for a total of 15 seconds, and record the number on the instrument's extraction grid as the "percent solids in the solution." Use that number in conjunction with an extraction graph—which has a "percent solids in the solution" line and a "percent of extraction" line—to draw intersecting lines on the graph. That's your extraction percentage.

The interesting fact is that this tool can greatly enhance the learning curve of any barista by allowing him or her to taste espressos at differing levels of extraction (low, medium and high) while noting the aromatic, visual and taste variations from cup to cup.

• *Neutral palate cleansing elements*
The palate must be able to distinguish among different elements and characters of flavor during the evaluation process.

The most important point to remember here is to limit the number of samples tested. Most people simply attempt to taste too many coffee or espresso samples and are unable to properly perform the tasting evaluation.

Second, please remember that having a clean crisp palate to start with (free from excessive flavors, cigarette smoke, spicy foods, onions, mustard, gum, sweet desserts, strong mints, toothpaste, etc.) is of immense importance if you want to discern between the subtle flavors of different coffees.

Finally, please make sure to consume some kind of neutral cleanser between each sample. Examples of a neutral cleanser include water, unsalted bread or apples.

• *Properly fine-tuned senses*

Prior to tasting espresso samples, make sure your senses are working properly.

Illnesses such as the flu, allergies or other viruses may alter your sensory tools. Your nose must be able to detect aromas properly.

Your hands should be free from lotions, perfumes and odors that can affect the coffee beans, the coffee grounds and/or the serving cups.

Your eyes should view all the controlling variables prior to, during and after the extraction. Watch such variables as lighting, types of serving cups used, the conditions of the beans prior to grinding, the actual pour of the espresso, and the important spent coffee cake after extraction.

Train your ears to listen for problems. How does the grinder sound? Does it sound crisp or flat? Do you hear any metals or rocks running through the grinder disks? Does the grinder make a different sound when the hopper is full of beans vs. when it is partially full of beans? Does that affect the grind quality? How does the water pump sound? The water pressure? How crisp is the sound of the solenoid valves when you open and close the group head?

• *Historical tasting record book*

Whenever you perform a taste evaluation, construct and keep a data record. This historical data will offer insight that, when reviewed and studied, will help your professional skills evolve.

The type of data recorded and reviewed is subjective and varies among individuals.

Following is the data I have chosen to record for my personal tasting records over the years:

- Conditions of the tasting environment.
- Availability, condition and accuracy of troubleshooting tools.
- Roasting date of beans, physical appearance of beans, feel and aroma of roasted beans.
- Optical roasting degree of the sample to be tasted.
- Caramelization percentage achieved during the roasting process; density and moisture of the roasted beans. (Equipment that tests for these two variables is available but expensive.)
- Known storage conditions of roasted beans.
- Espresso grinder conditions and cutting disk conditions.
- Quality of water flowing from the group heads of my espresso machine.
- Quality of water flowing from the Americano tap of my machine (if the Americano tap is drawing water from the boiler and not from the heat exchanger).
- Cleanliness of the espresso machine components and utensils.
- Water pump working conditions and water pressure delivery. (The ideal pump pressure setting is between 8 and 10 bars on the pressure gauge. The exact setting point will vary depending on the equipment brand and model and the brand and blend of coffee used.)
- Water temperature and control over equilibrium. (The ideal water temperature is between 193 and 197 degrees F. The exact temperature setting will vary depending on the equipment brand and model and the brand and blend of coffee used.)
- Thermic stability.
- Optical and physical test of the grind (size, evenness and quality).
- Amount of coffee grounds used for the extraction process, in grams. (The ideal for a single espresso is 7 to 8 grams.)

- Packing of the coffee grounds (pack pressure, number of times packed, and angle or slope of packing).
- Time spent placing coffee grounds in the portafilter basket, packing them and fitting the portafilter into the group head for extraction.
- Elapsed time between when the barista secures the portafilter in the group head and the moment water first hits the coffee grounds.
- Flow, color, depth, and density of pour (continuous, intermittent or pulsating flow?).
- Pre-infusion timing. (The time passed between opening the group head solenoid valve and the first drop of espresso appearing. The ideal pre-infusion time is three to five seconds.)
- Timing of complete pour. (The ideal pour is 25 to 30 seconds, including pre-infusion time.)
- Timing of complete pour vs. water volume achieved. (The ideal ratio of time to volume is 25 to 30 seconds per each espresso of 3/4 of total liquid volume.)
- Quality and stability of crema.
- Viscosity of crema (as represented by the extraction of the oils in emulsion).
- Density, depth and body of the crema (as delivered by the differences in the solids content of each extracted espresso).
- Results of sugar test. (I always place 2 teaspoons of sugar in one of the two single espresso cups just poured to test the time it takes sugar to float to the top of the crema.)
- Evaluation of the espresso's aroma, taste, character, and aftertaste.
- The condition of the spent coffee cake after extraction. (Porosity? Water coverage? Color and feel of grounds? Soft vs. hard? Does the cake fall apart or stick together after being dumped from the portafilter? Cake shape? Cake size and depth?)
- Condition of the broken cross section of the coffee cake after extraction. (Individual water channels of extraction vs. a more complete vertical extraction? Uniformity of the moisture content and color of the spent coffee grounds?)

You will need to record the above variables as a total system, over and over, until the evaluation process includes all the variables automatically. These variables will become part of the chronological taste and evaluation process.

• *Undisturbed focus time*
You need to allocate time for a proper tasting so you don't rush through the process.

The only way to perform a proper evaluation that will truly improve your barista skills is to make it a consistent and ongoing process. Most importantly, you have to do it alone, without interruptions, so you can completely focus, pay attention to details, and enjoy the process.

The Eight Most Important Variables of Extraction: A Detailed Look
Let us now discuss in-depth the eight most important variables of evaluating espresso extraction and taste.
1. Water: a big variable of coffee taste.
2. The greatest barista misconceptions of roasted coffees.
3. Understanding why different coffee brands and blends react differently to the extraction process.
4. Coffee storage considerations.
5. The art of grinding beyond the push of a button.
6. Extraction beyond the basics: becoming one with your machine.
7. The hidden dangers of *latté art*.
8. The importance of having a troubleshooting system or standard for all employees to follow consistently.

1. Water: a big variable of coffee taste

The quality of water will affect coffee taste, odor and color due to chemicals present in the water (nonvolatile and inorganic) and inorganic physical characteristics in each water's unique character. These characteristics are created by its turbidity, color, hardness, specific conductivity, and percentage of total dissolved solids.

Certain odor-producing chemicals present in some water may impart an odor through the actual extraction. This is because the chemicals are retained by equipment and other items used to serve customers.

Sodium chloride, manganese and iron, for instance, may make coffee taste bitter. Zinc and copper may offer a metallic taste, and sulfate will impart a medicinal bitter taste. The turbidity of the water, organic chemicals and organic matter in the water may affect the color of the coffee. Dissolved gases, minerals, chemicals, and household and industrial waste may affect the odor.

Water can alter the taste of coffee in many ways. How do you ensure you have good quality water for proper extraction? The answer is found in a chemical analysis of your water supply.

If you have Total Dissolved Solids over 300 parts per million, pH levels over nine, calcium and magnesium levels over 100 parts per million, sodium and potassium levels over 50 parts per million, and a total hardness over 150 parts per million, your water needs a filtering system appropriate for your individual needs. Should the results indicate you need to treat your water supply, make sure you find the proper treatment system (i.e. mineral softener, carbon filter, activated carbon, chemical softener, etc.) and that the system has enough capacity to satisfy your water volume needs. Make sure you replace the filter routinely and clean it at the intervals specified by the supplier.

If you use a water softener, make sure you don't soften the water too much, as excessive softening produces darker coffees in color but extracts only slightly more soluble solids. This over-extracts the coffee oils resulting in a loss of aroma and a bitter taste.

Don't forget to treat hot water within the boilers of coffee and espresso equipment as well. Scaling, liming and related deposits inside the boiler can harm the equipment and the taste of the brewed coffee. You can prevent this problem by combining polyphosphate treatments with the maintenance and cleaning intervals required for your boiler and brewing equipment.

2. The greatest barista misconceptions of roasted coffees

The flavor profile of coffee is directly related to the color of the bean's surface.

This is a misconception because we must differentiate between the "mechanical" chemistry of the bean and the "soluble" chemistry of the bean. While the first may relate directly to the color of beans (relative to appearance), the second doesn't correlate at all to the color, as it will depend on many more factors. The chemistry that produces pigmentation is separate and not related to the soluble chemistry developed in the roasting process.

Microclimates, agriculture and topology are the most important elements that control and direct the make-up of coffee constituents and their resulting flavors.

Not true. While minerals, for instance, appear in coffee from the above-mentioned variables, the 847 constituents in coffees (coffee is very complex; wine, by comparison, has only 257 constituents) are inherited from the coffee's genetics, which in turn control the soluble chemistry developed during roasting. We all need to be more aware that the marketing of coffee origins, varietals and estate coffees sometimes plays a much bigger role than the truth.

The prettier and bigger the coffee beans are after roasting, the better the brewed coffee will taste.

Absolutely not true. Correlating the look, size and shape of coffee beans to the end taste is simply a selling technique. The mechanical chemistry has nothing at all to do with the soluble chemistry that produces flavor and all of its attributes.

Lighter-roasted coffees deliver a higher caffeine content. And the more caffeine in a roasted coffee, the more bitter the coffee will be.

This common statement probably isn't true because caffeine is only responsible for eight to 10 percent of the bitterness found in a typical coffee beverage. In all reality, caffeine may be more responsible for delivering body, depth and strength to a cup of coffee than bitterness.

Darker roasts tame the acidity of coffees that may be excessive and unpleasant in some cases.

This statement is only partially correct. The roasting process does in fact reduce some of the acids found in coffees, but at the same time it increases other acids. The point is there are many types and kinds of acids in coffees, and the acidity found in a cup of coffee is a result of all these acids coming together during the roasting process.

The great aroma of coffee comes from the quality of green coffees and their freshness.

Absolutely false. The aroma is due to the formation and degradation of the 700 volatile aromatic compounds that have been identified in coffee. It is thus the marriage of different coffee roasting techniques (roasting time, temperature, etc.) that unleashes the mechanisms that create coffee aromas.

Darker beans have more oils on the surface due to higher roasting temperatures, and therefore the brewed coffee tastes richer.

This is another common misconception. It is true that the darker the roasted coffee, the more oils will be on the surface, but this phenomenon is not related to temperature. Rather it relates more directly to roasting time. The longer the coffee beans are exposed to heat, the more the oils will separate from the beans and the higher the internal hydraulic pressure. A rich taste is, of course, linked to many more elements than the roasting degree. In actuality, most darker-roasted coffees deliver less complex flavors and less rich taste profiles than lighter roasted coffees.

Lighter-roasted coffees will taste smoother (not as sharp as darker-roasted coffees) and will deliver an immense amount of crema, which is really the key to the best flavor.

70

Lighter-roasted coffees will most definitely produce an immense amount of crema. This is probably the first and most elementary concept learned by any novice roaster. However, just because an espresso delivers a shot glass full of crema does not mean it tastes good.

I have tasted some light-roasted espressos that deliver an immense amount of crema but are undrinkable due to extreme acidity, pungency and astringency. Remember that a complete balance of flavors does not usually come from any one given variable. Simply roasting a coffee light to achieve great amounts of crema may make it look good, but it doesn't guarantee flavor.

Some espresso blends have a higher yield of cups per pound, allowing the barista to use less coffee per shot.

While it is true you can achieve a higher per pound cup count by dosing less coffee into the portafilter basket, it is absolutely not true that you will extract a similar quality espresso. This will not deliver more total soluble solids or flavor components. You may achieve more quantity, but at the expense of quality—no matter what coffee you use. Never follow this path.

3. Understanding why different coffee brands and blends react differently to the extraction process

The complexities and characteristics of each coffee bean varies greatly. This variety is a gift from nature.

1) The origins, variations in botanical species, topology, climatic conditions, harvesting, picking, and selection methods all make an enormous difference in the character of the green product. The moisture content, size, shape, density, color, odor, and taste all contribute in different ways to the resulting coffee blend.

2) The roasting process greatly personalizes each roaster's coffee blend. Characteristics

are affixed to the coffee's taste and personality by the roasting equipment and how that equipment is used. Time, temperature and airflow all play an important role in either creating or destroying volatile and aromatic water soluble elements that will become the foundation of each blend. A darker-roasted coffee will, for instance, contain less fiber, and thus will deliver less viscosity and body in the cup. It will also feature less complex flavors and a less dense cup due to a greater loss of organic components.

But a darker-roasted coffee will also deliver a silkier, smoother texture and overall feeling because there will be less chlorogenic acids present after roasting. This coffee will also allow the barista to extract more flavor because of the existence of additional dissolving properties.

3) The blend is the signature recipe of each roaster, and is designed to deliver an orchestra of flavors built upon the different characteristics of each coffee varietal.

It is thus the combination of nature and the "travels" of coffee—as expressed by the roaster's choice of green coffee ingredients and his or her personal roasting and blending techniques—that deliver a vast selection of brands and blends.

We can only achieve the proper realization of flavor potential by adjusting our espresso extraction techniques to best fit each unique espresso blend.

4. Coffee storage considerations

Storage alters the nature of all foods by restructuring both chemical and physical compositions.

In the case of coffee, we are mostly concerned with chemical alterations. These can have direct and measurable effects on the volatile aromatic oils of coffees, which are easily destroyed through improper storage.

A roaster must retain the fragrances produced during the roasting process—which originate from the release of pre-existing volatile compounds—to maximize the resulting flavor components.

What coffee enemies do you need to fight through proper storage?

The enemies of coffee are water or moisture, oxygen, foreign odors, light, and temperature. Let's take each one of these and analyze the dangers they represent and how we may protect our favored coffees from their attacks:

• Water/moisture

Roasted coffees typically have a water content of one to two percent. If moisture levels are not kept below 3.5 to four percent, stale smells and flavors will develop. The coffee will age quicker than normal, resulting in a short shelf life for a very bad tasting coffee.

High moisture levels can also cause irregular extractions due to coffee molecules that "stick" together. In extreme cases—such as when the relative humidity exceeds 60 percent—water content within the beans may grow exponentially. The beans may spoil or mold. It is thus extremely important not to store coffees in the freezer or refrigerator. The moisture introduced by the freezer will crystallize and separate water from the other constituents. This will start "seeded oxidation," which in turn will promote stale and aged coffee.

The refrigerator, on the other hand, causes condensation that will increase the moisture levels to three to four percent. Those levels, as noted, are to be avoided. The best solution is not to put coffee in the freezer and refrigerator, thus allowing for a more natural decomposition. This will help develop the proper flavor curve. This "natural" method will also assure more consistency throughout the brewing and extraction processes.

• Oxygen

Oxidation will introduce a loss of aroma and flavor, staleness, and, in the long run, rancidity. Fresh-roasted coffees have a "natural" barrier to oxidation in the form of carbon dioxide formations.

71

Carbon dioxide is a by-product of the decomposition of all organic matter, and as such it is also found in fresh-roasted coffees as a natural gas. This gas is heavier than air, and while living inside the coffee bean, it fights the intrusion of atmospheric oxygen by providing greater positive pressure than the incoming air.

Owning a life cycle of its own, carbon dioxide will eventually stop releasing, and will then start a negative pressure process. It is during this stage that carbon dioxide welcomes not only air but many of the atmospheric gases that can harm the flavors of all coffees.

It is therefore imperative to store coffees in an airtight package after opening the original packaging. Tin and aluminum containers with gaskets meet the airtight requirements, but their metallurgic qualities will negatively impact coffees by acting as "oxidation chemical reactors."

Glass containers with gaskets don't allow oxidation, but they will harm coffees by allowing light to penetrate.

 The best solution is to store coffee in oven-baked, high-gloss-sealed ceramic containers, complete with gaskets and tie-down clamps. These will slow down oxidation and keep light out.

• Foreign odors
The porous structure of a coffee bean's cell walls—combined with the negative decomposition of carbon dioxide and the absorbing qualities of fatty substances found in the coffee oils—frequently allow foreign odors to penetrate and saturate the interior linings.

This exterior contamination will alter aromas and flavors greatly.

The best solution to this problem is to pay particular attention to the items you place near the coffee beans while brewing. Also store them according to the procedures described above.

• Light
Allowing light to shine directly on coffee will create "self-oxidative" reactions. Light rays will trigger these reactions and cause rapid exponential oxidation.

Once again the best solution is to follow the storage procedures described above.

• Temperature
Temperatures above 80 degrees F will greatly harm any coffee by degrading the carbohydrates, oils and sugars of the coffee beans. The beans' pores will be forced open, hydraulic pressure within the bean structure will increase, and immense amounts of oil migration will occur very fast. The coffee will age and turn rancid very quickly, resulting in a poor taste.

The best solution is to store coffee in an environment that ranges between 50 and 65 degrees F. Storing coffee at a stable temperature helps solve the problem.

In conclusion, be proactive by properly storing your coffees. Also remember that no matter what form of packaging your coffee is shipped in (or the storage method you use upon receipt), your customers should consume all coffees within two to three weeks of their original roasting date, even if your favorite roaster claims a longer shelf life.

5. The art of grinding beyond the push of a button
The reason you grind coffee is to increase the extraction surface of the coffee "bed" so that hot water can easily extract essences of flavor and aroma from the grounds. There is thus a direct and important relationship between the need to expose the extraction surface to hot water and—just as important for proper brewing—the rate the hot water flows through the extraction bed.

The specialty coffee community has spoken of "a fine espresso grind" for a long time, but it has placed no emphasis on the condition of the grinding components and of the actual mechanical grinding process needed to achieve this "fine espresso grind."

The reality is that most retailers simply look for "a fine espresso grind" and forget to check and maintain their grinder's mechanical components. Retailers must service these components frequently to properly grind these coffee beans. If the equipment isn't serviced, the beverage quality suffers immediately and the all-too-common results are "fine espresso grinds" with *uneven* and *inconsistent* grind particles. This situation will yield an uneven extraction that will in turn offer an unfavorable appearance, quality and taste.

It is thus of extreme importance to realize you need to grind coffee *evenly and consistently through the mechanical process of crushing and shaving.* In fact, because the geometric and cellular structure of coffee is varied and not homogeneous, the need for a fine-tuned and properly maintained grinder is an imminent reality.

The grinder must achieve a true "consistent shaved quality" through two steps: The grinder must *crush* the cellular structure of the bean into smaller fragments of 1 to 2 millimeters in size (which allows the water to flow properly through the extraction bed), and it must *shave* finer particles off the already crushed larger grind fragments. This *shaving* will allow the water to properly interact with the soluble/emulsifiable substances. This complete *crushing* and *shaving* process must be in place to yield the very best in coffee and espresso extraction. And this can only be accomplished with clean grinding disks that are in proper cutting shape.

You must inspect your grinding disks as often as possible for nicks on the sides of the cutting edges, irregularities, and dull or flattened cutting edges. You must immediately replace grinding disks with any such irregularities, regardless of the disks' age.

Retailers should also inspect the axle that turns the lower cutting disk of most professional grinders. This axle must achieve a level of 900 to 1200 rotations per minute. It must do so with a fluid, consistent and balanced movement. It is thus very important to check the rotating motion of the axle from time to time and to look for inconsistencies. Also check the axle's bearings and lubrication. It's also advisable to clean the axle's housing to free adjoining components from coffee grounds. Finally, the grinder's power supply must be of proper voltage and connected to a surge protector.

The last three areas of concern for proper grinder maintenance are: the hopper itself, which a retailer must wash and dry every week to eliminate oil and bacteria buildups; the magnet, which must be aligned at all times to attract damaging metal debris—present in all coffee blends—that could harm your grinder's disks; and the threaded components that hold the housing for grind adjustment, which a retailer must brush free of coffee grounds and heated oils that could easily "weld" the grind adjustment wheel in a single position forever.

6. Extraction beyond the basics: becoming one with your machine

It's great to master all the variables we've discussed so far, but to truly extract quality espresso time and again while a line of 10 customers stretches out the door, you've got to become one with your machine and grinder.

You must practice with your equipment behind closed doors, undisturbed. You must learn all you can about your equipment's thermic stability, thermic recovery and reactions to different demand loads.

Learn how to marry all your senses to the individual characteristics of your equipment, and to go beyond the basics of extraction. Lastly, you must practice, practice, practice. All techniques must become second nature!

7. The hidden dangers of latté art

Latté art has forged a predominant role in the imaginative expression of specialty espresso drinks.

The visual characters are beautiful and the art is very expressive. The milk is smooth and textured, and the barista can potentially develop and blend the flavors of the underlining coffees into the milk.

All of the above is absolutely fantastic for our industry, but only if the barista still focuses on delivering the highest quality espresso to beautifully complement the latté art.

Unfortunately, I have witnessed many baristas who place so much focus on the steaming and pouring of the milk for the purpose of creating latté art that they compromise the quality of their espresso. Ultimately, the beverage will suffer.

Latté art should remain a wonderful addition to the art of extracting, not a substitution for it.

8. The importance of having a troubleshooting system or standard for all employees to follow consistently.

In order to efficiently and successfully troubleshoot espresso extraction, we must follow a simple investigative plan. We must also implement a system that all baristas can easily apply.

But before we can construct any such system, we must decide which elements are relevant to our troubleshooting needs.

To achieve this, I have built a user-friendly checklist that will simplify our troubleshooting needs.

Relevant Input to Investigate

Equipment: Espresso Machine
Mechanical conditions
Does the pump not work?
Does water just trickle out of the group heads?
Does it not come out at all?
Are baskets cracked or indented?
Does the Americano tap not work?
Do you not have steam?
Is the water level in the boiler sight glass below the minimum line?
Is it above the maximum line?

Mechanical fine-tuning
Does the pump read below nine when activated?
Does it read over 10?
Does it sound weird?
Is the water temperature in the group head below 190?
Is it over 200?
Does water leak out around the sides of the portafilter gasket?
Do you hear any rattling, water-leaking or steam-leaking sounds when the pump is activated?

Regular maintenance
Do group screens look bent, broken or worn?
Do group screens not want to come out of the group head?
Do group gaskets feel hard?
Do portafilter flanges look worn?
Do the portafilter baskets look worn?

Regular cleaning
Do baskets, screens and portafilters look and smell dirty?
Does the water spreader look dirty?
Does the group head look dirty?

Espresso Grinder
Mechanical conditions
Do the grinder's cutting disks sound like they're touching when rotating?
Do they feel like they are stuck and not rotating?
Does the grinder's grind adjustment not turn?
Does it not regulate the grind when you act upon it?

Regular maintenance
Does the grind quality not look and feel uniform?
Does the grinder feel warm in temperature?
Is there a large variation in grind particle size between one adjustment notch/number
   and the next one?
Has it been longer than six to eight months since you last replaced your cutting disks?

Regular cleaning
Does the hopper have oily buildup?
Is there oily buildup in the area where the cutting disks are housed?
Has it been longer than two months since you last cleaned the grinding disks and the
   threads of the adjustment rotator?

Operator: The Barista
Fresh grinding
Are you not fresh grinding for each cup?

Proper dosage
Do you have more than 8 grams of coffee grounds per each single in the basket?
Do you have less than 7 grams?

Proper packing
Are you packing at a slanted angle?
Are you packing too softly?
Are you taking more than 15 to 20 seconds to dose and pack?
Are you packing inconsistently?

Proper temperature "cycling"
Did you forget to cycle your espresso machine's group head for temperature
   stabilization? (Remember that cycling group heads is essential, as it makes up for the
   engineering design of your particular espresso machine brand and model.)

Proper timing
Are you waiting to place the filled and packed portafilter into the group head?
Are you waiting to initiate the water irrigation over the basket?

Pre-infusion timing
Do you have less than three seconds of pre-infusion to the first drop of espresso?
Do you have more than four seconds?

Infusion timing
Do you have less or more than 3/4 to 1 ounce of espresso liquid in the cup (for a
   single) before your extraction has reached 25 seconds?

Do you have less or more than 3/4 to 1 ounce liquid level after your extraction has reached 30 seconds?

Do the coffee grounds look and/or feel too coarse or too fine?

Spent grounds in basket
Do the spent grounds look like they got "wet" unevenly from the water?
Do they feel spongy?
Do they show a screen imprint?
Do they smell funny?
Do they smell burned?

The environment
Is it a very hot or very cold day?
Is it a humid day?
Are there air currents in your environment (draft, fans)?
Are the temperature and humidity conditions changing a lot today?

Product: Coffee beans
Roasting date
Is the date on the bag older than two weeks?

Appearance of beans
Do beans look extremely oily?
Do they look scorched?
Are they much lighter or much darker than usual?

Aroma of beans
Is it strange, offensive or off?
Is it a burned smell?
Is it different than usual?
Is it flat?

Storage of beans
Are beans stored in cold environments?
Warm or hot?
Moist or humid?
Are they exposed to light, sun, air, or strong odors?

Water
Water quality
Does the water look cloudy, tinted or hazy?
Does it smell or taste funny when hot?
Does it smell or taste funny when it cools down?

Milk
Milk quality
Is it past the date on the carton?
Have you stored it improperly?
Does it smell or taste funny?

How to Use This Troubleshooting Checklist

Starting from the top of the checklist, if you answered *yes* to any of the questions, make note of it and do not continue until you have turned that *yes* into a *no*!

It is only by fixing these problems in a chronological order (as listed in the checklist) that we can begin to troubleshoot properly and answer our questions.

This system will not only find problems, but it will evolve the barista's skills. He or she will deliver quality and consistency at each encounter, and you will build on your successful long-lasting business relationships.

The physical product and its tangible quality can only be fully realized when it is married with a passion for details and thorough troubleshooting systems. The goal is to clearly amplify the consumer's ability to appreciate the specialty coffee experience in its full potential. Professional growth requires modesty and a humble attitude. This kind of disciplined professionalism takes a part-time job and gives it feeling, ownership, pride, and quality that can last for years.

There is a vast difference between having a job where one performs the basic routine duties of espresso extraction and a job where one's passion, care and commitment deliver the coffee experience at its very best.

Continued research, self-evaluation, hard work, on-the-job training, and education that never ends is the required fuel to achieve and enjoy a professional barista position in today's specialty coffee industry. This industry has grown and found its place in our communities and lives, but it still needs to act more mature, more professional and more dedicated to its final consumers if it wants to find a prominent place in the supply chain of "premium products." And believe me, most final consumers view specialty coffee as a "premium product" every time they pay you and I for an espresso-based drink! We have the luxury to provide great products for generations. Let us give our final end users what they deserve. They are worth it!　●

Kevin Knox

Kevin Knox is senior vice president and coffee buyer for Allegro Coffee in Boulder, Colo. He has worked at the highest levels of the specialty coffee trade during the past 20 years, specializing in roasting, coffee evaluation, training, and writing educational marketing materials. Knox is a frequent contributor to coffee trade journals and co-author (with Julie Sheldon Huffaker) of the reference book *Coffee Basics* (New York, Wiley & Sons, 1997).

79

Chapter 5

What to Look for in a Coffee Supplier

While this chapter is targeted towards retailers searching for wholesale coffee suppliers, many of the suggestions here are also applicable to people contemplating roasting their own coffee.

Becoming an Educated Buyer

What sort of coffee business do you want to be in? Espresso-based milk drinks are all the rage these days, but without a background in whole-bean coffee and brewing basics, it's easy for a specialty coffee retail store—which should represent the pinnacle of coffee brewing—to turn into just another fast food business. For most people I know, the key to staying inspired by the coffee business is to combine the appreciation of the people and lands that grow coffee with a connection to coffee flavors via such classic brewing methods as the French press and vacuum pot. Beyond divine inspiration, it's virtually impossible to make intelligent choices in coffee or equipment without first grounding yourself in coffee origins and a program of regular formal coffee tastings. If you're a newcomer to the business, the first steps I'd recommend are to join the Specialty Coffee Association of America (SCAA) and to attend its annual conference, then register for every seminar you can find. Second, I'd avail myself of several of the classic introductory texts, such as Kenneth Davids' two classics *Coffee: Buying, Brewing & Enjoying* and *Espresso: Ultimate Coffee*. These experiences will help enable you to make the evaluations outlined below.

Experience, Expertise and Passion

When evaluating suppliers, the first thing to look for is knowledge and experience conjoined with a genuine passion for the product. The people who actually buy and roast—notice I did not say "sell and market"—must treat coffee quality with reverence. Newer entrants to the world of coffee roasting usually have little or no background in evaluating the quality of the green coffees they buy, and often depend on their suppliers for quality control. This is the equivalent of letting wolves guard your sheep. Process control during roasting and packaging at such microroasters is also often seat-of-the-pants, leading to highly variable quality and freshness.

At the other end of the spectrum, coffee buyers for huge corporations that have every process control and buying tool imaginable at their disposal typically suffer from "quality paranoia." They typically make price the first and last consideration in sourcing, which precludes them from buying the really great coffees.

Avoiding these extremes, I suggest looking for companies that employ buyers who have at least five years hands-on tasting and roasting experience, an obvious passion for quality, and a commitment to consistently improving their products and processes. Pay attention to what your prospective suppliers say. If they talk about product rather than price, proximity or marketing "support," take that as a very good sign. If they take more pride in their training (of both their own employees and customers) than their brochures, you're probably in the right place.

Once you've honed your list of potential suppliers to a workable handful, you should arrange a personal visit—if at all possible—including a formal tasting (called "cupping") with the coffee buyer or master roaster. Look for roasting logs in the roasting room, consistent use of an Agtron roast color analyzer, and above all roasters who taste the coffees they're roasting and are eager to explain why a particular bean is roasted a specific way.

Take a look at the total menu of coffee offerings from various roasters as well, for it reveals a great deal about their goals and competencies. Is there variety in roast color and blends, or a monotone "one roast fits all" approach? How much emphasis is there on farm-designated or "estate" coffees versus proprietary blends (the latter being, of course, available only from that roaster)? Does the company claim to roast a custom blend for each and every customer? Because there are relatively few great coffee blends possible, this would mean the company is willing to sacrifice product quality in pursuit of a naive notion of good customer service.

Another telling test is the emphasis the company puts on the "unholy trinity" of Kona, Jamaican Blue Mountain and flavored coffees—the three products that sell in inverse proportion to the sophistication level of the consumer. A catalog that contains half flavored coffees, for example, is a sign that a roaster is pandering to a market rather than educating it.

How much emphasis does the company place on espresso blends, and are such blends formulated and tested by individuals with a real knowledge of and passion for the special requirements of this demanding brewing method? The proof is in the cup here, so make sure to do separate tastings of espresso and espresso-based beverages. Ideally, both the roastmaster and the sales and machinery service personnel will exhibit not only a love for coffee but a keen knowledge of the variables—from bean and roast to machine and training techniques—that are required to yield consistent excellence in the real world of retail. Flawlessly maintained machinery and well-trained baristas account for most of the quality of the finished cup, so make sure your supplier's capabilities go well beyond supplying fresh-roasted beans.

Partnership

Many times partnership in business is thought of as a form of back-scratching, where one's loyalty and volume is rewarded with special pricing, help with advertising, and so on. In specialty coffee, a genuine partnership between supplier and retailer is instead dependent on the ability of the roaster to help the retailer deliver the consistent excellence—cup by cup and pound by pound—that will keep the customer coming back for more.

Coffee is judged only as a beverage. To put it another way, as a coffee vendor, you're only as good as your last cup. In evaluating suppliers, take a good hard look at how much they know (or care) about water quality and filtration (98 percent of every cup of coffee is water). Do they know the difference between (and own) roller mill grinders for drip coffee and plate or "burr" grinders for espresso? What criteria do they use in selecting the drip brewing and espresso equipment they recommend? Do they view airpots as a "license to stale," or do they instead supply timers for every pot of brewed coffee their customers sell? What kind of training programs do they offer? How much understanding do they have of espresso bar design, menus and margins? Who staffs their service department, and what does the supplier offer in the way of preventive maintenance and emergency service? Most important of all, is their commitment to customer service commensurate with their passion for coffee quality? To find out, ask prospective suppliers for contacts among their current customers, and then ask the customers about the level of service they've received.

Freshness

While your nearest local roaster would have you believe freshness is a matter of proximity, it's really dependent on understanding the science involved and adhering strictly to procedures. Once roasted, whole-bean coffee exposed to air retains optimum flavor for only about two weeks. "Exposed to air" could mean a wide range of possibilities: open bins, plastic bags, stand-up pouches, even one-way valve bags that a roaster merely heat-sealed without removing the oxygen via vacuum or flushing the inert gas. One-way valve bag technology, rigorously applied, can extend a coffee's roaster-fresh shelf life from two weeks to perhaps three months, but no form of packaging eliminates the responsibility of the roaster (as well as the retailer) to be acutely aware of coffee's perishable nature at every stage.

Visit prospective suppliers, looking at cleanliness, order and quality control procedures. Ask questions! And remember that for great coffee, shelf life and freshness standards are based on comparing packaged coffee with beans right out of the roaster. In other words, the standard is excellence, not "consumer acceptance" (what one might be able to get away with). Also take a look at how prospective suppliers handle ground coffee, which without special packaging is stale in a matter of hours. Taste and compare, and pay attention to the quality of the coffee you are served.

Price vs. Value

The reality of the pricing structure in the coffee business—as in so many other retail endeavors—is that the last person in the supply chain, in this case the retailer or restaurant owner, has by far the best profit margins of anyone involved in the process. This isn't to say retailers don't need or deserve their margins; with the labor and real estate costs they face, most would argue they need every penny. But with gross profit on whole-bean coffees typically running 80 to 100 percent—and several times that for espresso drinks—there is a great deal of elasticity available to the retailer that coffee growers or roasters can only envy.

Green coffee follows the same sorts of rules as grapes for great wine and other similar foodstuffs, which is to say there is not a linear relationship between price and flavor. Some mediocre coffees (such as Kona and Jamaican Blue Mountain) are costly because of rarity and hype; some great coffees (e.g. estate Papua New Guinea or Yemen Mocha) are only moderately expensive because they are known mostly to the trade and not consumers. Finding coffees that deliver maximum pleasure per pound—value—depends on tasting expertise backed by a product-driven company culture.

For retailers or restaurants planning on being in coffee for the long term, they need to source not the lowest price but the best possible value from their suppliers. Suppliers must be able to supply the ideal coffee for the intended purpose, and that includes offering the comprehensive educational and marketing tools needed to educate staff and consumers about the special features of a product. On the retail side, this means the operator knows something about the farm on which the beans were grown; on the beverage side, it means the supplier helps ensure that everyone who operates a coffee-making device

83

does so with a thorough understanding of the requirements of brewing a great cup. Ultimately, the supplier who demonstrates a dedication to the process of delivering great coffee rather than obsessing over the price of a given blend is going to be a far better partner in profitability.

Taking the Business Personally

In my experience, success in coffee depends on combining a personal appreciation of the people who produce and drink it with a loving embrace of all the details it takes to achieve consistently delicious coffee every day. Coffee is an art form and social stimulant, a sensual pleasure and a means to tour the world vicariously. It's a virtual public utility for those who love it—easy to take for granted yet difficult to appreciate fully.

The model for this approach to coffee—which is so much more than business—is the classic Italian espresso bar, which even today is likely staffed mostly by its owners. I mention this example because I think it represents hope to independent entrepreneurs here in North America, who can sometimes feel glum at their prospects due to the pervasive influence of a handful of national corporate coffee chains. Formidable as these large chains are, by their very ubiquitousness and impersonality they create a hunger in the marketplace for the handmade and the personal. And in coffee, as in any other part of the food world, true artistry and excellence are largely the domain of the human-scale, entrepreneurial business person. Great coffee bars and stores reflect the passion and vision of their owners and tend to be successful precisely because they embody values that go far beyond dollars and cents. Ultimately, the right supplier is the one who can be most helpful in making your own unique vision real. ●

Chuck Jones

Chuck Jones' passion for coffee stems from his family's 140-year-old coffee plantation in the highlands of Guatemala. Although Jones was born and raised in Pasadena, Calif., he spends much of his time in Guatemala. Upon completion of his studies in marketing and journalism at California State University at Long Beach, he and his brother Larry began importing and marketing green coffee from his family farm, Finca Dos Marias, and distributing it to specialty roasters throughout the United States and Canada.

Jones is an active member of the Specialty Coffee Association of America, and, since 1994, has been on the Membership Services Committee. He's also an Annual Conference Committee Facilitator. He is the 1998 chair of the SCAA Awards Committee and an instructor for the Sensory Evaluation and Espresso Lab workshops. In addition, Jones was in the Sustainable Criteria Group II at the First Sustainable Coffee Congress in 1996, and has been a presenter on seminar panels for Family Businesses and Marketing Guatemalan Coffee.

87

Chapter 6

The Source of
Specialty Coffee

During its colorful history, coffee journeyed from its indigenous home in Abyssinia (now Ethiopia) to more than 50 growing countries worldwide. In this chapter, we will journey to one of these coffee-producing countries, Guatemala, where we will examine the roots at the origin of the perfect cup of coffee we enjoy in our local coffeehouses.

But first, let's look at the types of coffee available. Most specialty coffees are from the arabica plant, or *Coffea arabica*. Another common species is robusta, or *Coffea canephora*. Although robusta maintains a very high demand on the global market, it generally pertains more to the "commercial" coffee market. It is usually produced at lower altitudes (200 to 300 meters) and is more resistant to diseases and pests than the arabica species. The robusta bean is small, round and convex with a brown or gray color. The arabica bean is elongated and flatter and has a bluish, green color.

The mild and aromatic cup of arabica coffee is a pleasant relief compared to the sharp and bitter profile of robusta coffees. The caffeine content of robusta may be twice the strength (two to 4.5 percent) of the arabica (one to 1.7 percent) species. And most importantly, farmers can harvest robusta coffee with machines, which makes it much less labor intensive. Arabica coffee is meticulously harvested and selected by hand.

Although both species are seemingly different, each type of coffee is produced for a specific market. Some countries and cultures would wince at the smell or taste of a find Yemen Matari and instead serve their dinner guests demitasses of sharp Indian robusta. When coffee enthusiasts taste coffee, it is always important to keep the appropriate market or culture in mind.

This brings us back to our journey to the roots of the origin of the coffee that we roast and drink. To prepare quality coffee ourselves, we know we must consider the origins, location, altitude, and climate of the coffee farm, in addition to the culture of the growing region. To appreciate the culture at origin is to better understand the flavor of coffee in your cup.

Along the Pacific Slope of Guatemala's volcanic chain lies the state of San Marcos. My

89

mother was born here. Her great grandmother Maria Maldonado and her friends from her village traveled down the mountain to the lower edge of the cloud forest in the early 19th century, where they started planting a new crop called coffee. After long, hard, self-less work, the farm, now known as Finca Dos Marias (the farm of the two Marys—my great grandmother and my great great grandmother), prospered, as did the descendants of the original families. Today, the farm's story is the same story told around the world in finer coffee-growing regions. It embodies what is noble about the sources of estate coffee.

Finca Dos Marias is at the other end of a long, rough day's ride from Guatemala City. Whether ascending the mountain by foot, bus or truck, everybody in the region knows who's from which farm. As our farm approaches, you see more nodding heads, cleaner school uniforms, fewer muddy potholes and road debris, and a more uniform appearance and deeper green to the coffee. All are signs of the approaching farm. Finally the last sign: "Bienvenidos a Dos Marias, Los Hermanos Asturias."

At the bus stop is the store the workers' union owns and operates. Close by but some-what obscured by the steep terrain and fields is one of several landmark churches, the pre-school and elementary school, the medical clinic, and the championship soccer field. Unseen at the edge of the forest are the parcels of land deeded decades ago to the descendants of the original families.

Finca Dos Marias is considered an estate coffee. Its coffee is produced, harvested and processed for export on-site. The ideal soil, altitude and climate lend to the quality that makes this a specialty coffee. Every step of producing, harvesting and processing coffee requires careful and painstaking care and dedication.

Production

In the nursery, the propagation of the plant begins. Growers select seeds from the strongest plants in the fields to ensure consistency and quality. Other plantations can either purchase seeds from outside sources or forego the entire nursery process and purchase young plants. Finca Dos Marias maintains a variety of arabica plants, ranging from the traditional *bourbon* and *typica* varieties to the common *caturra* and *catuai* varieties. The seeds are carefully placed on beds of specially prepared soil and covered with straw to shade and protect them from natural elements. In about three to four weeks, the first pair of leaves will appear. During weeks four through six, we carefully transfer the seedlings to small bags of soil. This will be home until the plant is one year old. It's crucial to keep these young plants well irrigated and shaded during this first year. By this juncture, we know which plants will be strong enough to transfer to the fields.

The head planter already knows exactly where these new plants will go. We generally don't replace plants in a large-scale area, but instead on a case-by-case basis. Basically, the farm will replace plants that don't produce enough coffee. Age, disease or pests could all cause poor production. The maximum productivity of plants is between 10 and 20 years. After that, the yields tend to drop.

Because of the considerable moisture levels at Finca Dos Marias, fungus-based diseases are the biggest concern. The *Ojo de Gallo* disease is the most common. Up to 50 plants in any given area can be affected and require replacement. A pest problem, although not of major concern on our farm, is the *Broca*, a small bug that bores into the fruit of the plant and eats through the seeds.

Other important elements for basic coffee production include the soil and climate. Fortunately, Guatemala's numerous volcanoes provide ideal soil for coffee—rich in organic matter and porous for drainage. When we remove a plant, it is a good opportunity to revitalize the soil for the new replacement. Normally, we replace 12 cubic feet of soil with a soil blend that includes composted cherry pulp. The new plant will begin to bare a normal crop of cherries in two to three years. If everything goes well, we will nurture the plant for the next 10 to 20 years through pruning to encourage consistent yields and manageable harvesting. If we don't prune the plant, it could grow as tall as 15 feet.

The altitude at Finca Dos Marias is 4500 to 6000 feet. This is considered high-altitude coffee, yet another determinant of quality. The lack of oxygen at this altitude allows coffee to mature at a much slower rate. The beans thus become denser. This bean density is important to roasters who are looking for complexity in the flavor of the cup. Roasters expect a certain type of characteristic from these coffees. The steep terrain of Finca Dos Marias also requires a great deal of labor to cultivate and harvest coffee. This is the disadvantage of growing coffee at higher altitudes.

The ideal location for coffee production on a global scale is between the Tropics of Cancer and Capricorn. The plant grows best where the annual mean temperature is 70 degrees F. Coffee is very sensitive to frost and does not grow well above 6000 feet.

Coffee plantations also require about 70 inches of rain annually. After each rain period the coffee bush flowers. The frequency of rain determines the frequency of flowering. Rainfall dictates both the quantity and regularity of the harvest. Because Guatemala has distinct dry and wet seasons, coffee trees produce cherries once each year. Usually beginning as early as October and finishing as late as April, Finca Dos Marias' wet season produces an average of 120 inches of rain annually.

In addition to water, coffee needs a few hours of daily sunshine. In many tropical growing regions, clouds may provide a natural shade cover. Areas with less cloud cover must rely on shade trees to protect the plants and soil from over-exposure. Depending on the microclimate of a plantation, different types of shade coverage are required to effectively produce coffee. Some farms grow coffee beneath multiple layers of indigenous shade. Other farms will use no shade at all. There are advantages and disadvantages to every technique. Finca Dos Marias has constant cloud coverage year round because it is situated at the base of a cloud forest. Our managed shade system includes several types of shade trees that provide important nutrients for the soil, protect against erosion from the sun, wind and rain, and provide a good source of firewood.

Harvesting

Because the rains dictate the flowering, Finca Dos Marias harvests once annually. In countries where rain occurs throughout the year, one may find coffee branches flowering non-ripe and ripe fruit simultaneously.

The fragrance of the coffee flower is strong, reminiscent of jasmine. The flowering lasts only a few days. When it falls, it leaves the ovary, which develops into the fruit or cherry over a six- to 10-week period. This is when the color passes from green to red. As the cherry reaches full size and maturity, it is ready to harvest.

Picking is a very delicate and precise part of the harvesting process. The labor at Dos Marias provides us a great advantage in the quality selection process because the same families have picked coffee at Dos Marias since the early 1800s. They take great pride in the quality of their work.

The pickers are organized into groups with elected supervisors called Caporales. The head supervisor, called the Mayordomo, is elected by the Caporales. The Mayordomo works closely with the head planter and farm administrator in every aspect of policy. Administration of this type is unique to Dos Marias.

Each harvest is planned days in advance. Pickers know where they will pick before they start. Many will visit the fields in advance and admire the ripe cherries that will ultimately bring them their pay. When pickers go to the fields to harvest coffee, they pick only the reddest, ripest cherries. They know they will return later to pick the other cherries as they mature. Because cherries from the same trees ripen at different rates, pickers will harvest the same fields several times during a single harvest. The more times they pass the fields, the more selective the quality of the coffee.

Once they pick the coffee, it is taken to the mill or beneficio to be processed. On some plantations, the benefit of processing cherries on-site is not available. Subsequently, the cherries are sent to a contract mill.

It is important to process cherries immediately following the picking so the cherries don't over-ferment. Over-fermentation will hurt the quality.

Processing

There are two primary methods of coffee processing—natural and washed. Most of the countries in the Americas employ the washed method because they have access to plentiful water. Other countries, such as Yemen, employ the natural method because they lack water. Both methods, if done correctly, give coffee unique qualities.

The objective of both methods is to remove the green beans from the cherries. Most coffee cherries contain two dome-shaped beans, with the flat sides facing each other. Some cherries contain only a single bean, called peaberry, that is more round-shaped.

I will focus on the washed method of processing because this is the most prevalent with arabica coffees and is the method used at Finca Dos Marias.

There are two main components to the washed method of processing. There is the "wet mill," which removes the fruit from the bean, and the "dry mill," which grades the coffee for export. When coffee is received at the wet mill, workers weigh it and drop it into a huge tank of water. Any cherries that are green, moldy or infested with *Broca* will float to the top along with any twigs and leaves. The quality cherries, on the other hand, will sink. These quality cherries will then be transferred from the tank to be pulped by machines, which literally "pop" the beans from the cherries by squeezing them gently. These seeds, covered with fruit or mucilage, are then sent to another tank while the removed skins of the cherry are sent to a composting pile, where they become an integral part of the soil renewal process.

The second tank is charged with removing the stubborn mucilage from the seeds, usually by fermentation. Fermentation allows the enzymes of the mucilage to break themselves down. This may take two to four days depending on the air temperature. Some plantations attempt to accelerate this process by using high-pressure water or agitating machines. At Finca Dos Marias, Ricardo, the old man of the mill, will determine when the seeds are ready to be rinsed.

At this point, the beans from the fermentation tanks are emptied into long canals so they can be rinsed and washed. Again, small walls in the canals will allow the "floaters" to pass and the quality beans to sink.

After rinsing, workers empty the coffee onto large drying patios for sun drying. Because there is considerable cloud cover at Finca Dos Marias, we use mechanical dryers when necessary. Once the beans are dried, they have hard shells covering them called parchment. When dried appropriately, the coveted green beans shrink within the parchment, thus completing the wet process.

Growers store the coffee for at least 30 days in the parchment. The coffee is then prepared for export in the dry mill. Some plantations without on-site dry mills will send or sell parchment coffee to contract dry mills.

When a buyer is ready, the coffee is prepared to order. The parchment is hulled from the beans and they are graded for density, size and imperfections. Generally, the objective of grading coffee is to achieve even roast development. The more the coffee is graded, the more expensive it becomes.

The first machine after hulling is called the Oliver. This is a slanted table that shakes vigorously at an angle, causing beans of different densities to be sorted into different bags. A buyer may request that the beans make several passes through this machine. The next step is to screen the coffee for size in millimeters. Normally, Finca Dos Marias uses a screen size of 16. The final phase is to manually hand sort the beans, a labor-intensive task that requires skill and attention to detail. We inspect each bean for visual imperfections. Some dry mills have replaced the human eye with an electronic eye sorter that looks for discolored beans. At Finca Dos Marias, we believe that even this process should be followed by a visual hand sort.

Once the supervisor approves the preparation of the coffee, it is ready to be bagged for export. Although weights vary from country to country, Guatemala exports its bags at 152 pounds. The "marks" for the bags leaving Finca Dos Marias include: "Doña Mireya," which indicates the special preparation my mother demands, "Finca Dos Marias," which indicates the special origin of the estate, and the image of a Quetzal bird. The Quetzal holds a special place in the hearts of Guatemalans. This endangered bird is the national bird of Guatemala and is also the name of the monetary unit. Ancient Mayan warriors once used the vibrant green feathers of the Quetzal for ceremonial headdresses. Finca Dos Marias is a breeding ground for these resplendent birds and we are proud to share their land with them.

Social Programs

Finca Dos Marias is a model farm in Guatemala because of its social programs. The quality of life for its employees outweighs the value of the coffee picked.

Most employees are coffee pickers. Each family has an account. The family is paid by the weight they pick. The families receive their pay twice per month. Unique to Dos Marias is that both men and women in the family have access to accounts. This helps ensure funds will be available for the women to keep the households. Some countries pay pickers by volume rather than weight.

The Asturias family has always believed education is the key to progress in society. Initially, the farm built a primary school for students from ages five to 10 years old. The family then subsidized the construction of a high school in the nearest town of La Reforma. When these programs proved successful, we built a preschool for children of ages three to five years. Preschools are very unique in Guatemala; ours is focused on the basics of personal hygiene and nutrition.

More recently, we formed a new high school, or "Instituto Basico Privado de Finca Dos Marias," to include a trade-oriented curriculum. In 1998, its first year of existence, 77 students passed the exam to move up to this level. In addition to the required curriculum, the school offers courses on cattle, cheese, electronics, and home economics. Trade schools are very important to the future of these families and the region.

If a student demonstrates exceptional skills and gains admission to programs outside of the region, Dos Marias will continue its support. When it comes to picking coffee, children are not allowed to open their own accounts until they complete the required elementary school years. Parents whose children show poor attendance in school will be penalized financially. These educational programs are approaching their third generation of operation and have proved to be successful in improving the quality of life for students and their families. Finca Dos Marias boasts a 98 percent literacy rate.

Access to medical care is equally important for a healthy labor force. A full-time nurse operates a high-quality infirmary on the farm. A doctor visits the farm twice monthly. We provide preventative health exams on a regular basis. If care is required outside the infirmary, the medical program covers it.

Conclusion

Coffee farms across the world grow and process their coffees under a wide variety of conditions and with varying degrees of skill and passion. One thing remains consistent, however: Coffee is one of the most labor-intensive crops in the world, and the people who grow it typically spend their entire lives working on the process.

What does this mean to you? It means every cup of coffee you sell came from the efforts of a whole farmload of people. And as more and more consumers come to understand that specialty coffee at its best produces a wide variety of wonderful flavors, we owe it to producers and their workers to understand the processes behind the coffee. Without their passion and culture infused in every cup, there would be no such thing as a "specialty" coffee retailer. ●

section two

two
YOUR PEOPLE

Bruce Milletto

Bruce Milletto is the owner of Bellissimo Inc., a company specializing in education for the specialty coffee industry. Bellissimo has consulted with hundreds of individuals and businesses worldwide, primarily in the retail coffee arena.

After receiving undergraduate degrees from Phoenix College and Northern Arizona University, Milletto earned his master of arts degree from the University of Oregon. Prior to his involvement in specialty coffee, he worked for various art agencies in addition to The National Endowment. Milletto opened and managed four coffee operations in Eugene and Portland, Ore., and in the process became acquainted with the excessive employee turnover rate in the coffee industry and the challenge of training. As a result, he partnered with Ed Arvidson to create Bellissimo's first product—"Espresso 101," a video training tool. Bellissimo then went on to produce a number of other products, including "Espresso 501," "Spilling the Beans," "Evening with the Experts," and "The Art of Coffee."

Milletto, the publisher of *Achieving Success in Specialty Coffee,* is a frequent contributor to such coffee industry publications as *Fresh Cup Magazine, Speciale Caffè Italia, Fancy Food Magazine, Coffee Culture Magazine,* and *The Italian Journal of Food and Wine.* He serves on and is a former vice chair of the Specialty Coffee Association of America's Communications Committee. He and Arvidson co-authored *Bean Business Basics,* a definitive how-to manual for starting and operating a retail specialty coffee business.

97

Chapter 7

Taking Training of Your Employees to a New Level

The successful operation of any small business requires excellent systems. And the system you develop for training your employees may be the most important program you implement in your specialty coffee business. No matter how beautiful your decor or how much time and money you spend to market your store, if your employees cannot prepare an excellent product, you are missing the point of the retail coffee industry.

As this book goes to press, I believe more than 70 percent of all specialty coffee operations in the U.S. are missing this point. I visit hundreds of coffee operations each year, and I wish I could report that product quality is improving. Perhaps as our young industry matures, quality—not immediate economic gain—will motivate most operators. People need to realize that long-term profitability requires selling a superior product.

Two years ago, I was hired by an East Coast doctor who wanted to leave medicine, move to the mountains of Colorado, and open a specialty coffee business. He asked me to join him on a week-long tour of the state to find the perfect retail climate in which to start his new business. During our tour, we sampled brewed coffee and espresso beverages in dozens of operations. The brewed coffee was often adequate, sometimes even good. The espresso beverages were a different story.

On the last day of our trip, in a small bookstore in Steamboat Springs, a barista finally served me a nearly perfect single straight shot of espresso. A full week and dozens of stores. I was shocked.

Do you think I was shocked because it took one week to find a good espresso? Not at all. I was shocked I actually received one. It speaks poorly of U.S. coffee retailers that I'm awed the few times each year I visit an operation and receive a properly prepared drink. Why do so many U.S. operations have such a limited understanding of espresso? Because they've never learned how to properly prepare it. And, sadly, many consumers don't know the difference. American baristas typically camouflage their espresso with 14 or more ounces of milk, chocolate and sweet syrups. If they didn't, their espresso would be unacceptable to most people's palates, would prove undrinkable, and would never sell.

ACHIEVING SUCCESS IN SPECIALTY COFFEE

In Italy, the opposite is true: I'm surprised when I receive a beverage of poor quality. Is the raw product that much better in Italy? The water? Neither. The difference is in the level of respect people give to the coffee. In Italy, consumers know how good coffee can taste when prepared properly. Because of this awareness, few operations would survive if they did not meet their customers' expectations.

This North American/European paradox is also due in large part to the basic culinary expectations of U.S. consumers. Many people are satisfied with 99 cent gonzo burgers as long as they're fast and cheap. But if pre-made lattés were kept under heat lamps, they would not sell at any price. Even in this world of "quick, big and now," consumers still search for quality.

In the U.S., consumers often have no idea how good coffee can be. When they discover an operation where quality is paramount, they return. As an owner/operator, you need to understand this concept. It's what sets specialty coffee apart from the horrible institutional brew of the past.

The Good News
Many retailers do not realize that no matter how good their coffee, how intelligent their baristas, or how expensive their espresso equipment, it's all meaningless if they don't maintain excellent training programs.

The good news: You can produce high-quality beverages in the same time it takes to produce inferior ones. There is absolutely no excuse for improper beverage preparation.

Time after time, coffee business professionals spend enormous energy and resources to source, build and design their operations. They understand that some espresso machines work better than others. When sourcing coffee, they spend days talking to roasters and cupping their samples in order to choose the best and freshest coffee available. When it comes to hiring, they look for intelligence, honesty and personality. But when I ask how they train their employees, they say, "Our machine salesman came down to the shop for an hour."

You should never require your equipment salesperson to train your staff, because in many cases, he or she won't have the knowledge to do an effective job. There are only a few companies nationwide that give their employees the product knowledge necessary to train others. If you get your information from the other 90 percent, your operation is in jeopardy from day one. Ask yourself the following question: If you owned a small restaurant, would you ask your grill salesperson to teach you to cook? No? Well this is exactly what you're asking your equipment suppliers to do if you let them train your staff. And training is the cornerstone of your success.

In this chapter, I will help you identify and correct any training problems that exist in your present operation. Your goal as an owner is to teach your staff the importance of quality. You need to train your employees effectively, empowering them with the knowledge that your operation holds coffee and beverage preparation in the highest esteem. Make sure they spread the word to your customers!

The Ongoing Battle
People in the coffee business routinely discuss the "battle" of training. Yes, training is a battle. Why? Because training is not something you do only once and then never think of again. It's a never-ending process that takes time, strategy and dedication. The annual turnover rate for baristas in North America is 60 to 80 percent. In a small coffee operation, an owner may need to train new employees on a weekly or monthly basis. As an independent retailer, your bottom line will depend on how well you train these new employees and how effectively you monitor the habits of your existing staff.

Coffee can be wonderful and memorable or it can be undrinkable. Teach your staff to respect the bean. If all the baristas and coffee consumers worldwide could visit a working coffee plantation to see and feel the love and energy that goes into every pound of coffee they serve or purchase, they would begin to understand the importance of quality. After this educational tour, they would understand that improperly preparing coffee from hand-picked beans—each carefully sorted, thoughtfully processed, and sent to us from the furthest reaches of the globe—is absolutely unconscionable.

Developing a Program

The best way to develop a training program is to break it into segments, noting the many parts necessary for long-term success.

• Hire the Right People

It's extremely important to hire the right individuals to work in your operation. Your success is dependent on those you employ.

Personality is a must for any employee behind a coffee bar. A positive and helpful attitude can be worth thousands of dollars to your operation each year. Look for enthusiastic individuals. Allow job candidates to express themselves freely in interviews. Ask them if they enjoy and drink coffee. Probe deeper to determine why they're interested in coffee. Observe their behavior and decide if the questions *they* ask *you* are good ones.

As a rule of thumb, I usually don't hire baristas with prior experience. This may seem unfair, but time and again these employees have caused problems and were difficult to retrain properly.

Last year, a client brought me to Virginia to train nine new employees. The client said two of the new hires had prior experience at a local chain store. I was skeptical. I was familiar with that particular chain and had never been served a good beverage or observed a well-trained staff in action during any of my visits.

My greatest fears were realized on opening night. During the frenzy created by the several hundred invited guests, I heard one of the employees with prior coffee experience tell another new employee, "You don't have to go to all that trouble. After Bruce leaves, I'll show you a bunch of shortcuts." She was given her walking papers that same evening. This one bad apple had the ability to undermine an entire staff with her I-already-know-how-to-do-this attitude.

Hiring older workers is often good business. They're sometimes slower to learn, but once trained, they often become the bedrock of an operation. Mature workers understand responsibility and respect. Sometimes they have more flexible hours than students or younger workers. Older employees also don't change jobs as readily and can be with you for many years.

This book has an entire chapter on hiring employees so I won't go into great detail. No matter what your hiring criteria, interview thoroughly and wisely. Take your time and choose your staff as if your life depended on it, because the life of your business does.

• Develop Written Guidelines

You will save yourself time and prevent future problems if you develop written guidelines and a list of employee expectations. You should never surprise your staff members with their job responsibilities. Hold one 15-minute employee meeting every week and a monthly hour-long mandatory meeting. If you didn't distribute a list of expectations to your employees when they were hired, it's not too late. Explain to your employees that your operation will be taking a new direction in training. Tell them it's important they break bad habits and increase their skills.

Produce a list of expectations and post it in a break room or near lockers. Note or highlight any important points. Under "Customer Service," list such things as: Positive Attitude, Good Judgment, Friendliness, Eye Contact, Up-Selling, Sincerity, Helpfulness, and Customer Education.

Under "Productivity," key on such ideas as: Cleanliness, Honesty, Organization, and Timeliness.

Under "Team Play," speak to issues such as: Communication to Management, Flexibility, Respect, and Non-Discrimination.

You can even take this one step further and have each employee sign a contract stating the specific goals of your operation and the services he or she is to perform. By going through this exercise, no employee can ever come back to you with the excuse "I didn't know."

• *Large or Small ... You Can Win the Battle*
No matter how large or small your operation, it's essential to maintain a specific training program. If your operation employs only one or two people and you work most of the hours, a half-hearted training program won't impact you as much as it will a store with a larger staff. It's still important, however, that you diligently train even your one or two part-time employees. They are the face of your company when you're absent.

I have asked numerous coffee business owners at trade shows how many employees they have. They typically say 40. I then ask them how they train their employees. A standard answer oftentimes is, "Oh, we don't do anything special. We just go over the basics with our new people." It's unthinkable that someone would invest vast amounts of time and money in a business and not realize employee training is of utmost importance.

• *Use Video Training*
Considering that my company, Bellissimo Inc., created "Espresso 101"—the coffee industry's most respected and successful training video—it shouldn't surprise anyone that I recommend this training tool for operations of any size. Most coffee bar employees in North America were raised on television, and video is a natural and comfortable way for them to learn and assimilate information.

"Espresso 101" teaches viewers how to properly extract, steam, foam, and prepare espresso bar drinks, but it also teaches them about coffee as a product. It's important for all retail coffee employees to understand the origins of coffee and the subtle nuances of the roasting process. It is with this knowledge that they will better appreciate coffee as a product, show respect in its preparation, and have the ability to give helpful and reliable information to your customers.

A training video is invaluable. It will work for you tirelessly, time and again. It will ensure that each and every employee receives the same training. A video is easy to send home with an employee whenever he or she needs or desires a refresher course. If you do all of your training hands-on, you can save hundreds of hours each year by using video as your primary tool. Have your employees view "Espresso 101" and give each the test enclosed with the video. You can also use the testing procedure as part of your pre-hiring screening. If a potential hire watches the video and doesn't perform well on the test, consider hiring someone else. Best of all, you will train each of your employees to prepare the same product. Each employee will tamp the same, extract the same, and steam the same, all of which will guarantee consistency in your operation. Achieving consistency is one of the most difficult mountains for an operation to climb. Video, if used properly, can solve this problem.

Coffee books can help you train employees if they are extremely motivated and willing to use their own time to increase their coffee knowledge. These employees are rare. Let your trainers or managers know from the beginning you expect them to learn all they can about the product.

Nothing, of course, will take the place of expert hands-on training. But combining a hands-on approach with video will give you a great training foundation. Instead of spending dozens of hours with a new employee, why not teach him or her the basics with video and then spend only a few hours with each trainee? This has been the most effective method for my stores, as well as for the thousands of others who own Bellissimo's video training program. I know from experience that I'll have to dedicate only a few hours of my time to end up with a capable, well-rounded employee, provided he or she viewed the video first. I challenge anyone to train an employee better in 12 to 15 hours of hands-on training without using video.

- *Appoint a Training Manager*

If your operation has six or more employees, appoint a training manager. It might be your oldest and most stable employee or someone who truly cares about your product and will monitor each employee carefully. Even established and long-time employees can fall into old habits or develop bad ones. Appoint someone who won't be afraid to correct the mistakes of even your most seasoned employee. It's to your benefit to make another person beside yourself responsible for product quality.

- *Consistency*

Every coffee operation should strive not just for consistency, but for "consistent excellence." You'll never achieve this type of consistency unless every employee knows just how important and committed you are to this premise. Discuss excellence in every staff meeting; you can never stress it enough. Explain to your employees that quality is what makes your operation different. Encourage them to strive to be the best and to always prepare beverages of higher quality than your competition.

Teach your staff it's better to throw a drink in the trash and explain to a customer you're remaking the order than to serve a product that doesn't meet your high standards. When you train staff members to know and believe your product is the very best, they'll start to follow your lead. Pride is infectious. Your employees will achieve a new level of commitment if they believe few other operations, if any, can deliver comparable quality.

Beverage Essentials

This chapter does not go into the subtle nuances of espresso extraction or brewed coffee preparation. I have left these topics to my fellow professionals, Dr. Illy, Mr. Lingle and Mr. Cipolla. But I do need to touch briefly on the importance of each as they pertain to training.

- *Your Coffee Beverages*

The most important part of your training program will be teaching your employees how to properly extract coffee from your espresso machine. You will need, of course, to stress the importance of the grind—how the perfect grind will evolve constantly depending on climatic changes. You will need to ensure that everyone in your operation is tamping the same, dosing the proper amount of ground coffee, and above all, monitoring each and every extraction throughout the day. Some operations employ timers, and I see no harm in this. The main tool, however, should be a person's eyes. Once an employee knows how espresso should look flowing from a portafilter and can identify the proper color and density of crema, he or she won't need a timer.

Your employees should settle for nothing less than perfectly steamed milk for lattés and cappuccinos. Many espresso bar patrons have never tasted a properly prepared cappuccino. I rarely order them because I've been disappointed and disgusted too many times. Teach your employees to use their ears, recognizing the proper sound of steaming milk as it initially expands. Then teach them how it should sound as you finish the process, heating it to the perfect temperature. Make them taste over-heated milk, and emphasize how unpleasant it is to drink extremely hot milk. Have them explain this to customers so they will recognize the magnificence of a wonderful cappuccino, properly prepared.

When it comes to your brewed coffee, teach your employees the proper brew strength. Make sure they realize coffee cannot remain fresh indefinitely in pump pots. It's helpful if your pump or shuttle pots come with timers; they will enable your staff to monitor the age of each coffee you brewed. Never allow your coffee to grow stale.

Make sure when you prepare drinks such as mochas or flavored lattés to add syrup and chocolate in the proper order and amounts. You need the end result to be both profitable and to follow the recipe established by your suppliers.

Teach your staff the importance of clean and well-maintained equipment. Peter Kelsch and Joe Monaghan will give you the details behind proper care later in this book.

Training: Part Two

Once your initial training program is in place and successful, it's time for you to think about the second phase of employee training—customer service and up-selling. You shouldn't stress either of these, however, until your new staff member prepares consistently good beverages and has gained some initial experience behind the counter. After a new employee feels comfortable with his or her barista skills, then it is time to expand his or her training.

• Customer Service

No matter how great your beverages, they're only half the package. The other half is customer service. Your customers are looking for more than just coffee. In a frantic world, they're looking for businesses that make them feel comfortable and at home. Your employees should learn your customers' names and what they drink. They should also recall the regular customer who orders a blueberry scone every day and set one aside when the supply gets low. These are the types of customer service essentials you should drive home to your employees.

Once again, we've devoted an entire chapter of this book to the subject of customer service. However, it's so important to your success it can never be overstated. As the owner you must, once again, set the example. Greet each and every customer that steps up to your counter. Make each customer feel special and appreciated. When you're busy, teach your employees to look customers in the eye and acknowledge them by saying, "I'll be with you soon." Little things go a long way. A loyal customer will reward you with continued patronage and word-of-mouth advertising.

• Up-Selling

Another important skill you should teach a new employee is up-selling. "Would you like one of our fresh-baked muffins with your coffee today?" "If you like today's coffee of the day—Guatemalan Antigua—it's on sale this week." You can double your daily sales if your employees learn how to suggestively sell. Very few employees will take this task on themselves. They need to know it's not just appreciated, but required. Make them understand this is a fundamental part of their jobs. A large chain store I consulted gave monthly bonuses to employees who sold the most pastries and bulk coffee. Auxiliary sales are relatively easy to track with today's sophisticated POS systems. Make this a part of your employees' jobs while also making it a game and a challenge. Once again, lead by example. Show your staff how to properly up-sell when you're behind the counter.

• Program Success

To achieve overall long-term success, you must embody training in your daily and weekly activities. The old adage "we never stop learning" is especially true when applied to a complex culinary product such as coffee.

Once you have a well-trained staff, take it to the next level by making books and videos available that will expand their general coffee knowledge and introduce them to advanced principles in espresso preparation. Many fine books are available, including several by Ken Davids and Dr. Ernesto Illy. In video, Bellissimo recently released "Espresso 501," an advanced barista training film that compliments "Espresso 101." The information on this tape will be somewhat intimidating to a relatively new employee, but once he or she has mastered all the basics, it's the perfect learning aid to take your staff to the next level.

Organizations such as the Specialty Coffee Association of America (SCAA) and the National Specialty Beverage Retailers Marketing Association (NASBEV) sponsor a number of seminars each year. Once you join these associations, they will notify you when one is scheduled in your area. Take advantage of these and other learning opportunities.

Clip and post any coffee-related items you come across on a central employee bulletin board to keep your staff up-to-date on current news about coffee. Learning and training may never end, but in a positive sense, they never should.

You should never be satisfied with your training program or your employees' knowledge. Training is an immense uphill challenge, but the top of the hill is exactly where you want to aim.   ●

Bruce Mullins

Bruce E. Mullins is vice president of product development and training for Coffee Bean International (CBI), one of the nation's leading specialty coffee and tea companies with over 6000 active accounts throughout North America. CBI, which recently celebrated its 27th anniversary, is best known for the Panache® specialty and Café Tierra® organic brands of coffees, Panache Blender Latté® and Blender Mocha® iced beverage mixes, Panache cocoas, and the Xanadu® brand of exotic teas.

Mullins is the creative director for all coffee and tea products at CBI. He oversees the company's internal and external training and assists in marketing and public relations. In addition to his duties at CBI, Mullins serves on the Training and Education Committee of the Specialty Coffee Association of America and is vice president and a board member of the American Premium Tea Institute. Prior to joining CBI, Mullins was a specialty coffee and tea retailer, managing his own and other coffee roasting businesses. He is trained as a specialty coffee roaster, tea blender and cupper, and lectures and writes extensively on the specialty coffee and tea industries.

Chapter 8

**Brewing Up Great
Customer Service**

When I go shopping these days, I often come home feeling lighter in the pocketbook yet heavier in the heart. This feeling is not comfortable. In fact, after some trips to the mall, my dissatisfaction flares up like the lumbago of old age, making me ache in places I forgot I had.

An emptiness seems to surround shopping today. Regardless of the part of the country or the swankiness of the surroundings, the shopper often feels strangely out of place, as if the entire retail process was designed to satisfy the needs of someone besides the customer, perhaps someone hiding in the back room. Stores offer too many choices or not enough. Sales help is nowhere to be found or hangs onto your elbow like an aggressive panhandler. The store manager seems to be the same age as your paperboy only with less experience. Was it always like this or did retailing used to be more natural and fun? Is shopping an inherently unsatisfying experience or has it just been allowed to become that way in too many places by too many retailers?

In the traditional view of retail customer service, people give a lot of lipservice to King Customer. As many of you readers realize, however, you need more than lipservice to satisfy the stated (and perhaps even more importantly, the unstated) needs of your customers. In fact, I firmly believe the majority of specialty coffee consumers are shopping for more than just beans or brevés. They are searching for affirmation. They are hungry for recognition. And they are thirsty for affiliation. In short, they are looking for the rarest of commodities—a truly satisfying retail experience.

Specialty retailers who offer fantastic coffees yet fail to recognize and respond appropriately to the soft, non-product needs of their customers will never enjoy maximum success in their individual markets. We have seen retailers with great coffee fail due to too much emphasis on product. They simply turned a blind eye toward marketing, staff training and customer service. Ironically, specialty coffee consumers often seem more forgiving of average quality than of mediocre customer service. To their credit, many of the larger chain coffee stores understand and exploit this. Do you?

In this chapter we will explore some new ways to think about customer service. We will invite you to become a customer in your own store and see yourself anew through your customers' eyes. You will be challenged to rethink your attitudes and policies regarding customer service. By the end of this chapter, after we take you through our special (and fun) "12-step program," we hope you understand your customers are looking to you and your staff for more than just outstanding coffee—they are looking to you for outstanding service.

Step One: What are Your *Really* Buying?

You know your customers come to you thirsty for coffee, but have you ever stopped to think about the other things they're looking for? No, I don't mean a bagel with cream cheese or a half pound of French roast, ground for drip (although that would be nice). Your customers come to you seeking nourishment of a different sort. They are looking for a satisfying retail experience, their Recommended Daily Allowance of respect and appreciation.

Most retail experiences in this country are dehumanizing and depressing. Retail shopping is endured—not enjoyed—by most consumers. Smaller local or regional retailers that once dominated the American business landscape have become an endangered species, unprotected by the Sierra Club. Retailers were once people like us—in touch with the community and its needs. Solid and friendly. Sadly, in the rush to become "new and improved," we seem to have lost sight of the human side of retailing—exchanging it for lower prices or convenient locations—without realizing how much we missed real retailing until it was gone.

As all of us used to accept mediocrity in coffee as "normal," the majority of consumers still accept mediocrity in retail as inevitable. Thankfully, many of us have learned there is a difference between good and bad coffee, between the pre-ground stuff in a tin can and freshly roasted whole-bean coffee ground to order. Specialty coffee customers are typically a cut or two above the average consumer, as measured in intelligence, income, experience, and expectations. Unlike the majority of consumers, they do not accept mediocrity as inevitable. They are the first to grow dissatisfied by what passes for customer service in most stores. They're often in search of more than just a quality cup of coffee. They're searching for a rehumanizing retail experience.

Average quality coffee delivered in a superior customer service retail environment will outsell stellar coffee delivered in a mediocre customer service environment. Because of the active involvement of their owners (more on this point later), smaller retail organizations can have an advantage over the larger retail coffee chains in satisfying the non-product emotional needs of their customers. The retailer that recognizes the active (the product) and passive (the experience) needs of the consumer, and who designs his or her business to fulfill both those needs, has already traveled a long way on the road to success.

Step Two: What is Your *Custom* Customer Service Philosophy?

All retail coffee stores should have a unique personality that reflects the owners' and managers' beliefs and values. Most retail businesses start out the right way: They have a firm opinion on products, training and service. As a business grows and matures, however, the owner's values and standards often become diluted or even overlooked. This applies to many areas of the business beyond customer service, and can ultimately be fatal to the retailer if not recognized.

If it has been awhile since you started your business—or if you are in the process of opening your doors for the first time—you will find it valuable to sit down and formally survey your own likes and dislikes about customer service. What types of retail environments do you personally like and dislike? What is the most memorable retail store you ever visited? What about it made such an impression? Was the service and treatment of the customers part of the attraction? How do other successful retailers team with their employees so that product quality and attention to detail become part of the natural flow?

As part of this survey, ask yourself what sort of personality you want your store to have. Does your store meet this goal, or are you falling a little (or a lot) short? Are you looking for a warm and comfortable experience with lots of sofas and warm colors, inviting your guests to linger and be family? Or are you looking for something a little more cutting edge and trendy, with a younger crowd that's on the move? Different store personalities will require different approaches in delivering excellent customer service.

Analyze the results of your personal customer service study. As the customer, how does your business meet your needs (both product and non-product)? Are there areas that need improvement? Specifically, how can you begin to move your business in the right direction? How long will it take? What can you expect to get in return?

For a different point of view, ask several trusted customers or associates to visit your store pretending they had never been there before. How would they rate it?

As the store owner, make sure you maintain written customer service standards that you incorporate into staff training and the structure of daily store operations. These policies should be considered rock solid and fundamental, yet at the same time be organic and responsive to periodic improvement or change.

Step Three: Owner-ous Responsibilities of Retailing

As the store owner (or as someone acting on behalf of the owners), you have a responsibility to your staff and customers to set the standards for great customer service in your store(s). This can be an easy or difficult task, depending on the size and number of locations you have.

Logically, in a small retail coffee operation (defined as having one to three locations), the owner's approach to establishing excellent customer service will be different than in a large (four locations or more) operation.

In a small operation, your personal good example behind the counter is the best way to develop a great customer service culture. In most situations, your managers and staff members will try to emulate *your* actions. Are you aware of your role as teacher? How thoughtful are you of the needs of your customers? Are you consistent with your own level of customer service even when it is busy or you are getting tired? Do you allow yourself to do less (or more) for your customers than your standards mandate just because you are the owner? Do you allow your staff members to problem solve for the customers (empowerment), or must they get approval from management for everything? When you note a staff member that isn't offering the optimum in customer service, do you let it slide (not good), make an immediate big deal about it in front of everyone (even worse), or treat it as an educational opportunity you or your manager will handle later in the day (the best idea)?

Do you consciously try to set a great example in your customer interactions, or, because you work in a large operation, have you become so removed from day-to-day business that you are secretly scared of saying or doing the wrong thing in front of your staff or customers? (Sadly, many owners—even ones that once loved to interact with customers—have allowed themselves to get out of step with the operations in their own stores. It's easy to think of excuses, but letting yourself become too busy with the bigger picture is often the reason.)

If this describes your situation, consider how much more effectively you could run a profitable and healthy business if you got back in touch with details (not to mention with your employees and customers). Your staff members would probably help in any way they could, because they know having a boss who is "connected" with the business is better than having one who makes decisions in a vacuum.

Step Four: Store Design and Layout Come First

Planning for excellent customer service should begin with the rough draft of your store's layout. It is not too much of an exaggeration to say you should design your store primarily for your customers, not for yourself or your staff. If you haven't yet opened the doors of your specialty coffee business when you are reading this educational book (good for you!), you should take another look at your blueprints while wearing your set of customer service glasses. Even if your store has already been open for years and you aren't in a position to remodel the whole thing right away, some low- or no-cost changes are possible that will facilitate giving great customer service to your customers.

Remember that your customers are coming to you for more than great coffee. They are coming to you for a friendly experience, one as professional and competitive as any of the large chains can deliver, yet more individualized to the needs of the customer and the community.

How you "process" each customer visit will largely determine how your customers perceive your level of service. It's important to serve people promptly, consistently and accurately during your busiest times without making them feel rushed or unwelcome. Anyone who has worked behind a busy retail coffee counter (as we have) knows what a challenge that can be. You can determine the effectiveness of your "process" partly through proper staffing and training, yet all will be for naught if the store layout is awkward or works at cross-purposes to the flow of people and products.

One of the most common flaws in an otherwise attractive and functional coffee store is a disconcerting (to the customer) sense of ambiguity about where orders should be placed. In many instances, the designer placed the order taker and cash register in an illogical place. The register is either hidden behind an architectural facade or a display of biscotti. The counter is often unattended, with no one to smile and greet the new guest. The customer hasn't been in your store for more than five seconds, and she is already uncomfortable because she's lost.

An intelligent solution is to place the order station closer to the front of the store. Despite "common sense" design advice from architects (most of whom would make dreadful retailers) about making customers walk past lots of tempting products on their way to place an order, try to make your store customer-friendly first. Strong sales (especially from a staff trained in suggestive selling) will follow.

Another oft-overlooked component of a customer-friendly specialty coffee store is an organized and highly readable menu board that features well-illuminated, not-too-complicated choices and descriptions. I've been in stores recently that had virtually illegible menu boards, a result of poor design and placement. When you are hungry or really need a cup of coffee, a complicated menu that takes forever to browse isn't going to win an award for customer service. Resist the temptation to list every Italian-style syrup that you can pour into someone's drink. Offer a choice of sizes (four is ideal, yet it's not always offered for unknown reasons) for all filter-dripped and espresso-based beverages.

During your daily rush periods, do you offer multiple cashier stations (with backup staff) to speed up order placement and delivery without giving the customer the sense that you're "rushing" her? Or do you force your customers to wait in lines for more than a couple of minutes? I often hear of customers who try a new coffee place for a beverage and sandwich during the lunch hour, then walk away sadly disappointed because they had to endure a 20-minute wait to place and receive an order. They can't wait to get back to one of the large (read as "efficient") coffee retail chains. It may be cheaper to ignore "surge" capability in the short run, but it will kill you in the long run.

One staffing strategy to avoid (even though it's surprisingly common) is letting each person behind the counter do everything for everyone. The same person that takes the order fulfills it. Everyone is a cashier. Everyone is a barista. Everyone is falling all over everyone else. This is not to say that your staff shouldn't be cross-trained. Just realize that as employees specialize in certain parts of your business, they will become faster and more productive, and will begin to offer better-quality products to your customers.

How and where your customers sit has a surprisingly large impact on customer service. Giving your store multiple seating options—if it's well-thought-out and designed— will allow larger groups to feel comfortable and intimate while allowing singles or doubles to have privacy and quiet. If at all possible, avoid running your order lines through seating areas. Put yourself in your customers' shoes. Imagine trying to have a quiet, mate moment over a cup of coffee while seated at a table in a bank lobby next to the tellers' lines. Customers waiting in line would feel like eavesdroppers, while the seated patrons would lose their ability to relax and feel comfortable.

Pay attention to your customers' often overlooked emotional (non-product) needs in store design and layout. Design your store to offer a clear sense of welcome when the customer arrives (through signage, a staff member posted near main door, etc.). Offer your customers a sense of fairness by designing a "first-come, first-served" line. Instruct your staff to verbally verify orders with the customer; this avoids mistakes and ensures that customers have a high level of confidence in your operation. Teach your staff how to properly make change. It's especially important they know how to carefully and correctly count back change to a customer (most people hate to have their change handed to them in a lump). Institute a rigorous cleaning policy all through the day to guarantee the cleanliness of the store's tables, chairs, floors, displays, and condiment areas. Finally, pay attention to the quality of the background music in your stores. Make sure it is ASCAP legal, but, more importantly, make sure the music is appropriate for customer—not staff—enjoyment.

Step Five: Staff of Plenty
Learn how to schedule enough staff to meet your customers' demands, not your accountant's. Excellent customer service is enhanced by properly staffing the store at all times (especially during busy times when customers are rushed).

Your store can't offer superlative customer service when your superlative staff is nowhere to be found. As simple as this seems, this is one of the biggest potential roadblocks to satisfying your retail customers. Your customers will not mind a "normal" wait as long as it seems fair (you're waiting on people in the right order) and you appear to be fully staffed, with everyone working hard. If the customer has to wait unduly long because of your poor job of scheduling, she will remember her anger at wasting her time in your line more than the taste of your perfect latté.

To give you a perspective on this, can you remember the last time you were standing in line at the bank for what seemed like forever, all the while admiring the seven empty teller windows? The bank, in its scheduling wisdom, chose to open only one window at high noon, and the lone teller is seemingly afraid to make eye contact in case the other customers stampede. You still can't figure out what the other three people behind the counter—all with keys on springy things wrapped around their wrists—are doing. Bet you can't wait to get back there and appreciate their customer service again.

Ironically, it's nearly as bad to over-schedule your staff. Having too many people on the floor at one time is a sure bet for lousy customer service. People are generally happier when they have plenty to do; boredom amongst your staff is quickly telegraphed to your customers. If everyone moves as if sedated, the attractive "hustle factor" of a well-trained staff is lost.

Scheduling is half art and half science. You have to accept the fact that, during any given hour, you will almost always be a little under- or over-staffed. When in doubt, though, remember the bank example from above and pencil in that extra person. Although your labor costs may arguably be a little higher at the end of the year, you'll have purchased an extra measure of sales opportunities through up-selling and encouraging repeat business. Also, you should believe that in doing right by your customers, they will reward you with a stronger and healthier business, and will resist poaching by your competitors.

Step Six: Socially Adept Only Need Apply
Great customer service begins with hiring great people. They must have a knack for knowing how to work hard while using great people skills. Depending on which part of the country your business is located, finding these people may shift from being merely difficult to nearly impossible. And a strong economy can be a mixed blessing. On the one

hand, it pumps a ton of money and the time to spend it into the retail sector (including your business). On the other hand, good employees now have their choice of jobs at better-than-traditional wages, which forces a lot of marginally talented people into the workplace asking for top dollar. Why can't things ever be simple?

Hiring quality people takes more time and energy today than when the specialty coffee retail business began its dramatic growth in the early 1980s. One thing hasn't changed, however—managers still select many specialty coffee employees because of their willingness to work certain hours or to fit within a certain pay scale, not for their skills with food and people. With luck and a good training program (more on that soon), you can teach your staff members what they need to know about coffee. You cannot, however, teach your young employees everything their parents should have years ago. People skills, manners and good listening skills all seem to be in short supply these days.

During the interview process, spend time exploring the prospective employee's compatibility with your vision of excellent customer service. How will she interact with your customers? Does she share the same work ethic and desire to work with people as your best employees? How big is her ego? Does she find it demeaning somehow to wait on people and clean up after them? Perhaps she has a "whatever it takes" approach to life that she will bring to your business. Whatever your interview method, you need a clear picture of her ability to deliver satisfaction to your customers by the end of the interview.

Look to your existing staff members for employee referrals. Chances are good that your best employees hang around with people like themselves. Offer a signing bonus to your employees for referrals, 50 percent to be paid on hiring and 50 percent after the new employee has been with the company for 60 days. Look to your customer base as a source of unpaid staff referrals. Both ends of the age spectrum are worth soliciting; older or semi-retired people, as well as younger college-age people, are often great part-time workers. Interestingly, both groups seem to enjoy interacting with each other, if the chemistry is right.

A diverse staff with great people skills will enhance customer satisfaction and repeat business, allowing for greater sales and profitability—even if you have to pay more for quality labor than you think you should. (For more good information about hiring and managing quality coffee employees, please see Don Holly's chapter, page 121.)

Step Seven: In the Public "I"
Assuming you've done a good job finding and hiring staff members with good people skills, you will still need to teach your staff the importance of "I contact" with customers.

This isn't the typical definition of "eye contact." This definition encompasses how you expect your staff to interact with your customers. This is an often overlooked yet fundamental foundation for directing and evaluating the efforts of your managers and employees. Don't assume your staff will automatically know everything you deem important, even if it seems to you like it should be under the Webster's dictionary definition of "common sense."

"I contact" takes an abstract concept (that positive verbal and nonverbal contact between staff and customer is beneficial to the employee, the store and the customer) and makes it personal and compelling. How many retail stores have you visited recently where you wish the owner and managers had emphasized how important it is for every employee to take a greater measure of ownership in the business?

Here is the written foundation of "Keeping Good 'I' Contact With Our Customers"
- I am this company to our customers.
- I will talk with my customers. I will look my customers in the eye. I will try to make them smile.
- I will try to remember my customers' names, faces and favorite drinks.
- I will try to make each customer feel good, even when I don't.

- I will try to stay focused more on my customers and less on my co-workers and myself.
- I will remember to try and give $2 worth of satisfaction to my customers for every $1 they spend.

Step Eight: Keeping Your Training on Track

A central precept of delivering excellent customer service is to implement a basic two-phase training program in your store. Phase One should encompass all the fundamental knowledge that a new employee must master to begin working for you in a supportive position. The knowledge will vary from retailer to retailer, but it usually encompasses learning company policies, running the cash register, learning the basic beverages and menu items, and so forth.

Phase Two is typically an ongoing "in-service" training program designed for all employees that includes more information about coffees, teas, promotions, new products, and so on.

Surprisingly few specialty coffee retailers have devoted enough effort to their training programs. Without a doubt, training is one reason that large specialty coffee retail chains have been so successful, often at the expense of the independent retailer. (For more information on competing against chains, see Shea Sturdivant Terracin's chapter, page 157.)

It's crucial to integrate customer service principles in both training phases. You should give every new employee a thorough introduction to ring-up customer service during Phase One, for example. Consider, though, integrating the following "soft" customer service policies during the same session:

The cash register lead for each shift is responsible for:
- Ensuring the steady interaction between customers and staff (keep the line moving steadily, call out the orders, and verify the customer leaves the line happy with exactly what she wanted).
- Leading staff in greeting all customers within 15 seconds of their arrival in store.
- Acknowledging regret if line is moving too slowly.
- Repeating orders to verify accuracy.
- Making helpful (and profitable) add-on suggestions.
- Ringing orders carefully, making change correctly.
- Smiling and thanking customers, encouraging them to visit again.

You should train other positions in the store for maximum customer service as well. This training can be a part of the Phase One or Phase Two training scheme, as in the examples given below:
- Barista should make sure correct beverage gets to correct customer.
- Barista should be aware that people enjoy watching beverage preparation and should engage curious customers in conversation as time allows.
- Barista should smile and thank customers for their orders, then express hope that they enjoy their beverages.
- Other support staff should work to keep counters clean and stocked, tables wiped, chairs cleaned, garbage emptied, etc. Support staff should strive for good conversation with the customers.

Step Nine: Product Excellence and Consistency

Training for consistently excellent product delivery is a Phase Two topic. Because most specialty coffee retailers today rely on sales of brewed espresso and coffee rather than whole beans (as our industry started out), you must train for high-quality, consistent espresso and filter-dripped beverage preparation.

There are a number of excellent training videos and aids available to specialty coffee retailers. (Bellissimo, the publisher of this book, offers an outstanding selection.) Merely owning a good selection of training materials isn't enough, however. You must actively integrate these materials into your ongoing training efforts.

How do you currently train your employees? Do you have a regular training manual, with written procedures that cover everything from cash handling to backflushing the espresso machine? Do you have a regular schedule of mandatory after-hours training sessions (perhaps once a month) during which you cover some refresher subjects before holding a coffee tasting? Who manages your training? Have you established training as a critical part of your business, or does your old staff just show new employees the ropes during slow times? If you realize that your product and beverage training procedures are somewhat unorganized—or fear that you're not covering your customer service concerns adequately—it's time to evolve.

First, take an inventory of all of your training materials and manuals, and identify how much of your arsenal you need to overhaul or beef up. Chances are good that your business has grown and added products that aren't appropriately covered (such as frozen espresso beverages). You may have put other materials together on the fly back when you were working to get your doors open and haven't taken the time to double back and redo them.

Second, review your Phase One and Phase Two training methods. Are you covering your beginning and advanced training needs well, or do critical gaps in information exist because, sadly, knowledge osmosis defies the laws of physics?

Don't overlook training for other key products, such as breakfast and lunch items, hot and iced tea, baked goods, biscotti, and other consumables. These items *will* help develop additional sales, and they represent yet another opportunity to significantly enhance customer satisfaction.

Fielding a team that really knows its stuff is crucial to excellent customer service, but it represents an investment of both time and money, two rare commodities in most small businesses. Training becomes an eternal line item in each year's budget, because—like when painting a huge bridge—as soon as you are done, you have to go right back to the beginning and start all over again. You must continually train your new people. Even your veterans won't remember everything forever. No easy answer to training exists, but without it your business (and its people) will never reach their full potential.

Prepare to randomly and senselessly reward great examples of customer service you witness (or learn about) from your staff. Employees always appreciate gift certificates to prestigious retailers, along with certificates for dinner for two at a nice local restaurant. A little investment in positive feedback goes a long way toward employee satisfaction and retention.

Step Ten: Making Purchase-to-Person Calls
One important component of many large coffee chains—a component many independent retailers haven't delivered—is to offer a selection of high-quality coffee and tea merchandise. Quality specialty merchandise has become much easier to find than it was even a few years ago, yet many retailers don't know what to buy or how much to bring in. Even worse, due to the volume purchasing power of mass marketers such as department stores, large coffee chains or discount houses (10 years ago, who would have ever believed that you would one day find French presses for sale in most supermarkets?!), the small retailer usually pays significantly more for these items but can't afford to charge more.

Despite the negatives, however, offering an intelligent selection of specialty merchandise gives a coffee retailer another opportunity to deliver excellent customer service. So many consumers are interested in discovering new ways of enjoying specialty coffee and tea at home, and so few retailers are really telling them how to do it, coffee retailers who can deliver knowledge along with products have a great opportunity to gain a competitive advantage.

If appropriate to your store's retail selection, your Phase Two product training should include teaching about coffee and tea merchandise items, such as brewers and grinders.

Your staff must become "fluent" in every merchandise item you offer. Be sure to stock at least one of everything in the backroom, available for your staff to "check out" and take home for the weekend (along with some free coffee or tea for their experiments). If an employee likes a product, she will sell it for you. If she doesn't like it or doesn't understand how it works, she will avoid it like a cup of cheap instant coffee.

If your employees are proficient in all equipment, they should be able to match the correct brewer to the customer's needs and budget (a successful "purchase-to-person" call). You should offer equipment demonstrations on the spot using the backroom model. Make giftwrapping available to your customers at no extra expense (something the big chains often fail to offer). Encourage your customers to bring in coffee or tea gizmos they bought from your competitors so you can demonstrate how to use them successfully. Talk about inexpensive guerrilla marketing—you wind up looking like a hero because of the customer service failures of your competitors!

Step Eleven: Product Perfection: Guaranteed!

How do you guarantee your products? If you draw a blank on the question or believe you don't have a product quality issue, pay close attention to this step. An important part of delivering excellent customer service involves delivering excellent customer products (duh!). It doesn't matter how good you and your staff are, you should still have a proactive plan to deliver excellent customer service when you inadvertently deliver a lousy latté or a mediocre mocha.

Your store's product guarantee (covering both perishable and non-perishable items) should be clearly written, covered by your Phase One training, understood by staff, and posted for staff and customers to see. An occasional error or lapse in quality is unavoidable, and customers are usually understanding and forgiving in these instances. What they won't quickly forgive is a staff member who is either defensive or in denial about a customer's problem or one who feels the problem is (solely) the customer's.

Here are some customer-service-enhancing ideas for you to consider:
- The very best way to enhance customer service is to offer unconditional satisfaction with all purchases. Yes, you may get scammed once in a while, but the goodwill you generate should far outweigh your losses.
- Empower your employees to fix a problem immediately without seeking upper management's approval or help (Phase One training).
- Make customer comment cards that are preaddressed to the owner readily available at several locations within your store(s).
- Note detailed product or service quality complaints in the close-out report filed daily by the store manager for long-term customer satisfaction tracking. Don't stigmatize the reporting of problems, only the avoidance or poor resolution of them.

Step Twelve: Customer Service Beyond the Boundaries

To help develop and maintain a strong and healthy retail coffee business, look for ways to enhance your reputation for great customer service beyond the walls of your store(s). Admittedly, some of these ideas may tiptoe into the gray zone separating customer service from marketing, but do not limit your definition of excellent customer service to within the walls of your store:

- Use frequent buyer cards to enhance your customers' sense of appreciation.
- Ask for and use birthday dates on the reverse of frequent buyer cards (with name and address) to send birthday cards to customers with coupons for free beverages.
- Offer a signing bonus of a free beverage when your customers turn in a competitor's frequent buyer card. (Basically, offer them coffee asylum!)
- Teach coffee and tea classes during the evening (when store is normally closed), and donate the admission price to charity.

- Donate products and services—in the names of your customers—to local benefits or charities.
- Offer a bounty for the re-use of refillable travel mugs or tin-tie coffee bags to help the environment.
- Offer a reading hour every Saturday morning and afternoon for your customers' children, allowing parents the time to relax in privacy for a few minutes over a cup of coffee.
- Carry bags and parcels out to your customers' cars.

Conclusion

As I said in the beginning of this chapter, people give a lot of lipservice to King Customer in the traditional view of retail customer service. After reading and (hopefully) rereading this chapter and following its "12-step program," I hope you view customer service in your specialty coffee store a bit differently than you did before. Make this pursuit as important as a perfectly timed double shot of espresso. Remember that specialty coffee consumers—despite the product's growing mainstream appeal—tend to have unspoken higher expectations for products and service than other people. They are searching. They are hungry. They are thirsty. They are looking for the rarest of commodities—a truly satisfying retail experience. If you understand what they are really shopping for, they will reward you with their greatest gift: their loyalty. Don't let the big chains make you believe you can't compete with them on this point. Excellence in customer service is actually one of a small retailer's most potent weapons in the retail coffee wars. ●

Don Holly

Don Holly is the administrative director of the Specialty Coffee Association of America. Prior to joining the staff of the SCAA, Holly was elected to its board of directors as treasurer. His involvement in the specialty coffee industry began in 1982 as a principal in a coffee roaster manufacturing company and as a roaster-retailer in Southern California. Trained as a financial analyst and commercial banker, he was responsible for coffeehouse operations and strategic planning at Diedrich Coffee.

Holly has also been an instructor for the required course in leadership skills in the Restaurant Management Certification Program of the University of California at Irvine. He has written numerous articles on a broad range of topics for coffee trade magazines, and is the author of the SCAA's Espresso Lab Manual that is used as a training text nationwide.

121

Chapter 9

Hiring and Managing Employees

Operating a successful coffeehouse depends upon the proper execution of a million details in the right order. Certainly, the leader is responsible for determining which details to address and for allocating the appropriate resources so each is addressed properly. But the leader is also responsible for building and maintaining the team that will get the work done. Given that this book is aimed at specialty coffee retailers who have already opened their doors and faced some of the early challenges of leadership, what advice can guide them toward real success? Here are 10 key tasks that contemporary managers of a coffeehouse should dedicate themselves to perform:

1. Be an Expert
2. Defend High Standards of Quality
3. Be Passionate About Your Concept
4. Define Your Culture
5. Attract Good People
6. Train, Train, Train
7. Give Your Team the Tools it Needs
8. Observe and Reward
9. Attend to the Individuals on Your Team
10. Give Yourself Time to Think

Directing the operation of a coffeehouse can be the most rewarding managerial experience available. In my career as a commercial banker—a career I maintained while simultaneously growing a roaster-retailer business part-time—I had the opportunity to survey hundreds of businesses in many different industries. During that study, which included intensive interviews of the owners and managers of these businesses, I reflected upon the specialty coffee company with which I was involved. The interviews consistently reinforced my opinion that the operation of a coffeehouse had to be the most rewarding work that existed. Nowhere else can you add to your community's quality of life so positively and guide the development and personal fulfillment of a team of fellow human beings so gratifyingly than in the coffeehouse business.

Leadership is culturally interdependent, meaning the style of leadership that will be successful is sensitive to the character of the individuals involved and the environment of their interaction. You can't apply one specific leadership style in all circumstances successfully. Assuming the style of someone else is also usually unsuccessful. Every individual in every circumstance needs to find the words, tone, method, and purpose by which he or she will define his or her particular style of leadership. Given a different circumstance or a changing group of people, the leader must adjust his or her style to fit the new dynamics. This is part of the challenge and joy for an aspiring leader—to constantly evolve and grow in effectiveness with the ever-changing dynamic of his or her charge.

Be an Expert

The definition of leadership in every culture throughout history has included the concept of the leader as expert. Mentors, guides, teachers, and managers all tend to maintain the aura of knowledge—they know more than those they lead. It is a human trait to respect a person of authority—"the guru on the hill"—as long as his or her knowledge is genuine, relevant and humbly available. To consciously choose to be an expert on everything pertaining to your business—from equipment maintenance to payroll policies—is an important step toward developing your leadership acumen.

Becoming an expert requires an open mind and an inquisitive hunger. There are no absolute truths. Everything is relative. Approach the acquisition of knowledge with the understanding that for each question you answer, you will uncover two more. Every true expert I know is fairly humble, freely admitting there is more he or she doesn't know than he or she will ever know. This attitude, combined with the immense joy that comes from learning, will quickly drive you toward becoming an expert. Pick topics of interest relevant to your business. Read, question other experts, and personally experiment when appropriate. Recognize that what you think you know could be false and that personal knowledge is often based upon a limited set of facts or perspective. Trust in direct experience and never close down a new source of information. If you follow all these guidelines, you will soon become an expert.

The basis of the specialty coffee industry is that knowledge and skill will yield something of quality that is greatly appreciated by consumers. People have taken coffee for granted for so long that they apply more misconceptions and poor practices to its preparation than commonly known truths and good practices. In short, plenty of room for experts exists. Your capacity and effectiveness as a leader will be greatly enhanced if your team regards you as an expert.

Defend High Standards of Quality

Respect for nobility is another human trait. Despite the almost nihilistic attitudes of many "Gen-X" youth in the labor pool, an innate desire still exists in our culture to adhere to high standards of quality. Maintaining high standards is a noble purpose in which even the most pessimistic of the young generation can find meaning and value. By conspicuously urging your staff toward ideals in quality, the resulting pride in producing such quality will reflect clearly in their attitude about their work, their service to the customers, and their loyalty to you.

Alternatively, it is easy to predict the poor attitude, service degeneration and disloyalty that result from managers who talk about quality standards and then constantly compromise them. Nothing kills the effectiveness of a leader faster than hypocrisy. As soon as employees learn "quality" is nothing more than a freely used marketing term they have no "practical" means of accomplishing, their job becomes just another job and you become just another "boss." With true quality comes pride, fulfillment and loyalty. With false claims of quality come shame, meaninglessness and disloyalty.

Be Passionate About Your Concept

Your concept is the embodiment of everything about your business that you control—the company name, décor, menu, location, themes, style of service, recipes, etc. The development of your concept and its constant refinement is an important factor in your company's sustainable success. You must be passionate about your concept—it's the energy that your staff must rally around, like the battle banner of an army. Passion is infectious, and your staff and customers will quickly adopt and multiply the joy and commitment you exhibit. A trademark of great leaders is the passion they foment.

To be genuinely passionate about your concept requires that your concept be well developed. The details of design and creation must show craftsmanship. In typical "chicken or egg" manner, it's difficult to say whether craftsmanship comes from passion or passion comes from craftsmanship, but there's no doubt they are interrelated and self-supporting. Understand how important it is to hone and consider every detail of your business. The aesthetic quality that such well-refined details exude yields an atmosphere that promotes passion. And once you apply passion, your concept will continue to improve.

Because passion is an emotional expression rather than a physical one, it is not limited to the laws of physics and the limitations of space, energy and time. Instead, passion allows you to tap into a limitless resource for which there are no laws and sometimes no rational explanations. It has often been noted that leaders are capable of yielding the impossible from a situation, and I believe this is due to a generated passion. When everything else is in place, add a little passion and you will generate magic. That's when fun becomes fulfilling. At the end of the day you and your team will have smiles on your faces from the magical work you performed together.

Define Your Culture

Culture, from an anthropologist's point of view, is defined as the ideas, values and beliefs that members of a group share to interpret experience and generate behavior. Every culture has "rules," both conscious and unconscious, that it applies in a given context to guide activity and the interaction of individuals. The leader must take responsibility for defining the culture of his or her business, much like a conductor interprets the music for an orchestra. In effect, all leadership issues are related to defining the culture of your business, and it is inappropriate to treat this subject as a subset of the big picture—it is the big picture! But it's also important to approach leadership like a task, consciously choosing the desired result and the manner in which you will attain that result.

A team with a well-defined culture will perform better than a team with a poorly defined culture. A well-defined culture implies that everyone on the team knows the overall purpose of the group, shares the same goals and values, and understands the specific role that each individual plays in the performance of tasks. It could be argued that organizing the team into a well-defined culture is a leader's highest priority. But it does no good to organize for the sake of organization. You must reason and spirit the organizational activity in a way that is consistent with the shared purpose and personality of the team.

You will know you have succeeded at defining and cultivating a culture when your employees exhibit a tangible pride in belonging to your team.

Attract Good People

You attract good people by having a team of good people. The magnetism of a successful team draws recruits like moths to a light. Applications for employment flow in without a "Help Wanted" sign. Referrals come from other employees, business acquaintances, friends, and relatives. Everyone wants to work for a winning team. Sound easy? Yes, but you have to earn this laudable condition through some hard and diligent work, and it takes time to get there.

Hire on the basis of character, work ethic and intelligence—in that order. Unfortunately, you can't determine any of these criteria in a written application, and interviews are never as revealing as you hope. I recommend several interviews, if you can afford them, with several of your key staff sitting in on the process. Listen to their reactions and insight. I like interviewing in the "kitchen" during the hubbub of activity, because it reveals the person's comfort level and focus in the intensity of a work environment. Balance your intellectual judgment of the person's qualifications with your "gut" instinct. If both evaluation methods agree this is a person you want to try on the team then make the offer. But if one evaluation method suggests to pass, then pass.

After hiring hundreds of people over my career and developing a general confidence in my ability to judge character and evaluate qualifications, I also readily admit I am still vulnerable to misjudgments. With very few exceptions, you can tell within two weeks after hiring whether the person is going to be an asset or a liability. Do something about it! I evolved a policy that I would not give anyone the authority to hire who had not personally been involved in three terminations. It is easy to hire someone who wants the job, but it is a real trauma to terminate someone in the same situation. I have fired at least 100 people over the years, and none of them were easy or pain free. But nothing drags the team down like a few bad performers, so for the sake of your good employees let go of the bad employees as soon as you identify them. Every time you let someone go, you become more careful, and thus skilled, at determining whom you should hire next time. If someone is not working out, admit you made a mistake and let him or her go. Employing a team of universally good workers is a sure-fire way to succeed.

Train, Train, Train!

Whenever my former partner and I perceived that we had an extra dollar to spend in our business, we would ask ourselves where we should spend that dollar—toward advertising or training. We chose training every time. Over a 10-year period, our sales increased at an average annual rate of 65 percent, and yet we never spent any money on advertising (except for a small Yellow Pages expenditure). From this experience, I would argue that every dollar spent on training yields $100 in value, whereas I was always uncomfortable trusting we would get a return of any significant value on advertising expenditures (despite the contentions of ad salespeople).

Training yields value due to many factors. Easiest to understand is that training improves the quality of product and the efficiency of operations. Better product increases demand and better efficiency increases the capacity to satisfy that demand. But from a leadership perspective, training is a conscious and greatly appreciated investment in your staff. Worker surveys consistently reveal that employees value training above all other company "investments." Why is this? The fact that the company "invests" in the staff is seen as confirmation that the staff is truly valued. Also, making staff members more competent and knowledgeable gives them greater pride and fulfillment in their work. All of this translates into better morale and loyalty and higher performance. There is no better investment.

I have heard people argue that it makes no sense to spend a lot of resources on training because of quick turnover. This is faulty reasoning. Of course turnover is high when you don't make an investment in training! It's like saying that watering plants makes no sense because they will die anyway. Of course they're going to die if you don't water them!

Another argument says that if you train someone you must increase his or her wage. Oh no! I often asked my coffeehouse general managers a rhetorical question: Who would you rather employ on a busy shift—four $6-per-hour employees or three $8-per-hour employees? The economic investment is the same, but what's the expected output? The question assumes, also, that the $6-per-hour employees have less than six months experience and the $8-per-hour employees are a few of your highly trained, more experienced workers. Any intelligent manager would quickly answer that he or she would rather have the three $8-per-hour employees—the cost is the same, but output may be 125 percent greater than that of four $6-per-hour employees. This leads to the realization that a manager should want to develop his or her staff into more valuable employees. Without any doubt, training pays for itself many times over.

Give Your Team the Things It Needs

One of the leader's principal responsibilities is to equip the team with the necessary tools, materials and information it needs to perform. This fundamental task of "thing fulfillment" must always take precedence over optional activities. The lights and water must be on. Coffee must be in the bins, milk in the refrigerator. The staff schedule must be posted. Paychecks must clear the bank. Failure in any of these basic fundamentals immediately and fatally erodes the mantle of leadership. When your staff makes known that it needs you to do something, do it. Yes your employees will take it for granted, not recognizing the full cost of your effort. Instead, you will have to find fulfillment in the knowledge they would have roasted you had you not done what they asked.

Observe and Reward

One of the popular management styles of the '80s was Andrew Grove's (CEO of Intel) "Management by Walking Around." It was not a new technique. Grove simply gave a name to a leadership practice that has no parallel in effectiveness. The idea is that direct and personal observation is the only way you can develop anywhere near a complete understanding of what's going on. An additional benefit is that your presence proves your interest, again boosting the pride and fulfillment of your staff. They want to know you care, and nothing confirms that better than your physical presence. To see and be seen should be on your mandatory list of regular and purposeful activities.

What do you do with what you see? The worst possible thing you can do is to pull out a piece of paper and start writing down criticisms. Do this just once and your employees will cringe whenever they see you coming. This is not leadership, this is bullying, and the results are devastating. Your staff won't want you around. If you do give praise it will strike shallow. In our contemporary society, you must conduct criticism within the framework of the "hamburger" approach, the meat of which is carefully placed between soft, warm buns. You want to do some good? Observe what is going right and write it down without being obvious.

One of the best management tools developed in this century is the Post-It Note. Unassuming and convenient, they offer an excellent means of giving regular pats on the back to your staff. Place them on time cards or work stations, recognizing good performance or expressing general appreciation. Little gifts like cards or books are also great rewards. Think about ways of rewarding your staff that are communications of the heart or spirits of appreciation. Thoughtful rewards tend to mean more to the recipient than gifts of money. Money is okay, too, when appropriate, but it is not the foundation for building a strong team. That only comes from building a meaningful relationship.

Attend to the Individuals on Your Team

Employer paranoia and the belief that the "captain should be the loneliest person on the ship" has led many managers to disassociate themselves from their staffs. Such a philosophy is a shame. There is a lot of room between isolationism and perceived harassment. Frankly, unless you know your employees well, your opportunity to guide them effectively is limited. What are their values? What are their goals? Although your responsibility as a leader is to the whole team, it is important to understand that your team is made up of individuals, and individuals, at some point, like to be known and treated on the basis of their personal uniqueness.

Give Yourself Time to Think

With all the demands placed on you as a business person and manager—as well as by your own individual and family needs—it's hard to find time to think. The alarm rings in the morning and the day is a blur until you get horizontal again, and then you wake up and do it all over again the next day. You have to schedule time to *think*. People who practice meditation know they have succeeded in that practice when they can clear their minds of all thoughts or focus on one particular thing. What this really means is that meditation can yield solutions to everyday problems because with a clear mind you can focus on these problems and find answers. The exercise is meaningful and worthwhile.

Give yourself some uninterruptible time to *think*, where you can focus on the team and your responsibility as its leader. How is each individual progressing as a human being and as a contributor to the team? Do you have a plan of development for each individual? How are the relationships between team members and how can they be improved? It is your job to think about these things and come up with strategies and lists of tasks to make things better. Your role as a leader can only be fulfilled by such conscious focus. It will not happen accidentally, and planning "on the fly" will not be nearly as effective as planning that results from a concentrated effort.

Developing Your Own Leadership Style

Leadership is relative. What needs to be done and how it is done will depend upon a unique set of circumstances, including the genuine representation of your own character. Have the confidence that you can become an effective leader. Devote the necessary time to studying, planning and implementation. A common trait amongst great leaders is their ability and diligence in communicating; everything else is up to your own personal interpretation.

So dedicate yourself to developing your own personal leadership style. Of all the possible management venues, I am firmly convinced that none is more fulfilling than a coffeehouse. The balance of challenges and enjoyment almost always made me go home with a satisfied smile on my face. To be a successful coffeehouse manager requires a broad array of skills and a solid philosophy of altruism. Certainly, part of the joy comes from the wonderful role that a coffeehouse can play in enhancing the quality of life of your community, but absolutely the most rewarding aspect is the part you can play in guiding and developing the people who work with you. A successful coffeehouse leader is one who actively builds and manages a team of people who deliver high quality products and outstanding service effectively and efficiently, resulting in tremendous growth and profitability for the operation. In applying the directives of this chapter, I hope you find measurable progress in your own development as a leader, as well as fulfillment in life.   ●

section three

section three

YOUR EQUIPMENT

Joe Monaghan

Joe Monaghan has over 20 years experience in the specialty coffee industry, and is currently the vice president of sales and marketing for Espresso Specialists Inc. (ESI) in Seattle, one of the industry's leading commercial espresso machine importers. In addition to overseeing the training standards of a coast-to-coast distribution network, Monaghan leads ESI's direct sales to many of America's foremost specialty coffee retailers. His background includes owning a chain of espresso carts in Seattle and roasting and selling coffee in the early days of Seattle's Best Coffee. He is the author of the best-selling book *Espresso! Starting & Running Your Own Specialty Coffee Business*.

133

Chapter 10

**Truly Understanding Your
Espresso Machine
and Grinder**

The invention of the first "Italian-style" coffee or espresso machine is credited to Italian engineer Luigi Bezerra, who in 1901 patented a commercial bar machine that brewed a single cup of coffee on demand using water and steam pressure. It is at this point that true Italian coffee was born.

135

The next major development came at the hands of Achille Gaggia, who in 1945 devised the first lever-operated group, which used a spring and piston to provide a much greater brewing pressure than was previously available. This not only greatly improved the quality of the brewed coffee, it also significantly increased the speed of delivery, a feature that was received enthusiastically by impatient Italian coffee drinkers.

The next major innovation arrived in 1961 with the release of the famous E61 by the Milano-based Faema company. This machine was the first to use a motor-driven pump to provide brewing pressure. The machine also featured a heat exchanger and distribution groups similar to those used today. This machine's popularity grew rapidly in the European bar market due to its decreased brewing time (now only 20 seconds) and its less-strenuous operating style (baristas had to expend less energy).

By and large, today's commercial espresso machines operate much like the Faema E61. Most of the recent innovations come from companies introducing sophisticated electronics and microprocessors to help with operation and controls. Approximately 80 percent of the world's espresso machines are manufactured in Italy. Other producing countries include Spain, France, Switzerland, and the United States.

Espresso Machine Basics

Espresso machines are designed to accomplish two primary and basic functions:

1) Brewing espresso coffee, or "shots," by infusing hot water under high pressure through finely ground coffee.

2) Drawing steam off the boiler to whip and heat milk for cappuccinos and lattés, as well as creating steam to heat other beverages such as cider or chai.

Diagram of a Typical Espresso Machine

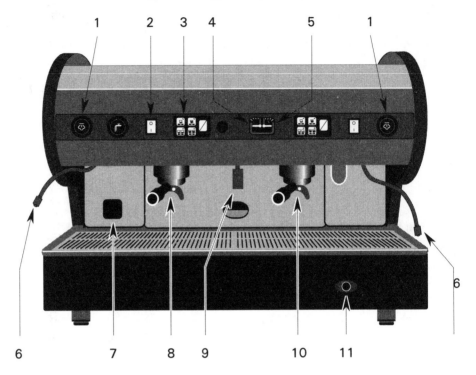

1. Steam valve
2. Manual brew switch *(overrides automatic)*
3. Brew button pad
4. Pump pressure gauge
5. Boiler pressure gauge
6. Steam wand
7. On/off switch
8. Double portafilter
9. Hot water nozzle
10. Single portafilter
11. Manual boiler fill valve

Illustration courtesy of Espresso Specialists Inc.

Other less central functions include dispensing hot water for steeping tea or making hot chocolates.

Although these functions are few and basic, creating a machine that delivers the correct balance of stable brewing temperature and adequate steam pressure requires considerable engineering.

Most espresso machines, regardless of manufacturer, are relatively similar in concept and design. All machines have some components in common, specifically boilers, groups and pumps. Differences among machines include the number and size of boilers, materials used in construction, and aesthetic design.

A vast majority of machines are single-boiler, heat-exchanger machines. The size of the boiler may vary depending on the number of groups and the output the machine was designed to provide. The boiler is typically made of copper or stainless steel, and it may or may not be plated with nickel or other material.

When the machine is operational, the boiler is approximately two-thirds full of water. This water is rapidly heated by a submersible, high-wattage heating element located inside the boiler. As the water reaches the boiling point, steam is created. The steam is trapped, or contained, in the boiler by the created internal boiler pressure. This pressure is regulated by a pressurestat. This pressurestat senses steam pressure inside the boiler, and when it reaches the desired pressure, it turns off the energy to the heating element. Likewise, when the pressure drops below the desired level, the pressurestat switches back on to bring the pressure back up. Most manufacturers design machines that run at an operating boiler pressure of between 1 and 1.5 bars (roughly 14 to 22 pounds per square inch).

Located somewhere inside the boiler is a smaller vessel that holds anywhere from six to 12 ounces of fresh water. This vessel is called a heat exchanger. The water contained in the heat exchanger collects heat from the boiler and then passes through the ground coffee during the extraction process.

Heat exchangers vary in design from manufacturer to manufacturer. Some are placed vertically in the boiler, others horizontally. The most popular models use a thermo-syphon process in which water circulates through the heat exchanger and group propelled by the natural convection of the heated water.

The boiler pressure regulates the temperature of the brewing water. As we all know, water boils at 212 degrees F (100 degrees C) at sea level. As atmospheric pressure is increased, the boiling point rises. The water contained in an espresso machine boiler set at 1.5 bars of pressure will actually boil at a higher temperature (approximately 225 degrees F). Therefore, by raising or lowering the boiler pressure, we actually raise or lower the internal temperature of the boiler, which in turn raises or lowers the temperature of the brewing water as it passes through the heat exchanger.

Another critical component of the espresso extraction process is brewing pressure. In today's espresso machines, a motor-driven pump provides the brewing pressure. Depending on the machine brand and model, the pump and motor may be located inside or outside the machine. When the barista activates the brewing process, the pump forces fresh water into the heat exchanger, pushing hot water out through the ground coffee. Most experts agree that the ideal brewing pressure is approximately 9 bars, or 125 pounds per square inch. The pumps are adjustable, and the pump pressure is registered on the gauge usually located on the front of the machine.

After the brewing water has left the heat exchanger, it is channeled through the brewing head, or group, where it is diffused for even saturation of the ground coffee. Groups are typically made of cast brass for even heat distribution.

The role of the group also includes stabilizing the brewing temperature. The best designs provide thermo-compensation for the groups by either circulating hot water through them or mounting them directly to the boiler. It is imperative that the group retains the proper amount of heat so that the brewing water does not cool too much as it channels its way toward the ground coffee. Most groups have a diffusion block and screen that causes the water to "shower evenly" onto, and through, the ground coffee contained in the portafilter.

In the case of double- or twin-boiler machines, brewing water is both controlled and heated in a somewhat different manner. Rather than placing a heat exchanger within a single boiler, these machines use a completely separate boiler or tank to hold brewing water. This completely separates the brewing water from the steam. An actual thermostat controls this second boiler rather than a pressurestat. Proponents of this system maintain the machine's brewing temperature will be both more accurate and stable, particularly in high-volume situations. The mass of water held at proper temperature is much greater in volume in a twin-boiler machine than the water contained in a heat exchanger. In addition, the high volume of milk steamed in American-style coffee bars has no impact on the brewing temperature of a twin-boiler machine. As in single-boiler machines, manufacturers of twin-boiler machines typically mount groups directly to the boiler, where water circulates for temperature stability.

After passing through the group head, the brewing water is forced through the ground coffee compacted in the device known as the portafilter (the technical name for the filter handle into which ground coffee is dosed). Like the group head, the portafilter is usually made of chrome-plated cast brass for even temperature distribution and contains a removable stainless steel filter insert.

Filter inserts come in single-, double- and triple-shot configurations. These inserts hold different amounts of ground coffee and have different numbers of holes on the bottom. Single-shot inserts are designed to hold approximately seven grams of ground coffee.

137

Espresso Machine Group Components

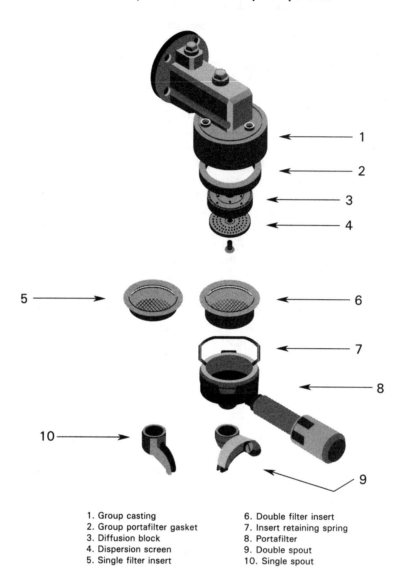

138

1. Group casting
2. Group portafilter gasket
3. Diffusion block
4. Dispersion screen
5. Single filter insert

6. Double filter insert
7. Insert retaining spring
8. Portafilter
9. Double spout
10. Single spout

Illustration courtesy of Espresso Specialists Inc.

Double-shot inserts hold approximately 14 grams and have twice the number of holes, and so on for triples. During the extraction process, the force of the brewing water must meet with the proper resistance to provide the proper flow rate. This resistance is provided by the ground and tamped coffee bed combined with the filtering action of the insert.

Volumetric vs. Semi-Automatic

With the exception of older-style lever machines and the more recently developed super-automatic machines, espresso machines come in either semi-automatic or volumetric configurations. A semi-automatic machine requires the barista to begin the brewing process by activating a switch or lever. The pump will push water through the coffee until the barista deactivates the switch. Volumetric machines automatically control the volume of brewed espresso through the use of sophisticated electronics. A flow meter measures the flow of water, then sends a signal to an internal microprocessor to discontinue the extraction when the predetermined volume has been reached. Users easily program the volume to personal preferences.

Milk Steaming

When a barista steams milk, he or she is actually drawing steam off the top third of the boiler. The machine opens a valve of some type, allowing the pressurized steam to flow out through tubing and a steam wand into the milk. Steam valves vary in type. Most are mechanical in nature, using a seat and gasket concept similar to a kitchen sink faucet. Some operators prefer a lever-type valve for ergonomic reasons, while others prefer a rotating knob-type valve for flow control. Some machines use electric valves that open and close, triggered by a switch or button.

Steam wands are made of either stainless steel or chrome-plated copper tubing, and are available in a variety of lengths and bend configurations. At the end of the wand is a tip, usually removable, with four to six small holes that create a spray pattern as the steam escapes. This pattern enhances the ability of the steam to whip the milk while heating.

Some manufactures provide temperature-sensing steam wands that automatically turn off at a predetermined temperature. Some manufacturers make milk-frothing devices that attach to the steam wand and dispense hot foamy milk directly into the cup.

Grinder

The importance of the coffee grinder is often underestimated, but coffee ground to the proper consistency is absolutely critical to the extraction process.

Espresso grinders perform two basic but essential functions:

1) They grind or mill roasted coffee beans into a powder form for brewing.
2) They dose and dispense ground coffee into the portafilter.

Although the role of the grinder seems basic and its practical functions few, it's crucial to grind and dose coffee with precision and consistency to maintain coffee quality. It's also more complicated than it first appears.

All commercial espresso grinders are constructed according to the same basic model: Whole beans fall from the hopper into the grinding area, where two textured plate burrs grind the beans evenly into a fine powder.

A grinder may use one of two types of burrs. The most common type of grinder uses flat burrs, one plate stacked on top of the other. The first plate spins while the other remains stationary. Centrifugal force pulls the ground coffee down through the burrs and into the dosing chamber.

The distance between burrs determines the fineness or coarseness of the coffee grounds. Less distance means a finer powder, while more space results in a coarser grind. Commercial espresso operations typically own flat-burr grinders; they are economical, reliable and meet most operators' demands.

A second type of grinder uses conical burrs. This grinder holds one burr shaped like a cone that sits inside the second burr. Conical burrs grind slower than flat burrs, so less heat is transferred to the beans during grinding. Because heat contributes to coffee staling, this has a positive impact on coffee flavor. In addition, proponents of conical-burr type grinders claim the ground powder has a more preferable particle distribution. However, in most cases and for most operators, neither the reduced heat nor the particle distribution contribute appreciable differences. Because flat-burr grinders tend to be less expensive and more time-efficient, they are more popular among espresso bar owners.

The grinder must not only grind evenly, but it must be responsive to the hands of the operator. Over the course of beverage preparation, the barista watches the rate of pour on the espresso machine. He or she can adjust the grind to help control the extraction rate, thus improving beverage quality. How do you adjust the grind? Deliberately and with care.

Diagram of a Typical Espresso Grinder/Doser

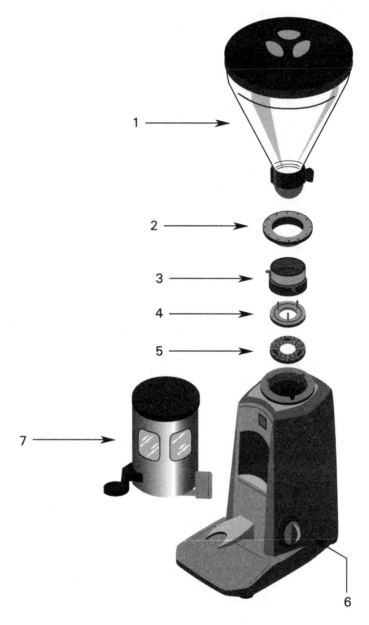

140

1. Bean hopper
2. Adjusting collar
3. Grinding burr mounting collar
4. Top grinding burr
5. Bottom grinding burr
6. Timer
7. Doser

Illustration courtesy of Espresso Specialists Inc.

Regardless of burr type, the grind is adjusted by rotating a collar at the base of the bean hopper. Rotating the collar either brings burrs closer together or moves them farther apart. Technically, only one burr is moving; adjustment brings the fixed or stationary burr closer to the moving burr or positions it farther away. Some grinders have click stops that work like adjustment stair steps to hold the grind in place. Others have fine thread enabling almost infinitely minute changes. Some operators prefer click-stop control because it's easier to use. Others, however, prefer to make fine-thread adjustments that allow them to finely tune for the perfect grind; they believe the click stops make too great a jump between clicks. Flat- or conical-burred, click-stop or fine-thread adjusted, grinder burrs are typically good for 1000 to 1500 pounds of ground coffee.

The grinder doser is usually a segmented or pie-sliced tray at the bottom of a holding chamber into which coffee falls after it passes through the burrs. This tray rotates inside the dosing chamber by virtue of a lever and cam mechanism. The operator triggers rotation with a handle or lever on the outside of the grinder. One pull on the dosing handle yields enough coffee to brew one shot; two pulls, two shots, and so on. The operator can adjust the amount of coffee released with each dose to between six and nine grams of coffee per pull.

As the ground coffee is dosed, it sifts through the bottom of the grinder and into a portafilter, held ready and waiting by the machine operator. Partial dosing—bringing the handle only partially forward or neglecting to allow it to fully return to its starting position after a dose—will throw off the volume of future doses. Similarly, "overdosing" refers to a portafilter into which too much coffee has been dosed. This will also have a negative effect on brewed beverage quality. ●

141

Peter Kelsch

Peter Kelsch is president of Espresso Services Inc. (ESI) in Minneapolis, Minn. Founded in 1989 as a technical service company, Kelsch has built the organization into a full-service provider of quality coffee equipment, products and technical services while providing training and consulting on the specialty coffee industry.

Considered an industry expert on espresso equipment, Kelsch has served as an informational resource for many foodservice and coffee industry publications as well as a presenter and lecturer at such events as Coffee Fest, the Specialty Coffee Association of America Conference and Exhibition, and numerous foodservice trade shows.

143

Chapter 11

Periodic Maintenance Schedules for Your Equipment

Unlike many people involved in the specialty coffee business, my introduction to espresso machines came about somewhat by accident. As a teenager, I was an avid consumer of espresso drinks. I was curious about what went on inside those interesting-looking boxes to produce such good-tasting coffee. But instead of seeking out a job working behind one, I fed my daily habit by waiting in line as a customer.

My introduction to the other side of the business occurred when I was in college. One day while I was studying in my favorite coffee shop, the espresso machine blew up with a pop and a flash. This created quite a bit of excitement among staff and customers alike, including a good friend of mine who was working behind the counter. Knowing I had some electrical experience, he asked me to help him get the machine working again. Screwdriver in hand, I figured out how to remove the panels, discovered the problem, twisted some wires together, and enjoyed the free latté my services had earned. Inadvertently, I also received my first introduction to the espresso coffee machine.

In retrospect, my experience that day illustrated the importance of espresso machine maintenance. The explosion resulted from a slow leak that had developed inside the machine, causing steam to condense on one of the electrical switches. Eventually, enough water built up to short out the entire electrical system. When this incident occurred in 1989, there weren't any companies in the city that repaired coffee machines. Without the successful intervention of my friend and I, the coffee shop could have shut down for several days until the owner was able to repair the problem himself. The owner could have avoided all this, however, if he had understood and followed good preventive maintenance policies and procedures for his machine.

Because the specialty coffee industry is relatively young, many new independent retail coffee shop owners run the risk of similar problems. Most have purchased new machines from distributors who are also new to the business. They assume if they haven't had problems in the first few years, all will be well in the future. Unfortunately this is not the case. Most retail shop owners are in for a few surprises as their machines begin to age. If they have not followed regular maintenance procedures, their product quality has suffered and they're facing the potential of serious consequences down the line. Because the performance and reliability of the espresso machine has a direct link on the quality of coffee drinks one serves—and thus to the main income of most shops—the reasons to schedule and practice regular espresso machine maintenance routines far outweigh any reasons to avoid them.

In addition to performance, there are other reasons to maintain an espresso machine. Unlike any other piece of foodservice equipment in the world, the espresso machine is designed for aesthetics as well as operation. In some cases an espresso machine is a piece of functional art.

The history of the equipment is also quite interesting. As with many products on the market today, all espresso equipment initially shared similar internal mechanisms. This, combined with the fact they were usually located at the front of a bar where customers gathered, meant the only point of difference was often the external appearance of the equipment. This industry trend has continued for nearly 90 years as manufacturers continue to create unique designs that set their machines apart from others. This unique piece of foodservice equipment is a valuable work of art. Good maintenance practices will protect your investment.

In the following chapter, I will discuss the technical elements of regular espresso equipment maintenance aimed at preventing poor quality product and equipment breakdown. By discussing how the machine works—I'll describe each section of the machine and what can go wrong with it—I hope to educate the reader enough to promote a stronger interest in retaining overall quality through preventive maintenance.

Basic Problems

An espresso machine is like the car you drive—not only does it cost a lot to buy, but it also needs scheduled maintenance. Take care of it and it will last a long time. Ignore it and not only will it perform less efficiently, but it will invariably break down at the worst possible moment and cost you dearly to fix.

From the day you plug the machine into the wall, four factors contribute to its depreciation and affect the quality of coffee it brews: water, coffee, people, and time. All these factors have a negative impact on the machine. Some are not avoidable, but some definitely are.

If the machine is getting good use, you will naturally cause wear and tear. Physical abuse, although sometimes excessive, is normal for an espresso machine. Although there are varying qualities of equipment—some can withstand much heavier taxation than others—for the most part all espresso machines can and do take some level of abuse.

Age is another area one cannot control. Every time you turn on the machine, it experiences a certain amount of age wear. Although it is very slight, over time it will—like each of us—begin to show its age.

Coffee also affects the machine. Every shot of espresso pulled leaves its own small mark of residue that can eventually build to a larger problem later.

Water is the last factor. This is the most difficult to control because you rarely actually see the effects it has until much too late. If I had to pick the number one cause of coffee machine failure, it would be the gradual effects of bad water. Water is so diverse and complicated one could dedicate a whole book to understanding it, treating it and using it to brew coffee. I hope to offer enough material in this chapter to at least convince the reader to pay attention to water.

I will revisit each of these areas as I discuss the internal and external workings of an espresso machine and how you can avoid serious problems through periodic preventive maintenance routines.

Understanding the Machine

To appreciate the value of preventive maintenance, it's important to understand the basic workings of an espresso machine. And to accomplish this, we need to make a few basic assumptions, all of which may not technically be true.

The first is that all machines work the same. This is true in as much as the technical parameters of espresso extraction have been consistent for nearly 30 years. The process they use to actually achieve the extraction is another thing, but regardless it is important to understand the guidelines the machines follow. The brewing parameters are very specific: Using 6 to 8 grams of finely ground coffee pressed with varying degrees of pressure into a metal portafilter basket, the machine pushes 1 to 2 ounces of water at 180 to 200 degrees F through the coffee at as close to 9 bars of pressure (or 130 pounds per square inch) as possible. The process should take roughly 20 to 30 seconds, and the resulting beverage should appear a dark caramel brown color and creamy on top.

Taking these parameters into account, there are many ways a machine can produce such a beverage, which brings us to the next assumption: All machines work exactly the same on the inside. This is not true. There are at least four types of internal workings for espresso machines on the market today, and each has several variations. There are single boiler machines with heat exchangers; single boiler piston machines with no heat exchangers; single boiler hydraulic machines with heat exchangers; and double boiler systems. The vast majority of the machines manufactured and installed in the market are single boiler systems with heat exchangers. General maintenance for all types, however, is similar and will have the same positive effects. Check with your distributor for more information on specific maintenance practices for your machine, as they could vary slightly.

This chapter will focus on single boiler machines with heat exchangers and the internal systems of this machine type.

There are four basic systems inside each machine: the steam boiler, the coffee group or groups (including a heat exchanger or separate boiler), the heating system (electrical or gas), and the control systems (electronic or manual). All of these systems work in conjunction with each other to make espresso. If one can grasp a basic understanding of each system—how it works together with other systems and how constant use and the aging process can affect each one—you will understand the need for maintenance.

The Steam Boiler

It's best to begin with the basics, and there is nothing more basic in an espresso machine than the steam boiler. It is a fairly easy system to understand both in form and function. The steam boiler is a large metal pressure vessel usually made of copper (for efficient heat transfer and flexibility). The boiler is sealed tightly and filled 2/3 with water. The machine supplies a heat source with either an electrical heating element or a gas burner underneath the boiler.

The machine applies heat and the water inside the vessel boils, thus building steam pressure in the last 1/3 of the boiler. The process is controlled by a pressure-sensing device, which turns the gas or electricity off when the desired pressure is reached. Because the pressure is also related to the temperature of the entire unit, the desired pressure is typically 1.2 bars.

In addition, all espresso machines have steam release valves to both heat and froth milk, hot water valves to take water from the machine, and a safety valve on top to ensure that if something goes wrong with the pressure regulators (which it sometimes does) the machine will release the steam pressure inside the boiler before it becomes dangerous.

Before discussing steam boiler maintenance, there are several facts about this system that may be helpful to know. Nearly all machines from large manufacturers are made to take gas and electric as a standard framework. In most European countries, gas is the most popular form of heat because the cost of electrical energy is high. Because of this, many

147

manufacturers have designed new machines with large boilers so they have a larger surface area to heat with the gas flame. This larger heat mass helps ensure a consistent brewing temperature.

Although it would seem logical that the main purpose of the steam boiler would be to supply steam to heat milk, this is not true. The main purpose of the boiler is to provide a large heat source to keep the coffee brewing group at a constant and controllable temperature, thus heating the brewing water.

There has been a noticeable trend in equipment sales focusing on boiler size as a premium feature. It is important to note that boiler size is nothing without an equally large heating element. An espresso machine performs best with a high ratio of heating power (in watts) to water in the boiler (in liters or gallons). This will not only produce more steam on demand, but it will also maintain a more consistent overall boiler temperature for making coffee.

Problems with steam boilers almost always result from untreated water and age. These problems lead to a depreciation in the quality of coffee the machine produces. The quality of water going into the boiler and the recycling of water once in the boiler will determine whether problems will occur in the future.

Preventive maintenance for your steam boiler is simple: filter and soften your water, and charge and replace the filters of your system on a scheduled and regular basis. It's well known that soft water is bad for drip-brewed coffee, but for espresso coffee it's almost mandatory. For drip-brewed coffee, soft water can add a slight salty taste if the water in its untreated state is hard or full of minerals. We can't detect this flavor in espresso because of the high ratio of dissolved solids in the beverage. Soft water also has the additional benefit of improving the crema or foaming effect of the brewing process.

If you have not had your water tested, you can purchase simple water test kits at a hardware store. Problems can occur even if the water is slightly hard, so it's best to treat the water regardless. If you don't, serious problems could result that will affect the performance of the machine, its working life, and the quality of the coffee it produces.

Bad water could eventually cause a problem with the boiler itself. Depending on the quality of the materials used and the engineering in the design, some of these problems can be worse than others. The whole boiler contracts and expands constantly as the machine cools and reheats (a main reason boilers are made of copper, a flexible metal). This process can loosen the seals and fittings attached to the boiler, meaning the boiler might eventually develop permanent leaks. This is aggravated by the fact that minerals in untreated water will re-solidify in areas that are hotter or colder than the temperature of the water itself. If the boiler begins to leak, the resulting mineral deposits will form on the external fittings and seals, which will intensify the leaking. Thus using hard water can prematurely destroy your machine by literally pushing it apart.

Hard water can lead to worse problems. As mineral deposits form on the inside of the boiler, they cover all surfaces. This displaces the water, thus lowering the volume in the boiler. These deposits will build faster on the hotter and colder areas. The hottest area is the heating element itself. As mineral deposits build up on the heating element, they slowly cover it and lower its heat output. This means the machine will have to work harder to boil water. The result: A 10-liter, 4500-watt espresso machine becomes an 8-liter, 3000-watt machine. Even worse, it takes longer to transfer heat to the heat exchanger, which results in a lower or very inconsistent brewing temperature for your espresso.

The potential problems go on and on. The problems usually peak as the heating element literally burns itself apart because so much of its heating ability is trapped inside itself. I will cover this more in the heating section, but this should give you an idea how poor maintenance in one area can affect another. Overall, I would estimate that as much as 50 percent of all espresso machine service is related to water issues, specifically scale build-up.

A less serious problem inside the boiler is sediment. If a machine doesn't have a water filter, sediment from the city water supply will build in the boiler. Although it is rare for sediment to be so severe as to cause problems in the first few years, I have seen machines that had enough sediment to actually cause major performance problems over time. The most prevalent problems are related to the sight glass. Many machines have a visible glass tube so the barista can actually see the water level in the steam boiler. This feature was originally designed for machines that didn't have automatic fill devices; the operator could see when the water level was low and manually fill the boiler. Some machines also use this feature to regulate the water level in the machine. Over time, a combination of hard water, mineral build-up and sediment can plug up the lower fitting that supplies water to the sight glass. If this happens, the sight glass may indicate there is water in the boiler while, in fact, there is none. The end result is that the operator will eventually run the boiler dry and burn out the heating element.

All problems with steam boilers develop over time and can be absolutely avoided by incorporating proper water treatment systems in your operating business plan. It seems a logical thing to do—and it's easy to replace and check these systems periodically—yet it is rare to find retailers who integrate appropriate systems and are consistent with their maintenance.

One thing to keep in mind is that it's never to late to do it right. Most equipment providers sell both softening and filtering systems, and many offer scheduled call backs and services to maintain your water quality.

The first step is to have your water tested. Second is to install a quality foodservice water filtration system for your espresso machine (if you don't already have one). Third is to install a softening cartridge or small manual water softener made for espresso machines if your water tests out even slightly hard. Fourth, create a consistent and mandatory maintenance schedule for retesting, replacing and recharging your system. If you can't do it with any consistency, hire a company to do it for you. Finally, if you have owned your machine for some time and haven't used such protection, have the boiler de-limed and flushed to be safe. Most service companies offer such services and can do them on-site when you are having a system installed. Keep in mind that even major retail chains pay outside companies to schedule, automatically ship, and follow up with on-site management to make sure water and its varied side effects are controlled. Both your time and your staff's time is best spent on customer service issues, not technical issues.

Another cause of boiler deterioration is time. Again, because boilers come in different qualities of design and engineering—and because boilers are constantly expanding and contracting as they heat and cool—eventually this movement will have an effect on the boilers themselves. This is obviously a quality issue. The better designed the boiler, the less likely it will have problems over time. But in machines of lower quality that are assembled with low-quality fittings and gaskets, this stretching and slight movement will cause areas to leak. If it does, depending on the situation and the age of the machine, you should either have the machine rebuilt or replace it. Regardless of the boiler quality, manufacturers recommend you replace gaskets and seals on a set schedule of usually four to five years. This prevents any potential for leaking or rupturing, and is a good safety measure if you can afford to have it done.

We also need to discuss the steam outlet and valves. All machines have either electronic or manual valves that allow steam and hot water to be released from the boiler. In the steam boiler system, steam valves are used more than any other part, making them a deciding factor for many people looking to purchase a new machine. Depending on the machine's valve design, preventive maintenance can be critical. There are two types of mechanical steam valves: cam-operated lever valves and rotary knob valves. In addition, there are many machines on the market today that have electronic solenoid steam and hot water valves. For the sake of simplicity—and because they are in the vast majority—I will focus on mechanical valves.

As with most other areas of the machine, no valve type is better or worse, but design

149

and engineering is everything. Poorly designed mechanical steam valves can not only be problematic, but they can be one of the most expensive regular service costs a shop can incur. Most valves need service over time, and every six months is not uncommon. But the differences between one valve and another and the costs to service and maintain them are dramatically different. The main factors are whether the valve was designed for heavy use and whether it's serviceable without taking apart the whole machine. Sometimes you don't have to remove the complete valve to service it.

Heavy use and human abuse are the biggest issues with valves. Heavy use requires more maintenance. Heat, time and use all wear and harden the seals inside the valve. As with any standard water faucet, the rubber gasket or seal will harden and deform over time. As a result, the valves leak.

Many times the valves are also abused. Highly caffeinated employees over-turn and over-tighten the valves. On lever-type valves, they sometimes hit them excessively. All these actions cause excessive wear and will lead to an eventual breakdown of the valve itself.

These problems can be costly to fix. Many valve designs are poor and outdated; they require the operator to remove the complete valve body from the machine to change a simple rubber gasket. To complicate matters, many times it's difficult to get at a valve. Occasionally it requires a near complete disassembly of the machine body to remove a broken or problematic valve. Costs can be excessive. They can also be completely avoided if the machine's valve allows access from the front panel or has a removable center so the operator can change the gasket without removing the whole valve body. The risks of valve problems are especially intensified if you have an abusive staff. Complete valves are expensive and their removal and replacement can cost even more.

Maintenance is the only way to reduce these costs. When rotary valve gaskets begin to harden, they require a harder twist to tighten. When they begin to leak, employees tighten even harder to stop the dripping of condensed water. This combination causes excess wear on the metals; over time, the whole valve may need to be replaced.

Lever valves are sometimes more problematic because they're either on or off; they have no middle ground. It is common to see them constantly dripping water on counters. Additionally, levers wear on the inside, which eventually lowers the steam pressure they release. Scheduling regular maintenance service calls and having your steam valves rebuilt on an annual basis is a smart and cost-effective way to save time, money and ensure the maximum steam pressure from your machine. Again, some machines feature valves that can be rebuilt without removing the valves themselves. This simple feature can save you hundreds of dollars and hours of downtime. The cost difference can be $150 in parts and labor compared to $250.

Finally, the steam boiler has a safety release valve screwed onto the top of the boiler. This simple device is mandatory as a precaution against the heating element on the machine malfunctioning. This mechanical spring pressure valve is set to release the steam pressure from the boiler at 1.5 bars. Over time this device can age and fail. If it does, you will know, as the release of steam from the boiler at this pressure is both loud and dramatic. Most manufacturers recommend replacing the valve every four or five years. Replacement will cost around $50 during a regular service call.

In summary, steam boiler maintenance consists of treating your water appropriately, having your steam valves rebuilt on a regular basis, replacing your safety valve, and looking into and fixing any mysterious leaks and drips from under your machine. Although the cost will vary greatly from machine to machine, your annual cost to maintain the boiler and valves should not exceed $300 to $400 per year.

The Espresso Brewing Group

In terms of performance, the most important area of an espresso machine to maintain is the coffee brewing group. Although it looks simple, this area has very specific tolerances for brewing espresso. Small changes will produce dramatically different qualities of espresso, especially in the brewing area.

To understand the brew group is to know how to maintain it. We can break the brew group into two main parts, best described as the internal and the external. Internally, the coffee machine has a heat exchanger for the group. This is typically a separate sealed chamber or tube inside of or passing through the steam boiler. This chamber is full of water. The heat produced from the steam boiler heats the water inside the chamber to a near boiling temperature. Externally, all espresso machines have a brewing group head. This is where the operator locks the coffee-filled portafilter into the machine. The external group is a large piece of solid brass designed in some way to absorb and maintain a specific temperature. All group heads are connected to the heat exchanger either directly or with copper tubing stretching from the boiler to the external group.

The brew group can be strictly engineered to meet precise temperature requirements, heat transfer scenarios, and complicated water pressure and flow conditions. I say "can be" because many machines on the market today still use brew group technology designed as far back as the 1950s. A very popular concept among contemporary manufacturers was designed in the early 1960s.

As science and technology has progressed, many successful manufacturers have invested in the design and construction of better brew groups. What can improve? Quite a bit, as the last 30 years has shown. The fact is the brewing groups of all espresso machines are still designed to simulate the early metal piston-type machines designed in the late '40s and early '50s. It was during this time that all early successful manufacturers applied empirical scientific methods for the first time to the study of coffee roasting and blending and to the brewing of espresso coffee. Interestingly enough, no matter how much technology has been applied to the basic principles of making espresso, the designs of the early metal piston espresso machines (when the correct standards are met) still make the best espresso coffee. The community of manufacturers and coffee roasters in Italy define the "best" by measuring the strength of the coffee, or, more specifically, the solids dissolved in the water.

In the early machines, a large metal piston forced the hot water through the coffee at a pressure set by a mechanical spring. When working correctly, there is no room for error. Manufacturers discovered that this brewing system is nearly perfect except for the cost and complexity of manufacturing such bulky metal groups. Companies then invented machines with electronic pumps that pushed water through the coffee, simulating the original design. Thus was the modern brew group born.

If this all seems redundant, read on. The goal of every brew group is to control the pump flow output and pressure and to set to the desired parameters in all situations. The difficulty of using a pump is controlling the water pressure and temperature, and this is where maintenance makes a difference. The brewing system is best understood as a small pressure cooker. You're going to cook a small amount of coffee for a very short period. Too much heat and it overcooks. Not enough and it is undercooked. And if the seals and pressures are not correct, some areas are overdone and some under.

The problems that can occur are numerous. Assuming you have placed the proper amount of coffee in the portafilter basket (7 grams for a single, 14 for a double), the grind is correct, and the tamp is of proper force, the machine now has to function the way it was originally designed. Once the activation switch is pressed, water pumped into the heat exchanger displaces already hot water inside and is thus forced to the exterior group through a small hole inside of a solenoid, or mechanical water switch. When the water reaches the upper inside of the brew group, it is spread out in a circular pattern by what is commonly referred to as a dispersion screen or block. From the dispersion screen, the water is forced out onto the upper screen in the group (commonly referred to as the shower screen). If you're confused, take the handle out of the machine and turn on the group. Look into the group for the source of the dripping water; this is the shower screen.

151

The portafilter basket is also an integral part of the process, as the holes in the bottom are of a very specific number and size, usually a few millimeters wide. After the coffee is fully wet and the pressure has built, the holes in the basket supply a specific amount of back pressure for brewing.

Now the pressure cooking takes place. The coffee swells inside the basket, the pressure levels off at the set pump pressure, and the combination of the temperature and pressure cause the extraction of dissolved solids, oils and small coffee particles, all of which are forced through the small holes on the bottom of the portafilter and flow into your cup. If everything has been set up correctly and is in perfect working condition, you should have a very pleasant tasting cup of concentrated coffee and a measurably high-quality one.

More important from a maintenance perspective is what happens after the brewing process stops. The water that is pumped under pressure on top of the coffee has to go somewhere, so the mechanical solenoid is turned off at the same time as the pump. This opens a path between the coffee (where all the pressure resides) and an outlet tube, which usually bleeds the water down into the drain pan of the machine. This release of pressure is a common noise in a coffee shop if you pay attention. Important to note here is that in addition to releasing the back pressure of water, the release draws coffee particles and extracted coffee back into the group. This is where the problems begin: Over time the release of back pressure in the group plugs the shower screen, the dispersion block, and the solenoid.

Wet cooked coffee is like tar. When you consider all the small chambers, paths and screen holes in the group, you can imagine what happens when coffee is packed and pushed back through the group and the small holes and chambers become plugged. In summary, the water flows in forced directions and pressure builds in some areas more than others. The coffee is therefore over-extracted in some parts of the group and under-extracted in other parts. Over time, you won't be able to get a good foam on the espresso, it will look weak, and it will take on a bitter taste. The solution is to backflush the group daily to clean all the coffee particles and oils off internal parts.

Most operators backflush their machines weekly, if not daily, and understand the basics of why they need to do so. For those who do not backflush, the process is simple. All you need is a blind filter basket or rubber basket plug and some cleaning detergent made for espresso machines. I highly recommend staying away from detergents that have vapor breathing and skin irritation warnings on their labels, as they can eat away some metal coatings on components. There are plenty of suppliers selling safe, non-caustic detergents that work very well.

If you have been backflushing regularly but continue to have group blockage, you may not be doing it right. To backflush, place the blind filter in the group handle and a teaspoon of detergent in the basket. Place it in the group and start the machine as if pulling a shot. The water will have nowhere to go, so you only have to wait for the pressure to build in the basket, which takes two to five seconds.

Now as you turn the brewing switch off, detergent is flushed through the inside of the group down the same path as the coffee residue. Activate and backflush the detergent eight or 10 times—that's usually enough to clean the group components, especially if you do it every day. If you use extremely oily coffee, you'll need to backflush more frequently as the oils act as an agent for residue build-up.

It's also helpful to clean the group gaskets while backflushing. To clean the gaskets, activate the brew cycle without sealing the handle tightly in the group. Once the pressure builds up and the soapy water begins to leak around the handle, pull it into place to stop the leaking. This will run soapy water into the rubber gasket in the group head, thus clearing any residue that may have built up during operation. Many distributors also sell group gasket brushes to help further clean the gasket.

Maintaining the brew groups of your espresso machine is by far the easiest way to ensure high-quality espresso for your customers. Every area of the brew group is subject to wear and tear because of hard water deposit or coffee residue blockage or the changing shape and effectiveness of the components. It's important to replace gaskets if and when they become hard and start leaking. It's even more critical to replace group baskets and shower screens. These two parts create the specific pressure environment required to produce good coffee. Both parts will stretch and compress during brewing, thus losing their initial shape. The small holes in both components are also critical in size and will change over time. The end user who is friendly with a screwdriver can change both, and the cost should not exceed $10 each. Replace both parts every six months to a year. Many retailers schedule biannual or annual tune-ups, but don't be afraid to do it more often.

In summary, keep in mind that every part in the group that coffee touches is subject to wear and residue. This will change the way the machine produces espresso. In addition, I cannot stress enough the importance of soft water. Treating your water will prevent major problems later in the life of the machine. I have seen the insides of heat exchangers that looked like someone had poured cement in them. Changes in the water volume in such areas will change the brewing temperatures, which will ultimately reduce the quality of coffee.

One last component you should eventually change is the group solenoid. Over time this device will lose its initial tolerances and begin to leak. When it does so, the pump will not hold the proper pressure on the coffee and the machine will consistently produce weak espresso with little or no crema. It's a good idea to replace solenoids every two to four years. They are expensive items—they run from $75 to $150—but you can test them to make sure you're not throwing away good money. As with all areas of the machine, better safe than sorry.

The Heating System

A less critical but still important espresso machine feature is the heating system. You can't maintain the heating system on a daily basis, but it's still valuable to know what it does and how it works so you can anticipate problems before they occur. Unfortunately, if you do have a problem with your heating system, it generally means your machine is already down and won't work. This is obviously the wrong time to learn how you could have prevented a problem. Regardless, there's still a lot you can do next time.

As I mentioned earlier in the chapter, espresso machines are designed to be heated two ways: gas and electric. In the last 40 years, most European manufacturers have designed equipment that relies on both power sources—electric power controls the operations of the machine and gas power heats the boiler. Because energy in the U.S. and many other areas of the world is inexpensive, many manufacturers have used electric heating elements on export machines as the primary means of heating the steam boiler. This has caused some maintenance challenges because European machines do not rely on electric power as much.

The long-term potential problems of electric heating occur when high-voltage power is drawn through the high-voltage components that make up the heating system of the modern machine. The components a retailer should most concern his or herself with are the power switch, the pressurestat (which turns the heating element on and off), and the heating element itself. We can also include the power switch on the wall in this category, as it is also a heat transfer area that can be affected over time.

The primary reason a heating system fails is age. As with any electrical device, the more you use it, the more likely you can expect long-term problems. This is especially true of high-voltage devices like espresso machines. Also, any time a device produces heat, it's vulnerable to the same failures.

When you turn on your machine, it draws power from the outlet on the wall through the power switch and the pressurestat to the heating element, where it meets resistance and heats the coil on the inside of the machine. Every component along the way creates heat. This heat will slowly cook the components over time, especially in areas that have

153

a break in the solid wire. The components thus deteriorate and grow more and more fragile, eventually failing or breaking.

Again, this is especially common with lower-quality machines. Manufacturers can completely avoid all problems with electrical components and related wiring by designing the machine to handle unlimited use. Unfortunately, manufacturers are in business to make money. They don't always intend for their machines to receive heavy use so they do not spend the extra money for better components. Further, many of the machines on the market today were designed with smaller heating elements to pass U.S. safety requirements and were upgraded later to produce more steam. This often challenges the whole electrical system down the road, causing a literal meltdown. Unless you know how your machine is designed and whether it can handle high volumes, there isn't a lot you can do but follow your maintenance routines religiously and hope no failures arise.

There are a few other potential problems I should also note. I already discussed what happens when hard water deposits accumulate on the heating element. Because the whole heating system will stay on longer, this will cause more overall heat stress. In my 10 years in the industry, I have seen melted plugs, power switches and internal wiring cause severe downtime for many operators. You should look at all these components yearly and replace them if you detect any heat stress. The pressure switch will also wear over time, and you should replace it every two to four years. If it fails (which it eventually will) it can cause a major electrical short and blow fuses. If you're in the market for a new machine, look for one that has a low-voltage pressurestat and uses low-voltage controls. These will generally last forever and reduce your maintenance costs and risk of failure. In terms of safety, there is no more important area of the machine to maintain.

Control Systems

Having reviewed the three major systems of the modern espresso machine, we now come to the area that makes them all work together. Control systems for espresso machines can be very simple or very complex. They are best defined as the electronics, switches and solenoids that start and stop water flow, turn the pump on and off, fill the boiler when needed, keep the machine hot, and allow it to make coffee. As with the heating system, there aren't many daily maintenance routines to follow for control systems aside from cleaning the outside of the machine and replacing external parts that look worn.

The type of espresso machine you own will determine the level of concern you should show for control systems. If you own an automatic espresso machine, it probably has a small, low-voltage computer system that controls all electronic operations. If you own a semi-automatic machine—meaning you have to turn the brewing cycle on and off manually—it probably uses a high-voltage switching system to control all the electronic functions. Either way, you should be aware of a few things to ensure a safe and long life for this system.

The reliability and quality of electronics used in espresso machines for control systems is wide ranging. The simplest and most reliable are found in semi-automatic machines. These are simple systems for which very inexpensive and durable components are available and commonly used. Different manufacturers often use the same on/off switches and solenoids, and all you really have to do is replace them at the factory-recommended times—usually in four- or five-year intervals. Again, replacement is recommended because the systems use electricity. And even though these systems consume a major amount of power, components will age and wear with use and eventually fail. I advise replacing external switches more often, but only when there are noticeable changes in the look or action of the switches.

Fully automatic systems are another matter. The design and quality of automatic control systems vary dramatically from one manufacturer to the next. Some are very sophisticated and others fairly simple. All the top manufacturers use custom electronics and high-quality components, but not everyone can be a top manufacturer. Regardless, there is little you can do to maintain this area except treat your machine well. Most problems that occur have to do with neglect—enough water or steam has typically collected or dripped on a component to short it out. Over time, automatic systems have a higher risk of failure, but again there is not much an operator can do once the machine is installed.

While shopping for an automatic espresso machine, look for models that have complete low-voltage internal control systems. They may cost a little more in the beginning, but the failure rate for such systems is dramatically lower than for typical high-voltage types.

Conclusion

It's always difficult to decide when you should quit maintaining and fixing your current machine and buy a new one. Retailers usually purchase new equipment when they have experienced enough headaches and excess service costs that it would be cheaper just to pay someone to impound the machine. Others upgrade when they can afford it or need a larger and better machine. You should reach these points through a combination of actions that include not only good business practices but much care and consideration for the quality and consistency of your espresso. Like the car you drive, the more you pay attention to your espresso machine by giving it biannual tune-ups, annual checkups, and four-year rebuilds, the longer it will continue to run.

A final note regarding your espresso grinder. Second to the performance of the machine itself, the main cause of poor-quality espresso is dull grinder burrs and dirty grinders. Change grinder burrs every 500 to 1000 pounds of coffee, depending on the quality of the burr and the hardness of the coffee. Every six months when you're having your machine tuned up, it's a good idea to replace your grinder burrs and have your grinder cleaned thoroughly. This will ensure your maintenance investment is worth the time and the quality of your espresso is as good as it can be. ●

155

Shea Sturdivant Terracin

Shea Sturdivant Terracin, recognized internationally as a specialty coffee consultant, writer, educator, and speaker, is the 1997 recipient of the Specialty Coffee Association of America's prestigious *Distinguished Author Award*. Her column "Grounds For Discussion" is circulated worldwide in *Tea and Coffee Trade Journal*, and she is co-author of the internationally distributed book *Espresso: Drinks, Desserts, and More!* Her travels as a writer and speaker have taken her to over 40 states, as well as England, Germany, France, Italy, Costa Rica, the Netherlands, Switzerland, Austria, Belgium, and the Czech Republic.

Sturdivant is a partner in The Coffee Associates, an international consulting firm bringing coffee solutions to the marketplace, and chair of the Business Administration Department at Bauder College in Atlanta, Ga. She is a former officer of the SCAA and former vice president of the Specialty Concepts division of DAKA International, a Danvers, Mass.-based restaurant company. Sturdivant also was business development manager for gourmet coffee for Continental Coffee Products Company, a division of the Chicago-based Quaker Oats Company, and president and co-founder of Coffee Roasters of New Orleans Inc. She first became interested in specialty coffee as a marketer and consumer in 1976.

159

Chapter 12

Competing With Chains in Your Area

Once hard to find, specialty coffee—or some version of it—is now available just about everywhere. Gas stations, convenience stores, white tablecloth restaurants, and even hamburger chains advertise the quality of their special coffees and delicious cappuccinos. Americans' love of fast food has caused the genre to include coffee shops with drive-thru windows that offer donuts, bagels or muffins to go. Although the "special" aspect of their coffee can be suspect, nontraditional locations are selling their version of specialty coffees in many convenient locations.

Whether the beverages offered are truly specialty, special premium or special instant, the American consuming public is increasingly fascinated with coffee. Consumers want the beverage on their terms, however, which means fast and convenient. Specialty coffee has adapted to this demand and its popularity shows no signs of diminishing.

Coffee and juice are the second most popular beverages in the United States after soft drinks. Almost half the U.S. population are coffee drinkers (49 percent), and on average consume 3.3 cups of coffee per day. While 57 percent of all coffee is consumed at breakfast, a respectable 34 percent is enjoyed between meals.[1] Some of this between-meal coffee is consumed at the office from an office coffee station, but a good percentage of it is purchased from one of the many coffee retailers in the U.S.

Specialty coffee has graduated from niche market to big business. In 1996, specialty coffee retail sales represented just over $2.2 billion. Of the 3500 coffee bars projected to have opened during that year, approximately 2000 (60 percent) were owned by chains of 40 units or more and 1500 (40 percent) were independents with their business concentrated in a small geographic area.[2]

The many facts and figures available on specialty coffee combine to tell of a still-burgeoning market. Started by entrepreneurs with a passion for "special" coffees, the specialty coffee industry now represents billions of dollars, and the mom and pop businesses that gave birth to the segment no longer dominate it. At the same time, they need not be dominated by the large businesses that do.

This heady information should come with the proviso: *Warning: for maximum effect, combine this information with experience and common sense.* While statistics effectively document past history, current trends and possible future trends, their value as decision-making tools increase when combined with practical experience and common sense.

A consolidation process has begun. Because specialty coffee is no longer considered a short-term trend and has demonstrated both profitability and staying power, large companies are acquiring single and multi-unit coffee cafés concentrated in favorable geographic areas. Big business' interest in specialty coffee proves it is here to stay. Do not take their presence lightly. While large companies have never been known as industry innovators, they are fierce followers of successful trends and have a take-no-prisoners philosophy. Large businesses are after maximum profit; they want your customers.

Well-funded companies can purchase several strong independent locations or regional chains and instantly own a national chain of stores with an established customer base. By purchasing existing companies with successful and profitable locations, a large company drastically reduces its learning curve. It doesn't want to reinvent the wheel; it just wants to buy it.

To illustrate the amount of money at stake, ration the $2.2 billion in projected revenue by the 60-to-40 chain-to-independent ratio. The average annual gross revenue per independent store is just under $587,000; the revenue per chain store is $660,000.

On the surface, it seems that a small independent making over a half million dollars in annual gross sales looks to be doing just fine, but keep in mind these are just averages. The companies that hit that mark are greatly outnumbered by the companies that don't, and even if a company achieves this large gross margin, its net profit is considerably less.

Small coffee bar owners face daily challenges from large companies in this increasingly competitive and crowded arena. The struggle for a piece of the specialty coffee pie gets harder every year as small shop owners find it more and more difficult to compete with the big boys.

One of the biggest challenges to the small company is the higher cost of inventory associated with smaller purchasing power. Unable to tie up cash in the large, long-term purchases needed to lower cost, independents practice "just-in-time" inventory management. Inventoried items are ordered "just in time" before they run out, and as a result, many independents pay top dollar for everything. Even if they have the money to tie up in inventory costs, most small companies do not have the luxury of owning large warehouses to store bulk purchases. Higher inventory costs and lack of storage space combined with an increasingly competitive environment usually means the independent is making much less profit per transaction than a chain store.

Chains, with their consolidated buying power, pay less for everything. This is in no way a reflection on the quality of their goods and products. Because of volume purchases, larger chains get discounts on green beans, paper goods, construction, furniture, equipment, brochures ... you name it, they probably get a discount on it.

Not only can chains negotiate a lower cost of goods, they can afford to create brand recognition of their products with professional advertising campaigns. Look at Starbucks. Its brand recognition is high and potential and current customers perceive the company's products as having a high value. Because of this perceived high value, consumers are willing to pay a premium price for products that cost pennies to prepare.

Is this the death knoll for small business owners in the specialty coffee business? Not in the least. Chains are merely competition, and competition makes everyone better. This dominance of large companies in the specialty industry does signal one thing though—small companies need to get real serious about their business if they are to survive and prosper. The secret of a successful small business is to think smart. Use your size to your advantage. You are not helpless against the competition presented by large companies.

While consumer demand for coffee products is at an all-time high, this demand, to a large extent, was driven by the high visibility and well-funded marketing campaigns of large chains. These large competitors are a reality in today's marketplace. Many chains do an outstanding job, have strong brand recognition, are forming alliances with food companies or grocery stores, are conveniently located, and are not going to go away. Therefore, independents in today's consolidated and competitive marketplace must be aware of the competition, knowledgeable of their companies' competitive advantages, and be able to communicate these advantages to their customers.

Small coffee bar owners may not have the money necessary to lower inventory costs through bulk purchases or drive a national advertising campaign, but they do have certain advantages over their large competitors. In smaller operations, owners and decision makers meet customers on a daily basis; in large chains, owners and decision makers are sometimes hundreds or thousands of miles away and keep in contact with individual stores through reports. This personal touch is a major competitive edge for small business owners and you should use it.

Treat Your Customers Like Welcome Guests
Personal loyalty goes a long way and customers who feel like welcome guests will likely be repeat guests. Remember your guest's name, favorite drink, birthday, and children's names. Thank the customer for his or her patronage by holding a "Guest Appreciation" activity during the holidays and handing out special invitations.

If you own a drive-thru location, keep treats for the children and doggie biscuits for animal companions. Even though they do not drink coffee, children greatly influence their parents' shopping habits. If you run a retail location with tables inside, keep books and magazines in a special play area for children so their parents can drink coffee and relax. You might even consider a special children's menu of delicious, non-caffeinated beverages. Make sure your menu is appealing to all age groups. In other words, use your knowledge of your customers to create a desirable destination for the whole family.

163

Buy the Best Coffees Available
A small company cannot go toe-to-toe with a big company on price alone and win. Too many small companies have mistakenly thought they could and have gone under from their errors. Make an adequate profit on each pound or cup of coffee you sell. If you have an excellent product and charge a fair price, your loyal customer base will support your business. One way chain stores have helped independents is by educating the consumer on coffee products and preparing them to pay a premium price for their purchases.

Don't assume your guests know you have quality products. Give them details about the coffees they're drinking. Many suppliers of green or roasted coffee sell informational pieces on their coffees—use them. Show your customers you use quality coffees by displaying the roast dates on the bins or bags. If a coffee doesn't sell after a week, pull it, donate it to a shelter, and make sure customers are aware of this. It is both philanthropic and advertises your quality.

Develop a Well-Rounded Menu
Many retailers treat their menus as afterthoughts. This is a big mistake. You should base your menu on the personality of your customer base and a practical assessment of your resources. How long will it take to prepare certain drinks? What's your inventory? What equipment do you own? How much counterspace do you have? Are your employees well-trained? Each of these should factor into your product choices. Your menu also needs to include more than brewed coffees and the traditional espresso-based beverages.

Create a flexible menu of beverages and give them unique, fun names. Pull the blender out and make frosty concoctions. Combine tea and juice, tea and flavored syrups, flavored coffees and flavored syrups, espresso and ice cream. Sell a special beverage with a special pastry. If you have a menu of food items, suggest different beverages to go with each one. Let your imagination run wild; show your personality.

Get your customers and employees involved in your menu development. Run a contest, then give free drink coupons or T-shirts to the person who submits the most creative name and recipe. Advertise these special beverages on a chalkboard or black Plexiglas sheet. Use colored markers to write vivid, colorful descriptions of each beverage. Give customers the recipes so they can make them at home from beans they buy from you.

Make your beverage presentation memorable. Serve espresso beverages with a créme-de-menthe wafer or a piece of chocolate on the saucer. Use toppings, colorful or crazy straws, unusual sugars, or paper umbrellas. Stick a cookie on top of a frozen beverage, or put a chocolate stirrer in a hot beverage. Ice cubes made with flavored syrups look great served in a clear cold cup and taste great with cold flavored coffee.

One of your biggest advantages as a small retailer is that you can be flexible and react quickly to customer likes and dislikes. Use your menu to set yourself apart. Giving a whimsical, sentimental or simply descriptive title to a drink quickly conveys your business personality to customers and sets your product apart in a crowded field.

You can name special beverages or blends in honor of holidays, local events, sports teams, colleges, or high schools, in addition to local people, places or things. Keep in mind, however, that while an inventive name might encourage a customer to try products, only a good taste will generate repeat sales. Listen to customer response; if someone doesn't like a coffee or beverage, make adjustments quickly.

Train, Train and Train Some More

Even though most large chains have in-depth training programs, they're still large companies with many employees who will forget or ignore their training once they are hired. Make sure you and your employees keep your skills current.

As an owner, you owe it to yourself and your business to train employees. Offer cupping lessons; let them taste the difference in the coffee and express the tastes in their own words. You don't have to make employees expert cuppers, but you do have to make them knowledgeable consumers. Give them a discount on purchases so they drink your coffee at home and use brewing equipment sold in the store.

Each employee should be able to describe the taste of the coffee he or she is serving. If customers are new to specialty coffee, the first question asked of them should be, "What do you drink at home?" Employees should then be able to suggest a coffee they would enjoy. On the other hand, don't make your employees coffee snobs. If a customer walks in the door willing to try specialty coffee for the first time, it should be a pleasant experience heightened by the expertise of a patient salesperson.

Market Your Business

Your business should reflect your personality. Building a loyal customer base includes making your retail shop a destination location. People should look forward to going to your store for the quality of the products, the well-trained employees, and the atmosphere of the shop itself. Market your establishment so that it appeals to not just your customers' sense of taste, but to their other senses as well.

Provide a visual feast for your customers. If you have a large front window, make sure you change the display with frequency so loyal customers will always have something interesting to look at and new customers are enticed inside. Post the hours of operation on the front door and make note of daily specials.

When selling whole-bean coffee, clearly mark the bins with the names of the coffees, descriptions and prices. Create special blends for customers, write the recipes on index cards and keep them in a file box near the whole-bean area. Create a "First-Time Buyer" menu of specialty coffees so the array of products won't seem as intimidating to newcomers. Display seasonal specials at eye level so they are easily seen. If you carry items that aren't moving, showcase them in an area near the cash register at a reduced price so they're easily within reach for impulse buys.

Provide reading materials for customers. Buy several subscriptions to major newspapers; expose customers to news from all over the world. Create a lending library and encourage customers to contribute to it. Publish a newsletter with educational material, social items on other customers, monthly specials, and recipes. Include a monthly calendar of events.

Make sure your establishment smells like a coffeehouse. Use cleaning fluids at night and do not allow employees to wear heavy perfumes. Take out the garbage several times a day. Frequently grind coffee and keep small displays of ground coffee on hand to show customers both the roast color and how the granules differ in size according to the extraction method.

Provide an atmosphere that is pleasant to the ears. Non-obtrusive music and the sounds of pleasant conversation soothes; raised voices and the clanking of dishes distracts. Use plants liberally, creating a pleasing atmosphere while helping absorb unwelcome noises.

Make sure the tables and condiment areas are not sticky. Wherever customers touch should be clean. This includes keeping the floors clean, the counters free of dust and glass surfaces cleaned of fingerprints. This also includes making sure glasses, plates and silverware are absolutely clean.

Run a Tight Business

No magic is involved in this one. Don't spend money you don't have or create debt you'll never overcome. Run a lean operation and don't create unnecessary overhead. Know the cost of every product and recheck the costs with every new shipment. Make the margins you need to survive and prosper.

Educate Yourself

Keep current on the specialty coffee industry through trade magazines, related periodicals and the many books and videos available on the specialty coffee industry. Take advantage of tremendous networking opportunities by attending educational events and seminars sponsored by the SCAA. Go to regional and national food shows and coffee events and look at trends in the restaurant trade. Visit your competition, make note of what it does well and what you can do better.

Statistics support the continued growth of the specialty industry, but common sense and experience tell you that success in this crowded arena will not come easy. A word of caution to small independents entering the business or struggling to stay afloat—you must have a burning passion for excellence that will sustain you through the hard times and not allow you to compromise your integrity. You also must combine this passion with a clear assessment of both your and your competitors' strengths and weaknesses. Play to your strengths, their weaknesses.

Know how much your product costs and how much you must charge to make a fair margin. Don't be afraid to charge a fair price for an excellent product delivered in an efficient and courteous manner. Free enterprise is a wonderful thing. If the products and services you offer are outstanding, you will not only survive, you will prosper.

Running a successful specialty coffee retail business and competing against large chains is not easy, but it is possible. If it were easy, everyone would do it. ●

165

1. *The National Coffee Association Winter 1997 Coffee Study, 110 Wall Street, New York, NY 10005.*
2. *FIND/SVP, 625 Avenue of the Americas, New York, NY 10011-2002*

Kate LaPoint

Kate LaPoint is owner of To The Point Business Imaging, a company specializing in marketing, public relations, writing, and editing for clients in the specialty coffee and foodservice industries. She has extensive training experience, teaching countless entrepreneurs how to effectively promote their businesses. She serves on the Specialty Coffee Association of America's Training Committee and is the former chief editor of *Coffee Talk Magazine* (now *Coffee & Cuisine*). LaPoint is a graduate of the University of Washington, with a bachelor's degree in editorial journalism.

167

Chapter 13

**Writing Effective Press
Releases to Promote Your
Specialty Coffee Business**

169

It's a business owner's dream, especially if you're the owner of a retail business: A write-up in your local paper, a mention of your company in an industry publication, or a feature article in a business magazine. As an entrepreneur, you probably have a list of questions about self-promotion as long as a kid's wish list for Santa. And you should. You spend all your time keeping your store running—from managing your inventory and balancing the books to training employees and ensuring quality in your products and customer service.

Following are some questions you may find yourself asking, along with some brief answers that will introduce you to the subject of this chapter—writing effective press releases to promote your specialty coffee business.

Question: Does the media really care about my company?
Answer: You bet! Whether you reach out to a community newspaper, an industry newsletter or a national publication, a newsworthy story is a good story. If you do your homework and approach each editor with an understanding of his or her publication's audience, you can find something of interest and value to those readers.

Question: How do I find time to promote my business?
Answer: You have to make time. This may require you to create a long-range plan and set aside time each week (or even each day) to focus on your promotional efforts.

Question: Are there creative ways to gain exposure in the media?
Answer: Your promotions can be as creative as you (and your staff). Generally, the more creative you are, the more likely you are to get noticed. For example, you can create a promotion or event that not only gains media exposure, but also benefits a charity. We'll discuss creative promotions later in this chapter.

Before You Begin

Press releases are excellent ways to gain immediate and long-term exposure for your company and/or product(s), both in your community and in your industry. In addition, they cost next to nothing to produce—merely the cost of the paper, the ink from your printer, the envelope, postage, and your (or a staff member's) time. Furthermore, press releases can lead to interviews and feature articles. Trade editors usually publish press releases in any of four sections, while community papers, club newsletters and association magazines often print them in a "brief" format. Follow these steps and you'll be off to a great start:

1. Determine your purpose

Are you trying to drum up new business? Do you want neighboring business owners to frequent your shop for their early morning lattés? Are you now serving light lunches in hopes you'll stay busy through the usual afternoon slump? Are you trying to gain recognition in the industry for your ongoing commitment to product quality? Do you want the world to know about your involvement with a local charity?

Before you write your press release, you must determine its purpose. It doesn't have to be incredibly specific, but the more detailed you are, the easier it is to get your message to the appropriate readers.

2. Match content with readership

Now let's learn how to create newsworthy content. We'll use the old standby *Webster's New World Dictionary,* which defines newsworthy as a subject that is "timely and important or interesting." Or—in terms we can use when writing press releases—news is anything of use or interest to the reader of a specific publication.

To a current or potential customer, it's news if you expand your menu to include full-service lunches. To your colleagues in the community and industry, it's news if your business is honored by an industry association for product excellence. To most people in your community, it's news when you host an event to benefit underprivileged families.

What is not news? To potential customers, it's not news that one of your baristas dyed her hair electric blue. To the industry, it's not news that you named one of your coffee blends after your dog. And to current customers, it's not news that you are now forcing all your employees to wash their hands after using the restroom (which you should have been doing all along). Be sure your news is of true value to the reader and that it sheds a favorable light on your business.

3. Talk to editors

Editors, just like you, are very busy people. They set deadlines for others while also having to meet their own deadlines—strict deadlines. Don't waste their time by sending press releases that are inappropriate for their readership, are poorly written, or that arrive past the deadline for a specific publishing date. The best way to make sure you meet each editor's specific criteria is to give each a quick call (e-mail works great for this, too). Simply ask for a minute of his or her time and pose the following questions:

- Do you accept press releases?
- What types of press releases, specifically, interest your readers most?
- What is the deadline for press releases?
- To whose attention should the press release be sent? (An editorial assistant probably handles news releases.)
- In what form do you prefer to receive press releases (i.e. mail, fax or e-mail)?
- Do you accept artwork? If so, which format do you prefer?
- May I call or e-mail to follow up on press releases I have sent?

If the editor says "No" to any of the above, don't take it personally. Remember that you are collecting information to help you get your press releases noticed and published, not to make life-long friends out of editors. Be sure to keep this information on file so you don't have to bother the editors again with the same questions. Editors have a strange way of remembering people who waste their time.

4. Set, and meet, deadlines
Once you've spoken to the editors of your target publications, set a deadline for yourself or the person in charge of writing and submitting the press release. Send the press release to each publication before its deadline, if possible. Most trade magazines close editorial about two months before each issue is published, so submit a press release to be published in the April issue absolutely no later than February 1. Much of the time, editors publish press releases on a first-come, first-served basis. If your press release is time-sensitive (i.e. if it announces you'll be hosting a charity event on October 11), include a "Do Not Publish After" (or "Publish Before") date at the top of your press release.

5. Use the talent of your staff
You never know when you have a great writer in your midst. If you don't have the time or skills necessary to write a press release, ask staff members if they would be interested in doing so. You can even reward them with time off the floor for an hour (if you can afford it), or by paying them extra to see the project through to completion. You decide the reward—weigh the value of the task (including time and skill) to the value of what you're receiving in return.

6. Create news about your company
So what if you believe you don't have anything "newsworthy" to say? Create news! Plan a charity event, apply for an award, do something extraordinary. This is another promotional realm where your staff can shine. Put your staff to work on creating an event or promotion that is interesting and important to people in your community and/or industry. I'm a big fan of shops that host charity events. Not only does it create tons of good press about the companies, but it also does a world of good for the charities themselves.

As You Are Writing
The most important words to remember when writing a press release are brevity, clarity and contact. Here are some guidelines to follow as you are writing your press release:

1. Be brief
Because each publication sets aside only a limited amount of space to print press releases, be sure to say as much as you can in as few words as possible. Not only will the published press release more closely resemble what you wrote, but you'll make the editor happy by not taking up his or her time with pages and pages of muddled text. As far as length goes, shorter is better. I try to keep press releases to one page, double-spaced. If you must take it to two pages, do so, but understand that busy editors may not read the second page.

2. Be clear
As explained above, editors are very busy people. We can all respect that. So do them a favor and write your press release as clearly as possible so they don't have to waste time decoding what you wrote. This will also minimize the chance that the editor will publish incorrect information due to faulty interpretation. Remember, you know your business inside and out. When writing a press release, put yourself in the shoes of a person who has neither experience running a business nor any professional knowledge of "specialty coffee." Use layman's terms and, if necessary, provide brief definitions (i.e. for "arabica" or "crema").

3. Focus, focus, tone, tone!

No, this is not the latest craze in aerobic training. As you learned in the "Before you Begin" section, you must think about who your readers are and what you want them to know. Perhaps you prefer to jot down an outline to maintain your focus. Not only do you have to focus on what you're telling readers, but you must keep in mind how you're telling them. This is referred to as "tone."

Are you telling families in your community about a charity event you'll be hosting, for example? Or are you letting colleagues in your industry know about an award you recently received? In either case, you need to write to your audience using the appropriate formality (or informality) and attitude, as defined by terminology and sentence structure. This simply means the spin you put on the announcement and the words you choose should say exactly what you want the readers to hear the way you want them to hear it.

4. Remain objective

When writing your press release or when speaking to editors, be positive but not too self-promotional. Fluff in a press release, often in the form of adjectives or superlatives, is almost always edited out. Furthermore, you will establish and maintain your credibility with editors if you speak professionally and honestly and cut out unnecessary hype. It's okay to get excited—just don't try to convince them you've invented the best thing since sliced bread.

5. Stick to the inverted pyramid diagram

What the heck is the inverted pyramid diagram? It's a form of writing used by news writers, editors and public relations professionals. Basically, it's a template for writing that calls for the most important information to be given at the beginning of the press release or news article. Less important background information fills the body, or middle portion, of the press release, and the least important, or filler, information is placed at the end. Following is my interpretation of the inverted pyramid diagram. It may be of use when writing press releases.

172

A. The beginning of your press release (the largest section of the pyramid) should state the most pertinent information. This includes your company name, a contact name and phone number, a title, and one or two sentences stating exactly what you want the readers to know.

B. The next portion of your press release should describe specifics about the announcement above. This may include the flavor, size or price of your new product, the requirements your company met to receive an award or the details of how or why your shop was expanded.

C. The further down the page you get, the less pertinent the information is to your press release. You might write about other products your company offers, other awards received, and so on.

D. The conclusion of your press release (the smallest part of the pyramid) should include a brief background paragraph on your company and/or products. This is often a standard paragraph you run on all press releases. The information is usually general enough that editors can cut it without affecting the content of the release.

E. If you still have space, you may include your company's slogan. Be sure, no matter where your press release ends, that you include (again) a contact name and phone number in your summary information.

An editor may cut your press release (as if with scissors) at any point between B and E, depending on how much space is available and how pertinent your press release is to the publication's readership. Never expect your press releases to be printed exactly as you wrote them (that's why clarity is so important).

6. Include contact information
It doesn't matter if you write the most clear and brief press release ever printed if you don't include your contact information. Keep in mind the purpose of your press release is to generate interest in your business as well as increase your sales. An editor may want to contact you with an important question about your press release. He or she may even want an interview. Readers of the publication may want to call for directions to your establishment or with questions about your product(s). If you don't include a contact name and phone number at the top of the press release—and in the closing lines—you won't receive any of the above.

7. Include artwork
Accompanying artwork is a great way to draw more attention to your press release. Publications usually print either color or black and white photos. Inquire with each publication regarding the preferred format (i.e. print, transparency or slide). Artwork will add to the cost of your press release, but if you have the budget for it, include a photo or two in your press packet. You don't necessarily have to submit professional photos, but if you take them yourself, make sure they look professional. Do not submit blurry or washed-out photos—they'll just add to the cost of the presentation and editors will rarely use them. Also don't send pre-printed graphics—such as brochures or color photocopies—and expect the images to be reprinted in the publication. The quality of pre-printed images deteriorates with each successive generation.

173

8. Look professional
Presentation counts! You should always submit press releases on original company letterhead. Don't send photocopies unless you will be faxing the press releases. The image you portray in every aspect of your promotion is the image you are presenting of your company, so always look your best. Double space your press releases and use a basic font for readability and editing purposes.

9. Note special requests
As stated above, be sure to include a "Do Not Publish After" date if your press release is time-sensitive. In addition to your regular business number, you may also want to include a toll-free number, noting that you would like it published. Supplying your regular number is especially important to trade magazines; many are distributed internationally and U.S. "800" numbers do not work when someone is calling from outside of North America.

10. Don't send too many
Press releases make your business look good, but sending too many press releases to a publication trivializes your message. Make sure your press releases have something to say and that you space them out accordingly. If a publication receives five press releases from your company every week, chances are the editor will grow so tired of your letterhead that he or she won't even open the envelope it comes in, no matter how brilliant the content. If the press release is filled with only slight variations on your previous release, the editor might even think you're taking advantage of his or her publication. This isn't to suggest all editors are this fickle, but you must be wary of overexposing your business in the wrong way. Public relations is incredibly important, but you must show at least some restraint.

Sample

Following is a sample press release that may serve as a reference when writing your own press release:

FOR IMMEDIATE RELEASE
For more information, contact:
Mama Joe at 206.985.0063

Friday, October 15, 1999

Hot Mama's Java Shop Kicks Off New Year
With Event to Benefit Local Charity

Javaland, WA—Hot Mama's Java Shop, located at 321 N. Coffee Street in Javaland, is celebrating the end of the millennium with an evening of food and fun to benefit the local organization Books for Babes. The event, to be held Monday, January 3, from 7 to 9 p.m., is open to customers, families and friends of all ages. The party will feature live music by local band The Coffee Drippers, as well as snacks and coffee beverages courtesy of Hot Mama's. A silent auction will be held from 7 until 8 p.m., with all proceeds benefiting Books for Babes.

Books for Babes is a nonprofit organization that provides books and school supplies to children of local families in need. The organization has been in existence since 1993. Local businesses donated several items for the silent auction, including beauty products, household appliances, gardening supplies, and more.

Hot Mama's Java Shop is a full-service coffeehouse that has been serving high-quality coffees, teas, lunches, and desserts for more than five years. Hot Mama's is proud to sponsor its third annual event to benefit a local charity. For more information on attending or donating to this year's event, please contact Mama Joe at 206.985.0063.

#

When Following Up

1. Contact the publications

If you have the time—and if they accept follow-up calls—contact publication editors to make sure they received the press release and to see if and when it will be published, as well as to answer any questions.

2. Track your promotion

Keep a file or scrapbook of clippings on your business. Not only can you show this to employees, customers and colleagues who are interested, but it will help you track your progress by noting which publications printed your releases and why.

3. Get feedback

Not only should you keep notes when speaking with editors, but it may be a good idea to keep brief customer (reader) response cards next to your cash register or on your tables. Ask customers to take a few minutes to answer questions such as: What publications do you read? Have you read anything recently about our company? Did you like what you read? Would you like to hear more about our company? If so, what? The answers to these questions will help you track the effectiveness of past promotions and plan future ones.

4. Use this information

When planning future promotions and press releases, be sure to consider what you did right and wrong during the last campaign. Was your press release too lengthy? Did you submit it too late? Was it inappropriate for certain readers?

Who To Target

Following is a list of industry publications to which you may want to send your press releases. You can obtain a list of community publications from your local Chamber of Commerce or your library.

Coffee & Cuisine: A trade publication for the specialty coffee and fine dining industries, available monthly in print and online. Accepts press releases three months prior to publication. 1218 3rd Ave., Ste. 1315, Seattle, WA 98101; Phone: 206-382-2112; Fax: 206-623-0446; www.coffeecuisine.com; editorial@coffeecuisine.com.

Coffee Culture Magazine: A trade publication covering coffee and tea in Canada, published five times a year. Accepts press releases two months prior to publication. 80 Spadina Ave., Ste. 205, Toronto, ON M5V 2J3; Phone: 416-703-6099; Fax: 416-703-0144; www.globalserve.net/ ~ coffeeculture; coffeeculture@globalserve.net.

Fancy Food & Culinary Products: A monthly trade journal covering the gourmet food and beverage and upscale housewares industries. Accepts press releases three months prior to publication. 20 N. Wacker Dr., Ste. 1865, Chicago, IL 60606; Phone: 312-849-2220; Fax: 312-849-2174; www.fancyfoodmagazine.com; fancyfood@aol.com.

Fresh Cup Magazine: A monthly specialty coffee and tea trade publication, serving retailers with print and online versions. Accepts press releases two months prior to publication. PO Box 14827, Portland, OR 97293; Phone: 503-236-2587; Fax: 503-236-3165; www.freshcup.com; freshcup@freshcup.com.

175

Specialty Coffee Retailer: A trade publication for specialty coffee retailers printed monthly and available online. Accepts press releases two months prior to publication. 2101 S. Arlington Hts. Rd., Ste. 150, Arlington Heights, IL 60005; Phone: 847-427-2003; Fax: 847-427-2041; www.specialty-coffee.com; sgillerlain@mail.aip.com.

Tea & Coffee Trade Journal: A coffee and tea trade publication available in print each month. Accepts press releases two months prior to publication. 130 W. 42nd St., 10th Fl., New York, NY 10036; Phone: 212-391-2060; Fax: 212-827-0945.

The Gourmet Retailer Magazine: A trade publication for retailers of gourmet foods and beverages as well as housewares. Published monthly in print and online. Accepts press releases two months prior to publication. 3301 Ponce de Leon Blvd., Ste. 300, Coral Gables, FL 33134; Phone: 800-397-1137; Fax: 305-446-2868; www.gourmetretailer.com; gourmetretailer@worldnet.ATT.net.

Specialty Coffee Chronicle: A bimonthly newsletter produced by the Specialty Coffee Association of America (SCAA) for its members. Also available is the more frequent, though brief, *Specialty Coffee Bulletin.* Accepts press releases as possible lead-ins to feature articles two months prior to publication. One World Trade Center, Ste. 1200, Long Beach, CA 90831; Phone: 562-624-4100; Fax: 562-624-4101; www.scaa.org; mferguson@scaa.org.

VirtualCoffee: A quarterly publication for coffee consumers that is available online. Accepts press releases one month prior to publication. 260 E. 15th Ave., Ste. D, Eugene, OR 97401; Phone: (541) 683-5373; Fax: (541) 683-1010; www.virtualcoffee.com; ciao2000@teleport.com.

I hope this chapter helps you begin (or continue) to promote your business with press releases. I wish you the best of luck in your business. More than anything, remember to have fun!   ●

Ward Barbee

Ward Barbee is secretary/treasurer of Fresh Cup Publishing Company Inc., whose products include *Fresh Cup Magazine* and the North American Specialty Coffee and Beverage Retailers' Exposition (NASCORE). He has spent most of his business life in the marketing, printing and foodservice industries. An accomplished chef, Barbee has operated catering businesses and river-guide services, co-founded the *Oregon Hospitality News* (now the *Northwest Hospitality News*), and reinvented the beverage trade publication business with *Fresh Cup Magazine*—"The Voice of the Specialty Beverage Industry"—now in its eighth year of print. Exhibitors and attendees alike have called NASCORE the best networking and selling show in the specialty beverage arena. Barbee brings a wealth of beverage and coffee knowledge to the table from the points of view of restaurateur, publisher, connoisseur, and industry spokesperson.

179

Chapter 14

Marketing Your
Espresso Business

A few years ago I was in Atlanta for a trade show. After a hard day pounding the floor at the convention center and a little tuning up at the hotel bar, three of us decided we needed a red meat fix and stopped by one of those national chain steak houses. You know the ones I'm talking about, where you get half the cow, a head of broccoli, a baked potato the size of Rhode Island, and some *very* expensive wine. When we had consumed enough food to keep a family of 10 alive for a week, we decided—because we were all in the coolest business in the world—to order a few after-dinner cappuccinos. Well, the waitress, bless her soul, told us the only coffee available at this incredibly expensive restaurant was some swill from a regional chain and that we would probably not find the coffee to our liking.

We paid our bill and headed for the door, not sure where we were headed but positive our final destination would be somewhere that offered a "gourmet" coffee. Sure enough, a few blocks away we passed a charming little seafood restaurant and noticed an espresso machine nestled on the back bar.

We looked at each other, nodded affirmative and bailed in, grabbing three bar stools hard by the steaming La Cimbali espresso machine. As the bartender was preparing our drinks, we had a chance to eye the bottles of after-dinner brandies, cognacs and liqueurs displayed so attractively on the back bar. Slyly the bartender slipped us the dessert menus. It was too much for any mortal to stand. The smell of fresh ground coffee, the hiss of the espresso machine frother, the dessert tray lurking at the end of the bar. Too much!

When we finally pushed ourselves away from the bar 45 minutes later, we had consumed, among the three of us, six cappuccinos, six assorted brandies, armagnacs, Benedictines, and cognacs, and a sinful slice of cheesecake, a pear torte and a death-by-chocolate something-or-other. And the tab? A tab that the chain red meat parlor *didn't* get? One hundred and five dollars, including a $20 tip. The chain had all the drinks, the desserts, the cups, saucers, and plates. What it didn't have was a plan to capitalize on specialty beverages to *sell* these other products.

181

Multiply this $105 by the 60 percent of the people (300 average covers per night) who the waitress at the red meat parlor told us asked for specialty drinks *each night* and you are talking about some serious money slipping right through their fingertips. The message? Add an espresso machine to your equipment list, develop some coffee drinks, teach your employees the difference between specialty coffee and the regular stuff, do some point-of-sale marketing (table tents, etc.), and rake in the dough. With a little bit of attention to marketing, you can turn your coffee service—which businesses have historically considered something that keeps them from turning tables a bit faster—into the most profitable part of your business.

I use this example to illustrate that the most important part of your business—after location and an adequate amount of capital—is *marketing*! Without it, you are doomed, whether you open a full-service restaurant, a sit-down coffeehouse, a juice bar, a drive-thru, or even a street cart. Even if you offer the best cuppa around, if people don't know about it, they can't buy it.

So where do you start? Your marketing effort should be part of your business plan. You need to avail yourself of every bit of knowledge about marketing you can get your hands on *before* you open your doors. There are many ways to attack marketing. One is to find the cash to hire a marketing firm to do all the dirty work for you. My preferred method is the "guerrilla marketing" style. This method basically puts you on the street and in the trenches to get in touch with the real world. This lets you put your fingers on the pulse of your customers and your market, an experience that no marketing guru can ever impart to you. There are lots of theories on guerrilla marketing, but this is mine. So after you've read all the books on the "right" way to market your specialty beverage business, here's the real story. It begins by watching what the "Big Boys" do.

The Starbucks Opening

Take Starbucks, for example. With over 1900 stores worldwide and one more opening every other day, the company must be doing something right. Long before a new store opens to the public, Starbucks has laid the groundwork for filling those tables. It begins by announcing, through press releases to local media, that it has leased a particular space in an area. Then the company advertises for help. How? By placing ads in local newspapers and on college billboards, and by posting "help wanted" signs in the windows of the as-yet-unopened shop. These posters create local awareness that Starbucks is coming, even if the company never hires anyone from the poster.

Then, as the store gets nearer to opening day and after the managers have pretty much selected their staff, Starbucks will stage a "press preview" night, where local politicians, TV, radio, and other media personalities are invited to see the soon-to-open store, marvel at the trendy products and services to be offered, and try their hand at operating this amazing new-to-them contraption—the espresso machine. This plays into the egos of politicians and the media, who are always looking for an angle to show themselves in a "community" light. Pictures of the mayor, the big-haired TV weather girl or the shopping mall manager frothing milk, pulling shots and mugging for the camera are sure to make the 11:00 news. This press preview also gives the new staff a dry run serving people in a real-life situation—always a good thing.

Now if Starbucks never spends a dime on advertising, and it usually does when opening a new location in a new area, it has already had its store featured on local TV, in newspapers, on the radio, and through the "coming soon" poster that replaced the "help wanted" sign in the window.

No wonder that when the store finally does open for business, the place is packed. The company has done its marketing homework, which usually results in a second spot on local TV showing how busy the store is on opening day, which brings even more consumer awareness. Remember, all this marketing effort began *before* the store even opened. So don't wait until you open to start thinking about marketing. Do it now!

Playing the Kiddie Card

One doesn't normally think of Southern California as a hotbed of espresso drinks. Smoothies, juice bars and Coors Lite come to mind when pondering what trendy SoCalers drink to slake their thirst. But a little north of downtown Los Angeles, a man opened a coffeehouse—the first one in the neighborhood—and marketed it in a unique way: He used kids. Here's how he did it.

After writing his business plan, getting his financing in order, selecting his location, and beginning construction, he started working on his drink recipes. His two pre-teen daughters were both active in school and in local soccer activities. After soccer practice, he would invite the kids and their friends over to test the frozen drink recipes he was working on. The kids became the "Cupping Committee." Each week they would pass judgment on several drinks—varying flavors, fruit additions, ice cream, the whole gamut. He even had them develop names for these drinks.

Soon the parents of the kids were stopping by to watch the fun. He asked the parents to sample his hot coffee drinks, which helped him develop the flavor profiles best suited to his particular neighborhood. Armed with this invaluable information, the owner created a menu tailored to his core customers. When he held the grand opening, guess who came? The kids, their parents, and their parents' friends, among others. And guess how fast word spread about this cool new gathering place down at the mall? He is now working on a second store and will again use the neighborhood kids as his guinea pigs. That's great marketing.

The Dome

During the first few years of *Fresh Cup Magazine*'s existence, I targeted the coffeehouse customer in addition to the operator. During those early years, I used to get in my VW bus and deliver *Fresh Cups* hot off the press to selected coffeehouses in the Portland metropolitan area.

One of the places I delivered to was a drive-thru location on a four-lane arterial in East County. The owner's husband ran a vintage used car lot and gave his wife the building to use as a drive-thru (he moved his office into a small house on the back of the property). To get to the location, you had to sort of thread your way through 1955 Chevys, '60s T-Birds and other interesting antique automobiles.

This, coupled with the fact that the store was located on the "wrong" side of the street— i.e. morning commuters had to cross oncoming traffic to purchase their cuppas—made for some pretty skinny sales days. One mid-morning as I was making my monthly delivery, she started crying the blues about how her business had never really taken off as she had hoped it would. As I looked at her small shop, a thought came to me.

She owned an Italian red two-group La Pavoni machine that she displayed in the window. She had the ability to serve drinks from both sides of the building as well as take care of the three small tables inside. I said, "It seems that people aren't drawn to your business because many don't really know what you're selling. You need something to pull them in. Your shop needs some real glitz to make a statement."

Having seen many espresso machines with big brass domes on them, I reasoned that a dome on her machine might just do the trick. The dome would shine through the window, alerting drivers of her shop's purpose. "Call your machine distributor and borrow a brass dome to put on top," I suggested, "then we can do a little comparison of your numbers without a dome and your numbers with a dome." She took my advice and made the call. The results? In one month, her morning sales increased from 90 to 100 drinks to 150 to 175 per day! Her sales of pastries, mugs and other goodies also increased. The lines of cars snaking through her husband's car lot grew longer and longer, which naturally attracted even more customers. Her husband even saw his car sales pick up. She was soon able to buy the dome outright, which made her distributor happy. And the volume of *Fresh Cup* magazines I delivered to her each month increased by 50 percent! What a win-

win situation! And all because she added a little dash of glitz to her window. Once again, Marketing, Marketing, Marketing!

The Press Release

The judicious use of press releases as a marketing tool can bring you a quantifiable increase in business. I say judicious because, as publisher of *Fresh Cup Magazine,* you can imagine how many press releases I've seen over the years. You can also imagine how many I've thrown away. There's just no way our file cabinets can hold all the press releases we receive in an average year. Here are a few tips on how to get the most mileage from the energy you spend preparing press releases. (For more detailed information on press releases, read Kate LaPoint's chapter on page 167.)

1. Establish a program

The best laid plans will *always* fail if you don't have a plan. You need to assign a staff person to be in charge of press releases. Find someone who has a little creative writing skill, an understanding of what's important and an idea of what sells. Remember, the media to whom you are addressing the press release receives hundreds each week, so yours *must* be interesting enough to make editors open it up, read it, determine if it has enough news or content to be interesting to readers or viewers, decipher how much editing it needs, and decide whether it contains useful photos or illustrations.

2. Create a signature "look"

We get releases all the time from the same companies with differing graphic themes. Sometimes we read through a ton of stuff only to find out the release is from a company that doesn't apply to our readership. If you are sending out really good information, the recipient will come to know your "look" and recognize whether he or she may be able to use it.

A lot of PR agencies spend megabucks creating different ideas—or "grabbers"—they think will attract the media's attention. Singing telegrams, balloons, expensive packaging, samples—PR companies have tried them all to gain a little advantage in the game of words. But for a restaurant or coffeehouse, inexpensive yet consistent graphics can be every bit as effective as the fancy stuff. Even the creation of a signature "look" can serve as a great press release; it alerts the media to your exciting new image.

3. Targeting the right media

There's no use going to all the trouble to prepare press releases if you don't have a plan for their distribution. If your coffee shop is in the trendy Park Slope area of Brooklyn, N.Y., you probably won't get a mention in *The New York Times* or on the local NBC Nightly News. Conversely, if your restaurant is in Timberville, Wash., and you're adding a gourmet coffee and granita program using a regional roaster and local supplier of granita and chai mixes, the chances your press release will appear in the *Timberville Times* are very good. It's probably even a better bet they will print your release if you are sponsoring a Little League team or your staff entry in the Fourth of July parade won a first-place ribbon. So try to keep your focus on local publications, and, if applicable, local radio and TV. Remember, your customer base is probably based in your neighborhood, so you should target media that your potential customers use to access community information.

4. What is good PR?

While some PR mavens still subscribe to the "I don't care what you say about me just as long as you spell my name right" school of publicity, the savvy PR person knows what sells. Winning a locally sponsored "best drink" contest is a sure-fire vote getter. Winning national association recognition for a "best small business" award is also an attention getter, as are winning "woman in business" or "minority in business" awards.

184

Don't think the "Promotions" and "People on the Move" columns are limited to the big boys. Hiring new managers or making other significant personnel changes are always news, especially in the local press. Your Grand Opening and subsequent openings of second and third stores is news, especially if you hire and promote locally. And don't be afraid to call on your local press outlets for public relations assistance, especially if you spend money advertising with them. The power of the advertising dollar is one of the most underutilized PR ploys. Cultivate your local press. Find out all you can about what the editors consider news. Invite your local newspaper staff in for a new specialty drink. Let the writers prepare them. This will surely get you some ink. Remember, always keep your thinking cap on when it comes to public relations. If you do, they will always spell your name right!

Market Research

A tavern owner friend of mine (who later became a two-term mayor of Portland) once told me that "market research" was the key to his success. By "market research," Bud Clark meant he spent a night every few months going around with a few pals to his competition. He and his buddies enjoyed a few libations and got a feel for what his competition was doing right—and wrong.

He learned several things from this night out: How his competition was dealing with changes in clientele demographics; the most popular drinks on the menu; how the bar used advertising displays and point-of-sale materials; and his competitors' level of customer service.

What a great idea! Don't be bashful about visiting your competition. You'll be amazed at how much you learn. Sometimes you'll have a hard time understanding how they stay in business because the drinks are so lousy, but keep an open mind. How are the drinks, really? Be honest. How are the displays? Neat, clean, organized? Is the shop crowded? How are the employees? Friendly, sloppy, knowledgeable? Are there any you think would make good additions to your team? Do you see things you can use in your operation that would make a difference to your bottom line? Take notes. Listen to the customers. How do they compare to your customers? The information you gather from this sort of market research will prove invaluable.

The attention you pay to your marketing will pay off many times over. You will have a greater feel for your customers, your neighborhood, your product mix, and your bottom line. Remember, a comprehensive marketing program includes PR, market research, support from your supplier, and the ability to keep your eyes open to any and all new marketing opportunities. I hope some of these unconventional ideas I've put forth help you attain your dreams and goals. Good pouring! ●

185

David Griswold

David Griswold is president of Sustainable Harvest Coffee Co., a company he founded in 1995 to provide small grower groups with greater economic incentive to harvest certified organic and shade-grown coffees. Prior to Sustainable Harvest, Griswold co-founded Aztec Harvest, a cooperative marketing and importing company for small farmer co-ops in southern Mexico.

Griswold serves as a board director for the Specialty Coffee Association of America and is chairperson of the SCAA Environment Committee. He is an advisory board member of the Coffee Kids Foundation and a member of the Social Venture Network.

187

Chapter 15

Marketing Organic and Socially Responsible Coffees

Beginning in the 1970s, the coffee industry witnessed a marketing innovation with the advent of specialty coffee—an alternative, more upscale brew than commercial coffee. Small-scale roasters on the West Coast began offering better-tasting, darker-roasted beans. In time, specialty coffee helped slow the decline in coffee consumption as coffee enthusiasts opted to drink smaller amounts of a stronger, higher quality beverage.

189

Three decades later, coffee marketing has evolved once again. Specialty coffee has become more competitive, and, to some degree, standardized or commodified. To gain market share, innovative coffee roasters and importers are offering coffees that carry unique or outstanding characteristics and environmental benefits. "Farm-identified" organic and socially responsible coffees satisfy new consumer values. These coffees often carry independent certification that validates their sustainable attributes. This chapter explains the market potential of these niches and specific ways to capitalize on them.

Coffee Makes Headlines

Judging from recent headlines, the media has finally discovered coffee. For many years, the only time coffee made the news was when a devastating frost wiped out Brazil's coffee crop, resulting in higher prices for consumers. Now dozens of publications have discovered a variety of angles that effectively illustrate the power of the "sustainable" coffee story.

Full-length feature stories in the media cover a new marketing niche for the specialty coffee beverage—organic and socially responsible brews. Reporters from *The New York Times*, the *Boston Globe*, the *Los Angeles Times*, the Associated Press, and National Public Radio have covered shade-grown coffee and its growing popularity with coffee drinkers, environmentalists, birdwatchers, and others.

This new kind of coffee marketing is more than cause-related. It is issue-oriented passion marketing—an innovative strategy that attracts a broad base of consumers. These coffees allow people to connect a daily, ordinary activity—drinking specialty coffee—to their concerns for personal health, social justice and the environment. This connection between a morning cup of coffee and the larger world has been approached from several angles:

- Many shade coffee hillside farms survived the landslides that destroyed other parts of Honduras and Nicaragua during Hurricane Mitch in 1998 (*Boston Globe*).
- Small coffee farmers face pressures to clear-cut their lands, effectively removing an important winter home for the Northern "Baltimore" Oriole and other migratory songbirds (*Los Angeles Times*).
- Many of Mexico's poor coffee peasants have formed cooperatives and learned to produce organic coffee, significantly improving their economic situation (American Public Radio's "Marketplace").
- Grass-roots groups are petitioning stores in Seattle—the home of specialty coffee—to provide consumers with shade-grown coffee (*The New York Times*).
- Many of Baltimore's bird-loving baseball fans handed out shade coffee information on mocked-up baseball cards, encouraging Orioles fans to drink shade coffee as a way of supporting their team's mascot (Associated Press).

Diagram 1

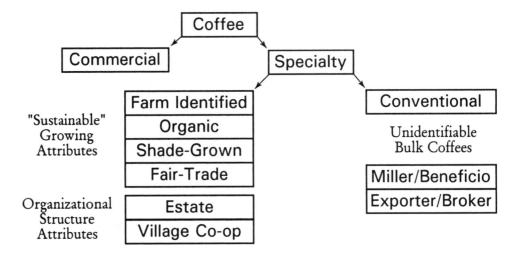

190

The Broader Marketing Picture

To understand organic and socially responsible marketing, one must first look at traditional coffee marketing. Commodity coffee is a mature market. About 70 percent of the U.S. coffee market is controlled by three commercial brands—Phillip Morris/Kraft, Proctor & Gamble and Nestlé. These three firms, along with the Colombian Coffee Federation, pay the bulk of the approximately $300 million spent annually marketing coffee to the U.S. consumer.

Despite these large marketing expenditures, American coffee consumption has declined every year since the 1960s. In the early 1960s, three-quarters of all adult Americans drank about four cups per day. It was during this time, however, that product quality dropped, turning American coffee into a hot, watered-down beverage served in a Styrofoam cup. Coffee was convenient but uneventful. It fulfilled a basic morning necessity, becoming as exciting as brushing one's teeth.

U.S. coffee consumption has dropped dramatically. Today about half of American adults drink just under two cups per day. Facing more sophisticated marketing campaigns from the other beverage segments, coffee has lost significant market share to soft drinks, milk, beer, and other bottled beverages. Specialty coffee is helping turn back this trend.

The reemergence of coffee began when a handful of West Coast entrepreneurial roasters began to sell coffees hailing from exotic places. They roasted these coffees in small batches to a darker, richer-tasting level and served them in living room-style cafés in boutique ceramic mugs. From 1970 to 1999, specialty coffee lured almost one-third of the coffee market away from the multinational firms. Recent studies estimate specialty coffee is a $3 billion per year industry.

Specialty coffee costs more, but its consumers are willing to pay more. Targeting the 25- to 39-year-old demographic, specialty coffee appeals to both the "Me Generation" of the 1970s and the "Yuppies" of the 1980s. It gives choices to people seeking individuality *and* offers a superior product.

What a difference for people who grew up thinking the only choice was between black or with cream! Consumers can blend beans from all over the world. Café menus now list dozens of drink possibilities. One can order a French-vanilla-flavored-double-decaf-skinny latté with legs. Status-seekers can opt for a $40 per pound Jamaican Blue Mountain estate coffee.

How Did Specialty Coffee Become Less Special?

As with all maturing industries, specialty coffee has become commonplace. As coffee chains have consolidated and standardized their operations, specialty coffee is moving toward commodification.

Diagram 2: Typical product life cycle

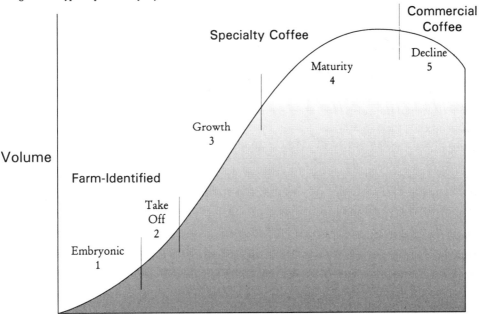

191

If one looks at the U.S. coffee industry, the commercial coffee segment has reached a period of decline. Specialty coffee, now three decades old, is moving up the front half of the curve. At the embryonic stage are the farm-identified coffees. These include estate, organic, sustainable, and socially responsible coffees.

At the beginning of 1999, Starbucks had approximately 1900 stores throughout the U.S. and beyond. Dark-roasted beans no longer separate one roaster from the rest. It's easy to find flavored espresso drinks in small towns and suburban communities, as well as in urban centers. Automatic espresso machines churn out lattés at roadside gas stations. The competition for accounts and new customers is fierce.

Not surprisingly, finding a marketing edge in the modern specialty industry is critical.

ACHIEVING SUCCESS IN SPECIALTY COFFEE

While good quality, friendly and knowledgeable customer service, and competitive pricing are the minimum requirements to stay in business, specialty coffee success demands a more creative marketing strategy.

The new coffee marketing—issues marketing—does not mean simply supporting the cause of the day. It means making a long-term commitment to an issue important to you, to the people who provide your coffee beans, and, most of all, to the people who drink your coffee.

This kind of marketing takes a serious commitment and a thorough understanding of the issues behind your cause. Not surprisingly, it also takes a bigger investment in a relationship with a coffee supplier thousands of miles away. But it's also one that generally pays off in customer interest and loyalty.

Organic and Socially Responsible Market Niches
Organic Coffee
Organic coffee is one of the hottest new categories in the beverage segment, and is the fastest growing segment in specialty coffee. Its growth rate doubles that of conventional specialty coffee. Organic coffee imports have increased by 245 percent in the U.S. since 1990. While organic coffee represents less than five percent of all specialty coffee, current sales in the category are estimated between $100 and $150 million, according to the Specialty Coffee Association of America (SCAA).

Organic and socially responsible coffees tap into the consciousness of many Americans. In one simple purchase they can protect the environment, maintain personal health and address social justice issues. Organic coffee will continue to enjoy strong growth for several reasons: consumer health interest, the growth of the natural foods industry, and better regulation of organic claims.

Coffee drinkers choose organic coffee because it provides them with both health and environmental benefits. People who consume chemical-free foods appreciate the opportunity to apply the same criteria to their coffee. Organic coffee also addresses people's environmental concerns. Why? Because coffee is one of the most chemically intensive crops in the world.

The regulatory power of the 1990 Organic Food Production Act helps maintain product integrity and price premiums. All processors of coffee, including roasters, are required to carry independent certification. The USDA is expected to soon provide stricter enforcement of the organic regulations, thus eliminating more uncertified organic products from the market.

Shade-Grown Coffee
Shade-grown coffee comes from specific farms where coffee trees are shadowed under a canopy of taller native shade trees. Shade-grown coffee provides a foundation for biodiversity, including habitat for migratory songbirds.

Shade coffee contrasts with clear-cut coffee, which is the best way to describe a modernized coffee farm. In this system, farmers deforest the canopy of trees on their coffee plots. Of the six million acres of coffee lands in Central and Northern Latin America, scientists estimate that 60 percent have been stripped of shade since the 1970s (Smithsonian Migratory Bird Center).

While precise definitions of shade coffee are hard to clarify, the sales of shade-grown coffee comprise one percent of the specialty market, or $30 million annually (SCAA).

Fair-Trade Coffee
Fair-trade coffees focus on the economics of the coffee harvest. Fair-trade companies attempt to provide workers with fair wages and healthy working conditions by setting minimum prices above the cost of production and by paying a premium price to small farmer cooperatives.

192

Within the commodities market system, the world price is determined by supply, demand, and, to a far greater degree, the investor/funds that profit from commodity speculations. In the span of a few years, world coffee prices have fluctuated between 50 cents and $3 per pound. These vacillations create a very unstable economic situation for growers who depend on coffee as their primary source of income. Fair-trade proponents believe their system of trade, based on respect for workers' rights, can help combat the economic inequities and worker degradation found in many coffee-producing countries.

Understanding Your Market

The first step is to assess your market. Do your customers value generic conventional or farm-identified coffees? Are they focused on price, convenience, quality, or a good story? What separates your operation from other cafés and roasters? Look closely at:

- The product—Which products do your customers value?
- The consumer segments—Who is your target audience? What issues are most important to this audience?
- The delivery system—How will you serve the product to the user?
- The communication strategy—How will the buyer be induced to try and re-buy?
- The price—What is the relative cost compared to alternative product choices?

Some roasters and retailers choose conventional coffees, hoping to obtain market share using a ho-hum marketing approach. They posit they have the "best-quality coffee." Yet nearly everyone in coffee adopts this same slogan. No doubt you need great quality, but this statement by itself doesn't carry much weight anymore.

Other roasters tell their customers they search the far reaches of the globe for the rarest beans. But they don't explain the interesting characteristics of the beans they discover. Their experiences on the coffee farm should certainly be of general interest to the consumers. Consider developing materials, including brochures and posters, that educate consumers about the sources of your beverages.

193

Think about your market-building opportunities. What are the popular pastimes of the customers you serve? Are they birders, wildlife conservationists or fishermen? Is there a local network of businesses or church groups that would support coffee that provided better incomes to farmers in the developing world? There is probably some way to connect their passion to a coffee origin you carry.

Because a growing number of American consumers make purchases based on socially responsible criteria, a roaster can differentiate itself by supporting these types of issues. Seventy-eight percent of adult American consumers said they would be more likely to buy a product associated with a cause about which they care (Transfair USA). Using creativity and reliable information, savvy roasters can connect their coffees to issues that are important to their customers.

For example, some Costa Rican and Colombian coffee farmers "wet-process" their coffees in ecological ways that protect their local streams. Wouldn't fishermen in your community choose coffee that supports their passion rather than choosing a non-descript blend? Many shade-grown coffees can be sourced from farms that protect the habitat of a particular bird species found in specific U.S. regions. Could this bring in new customers or build a more loyal base of consumers?

Farm-Identified Coffees

There is significant marketing power in offering "farm-identified" coffees. Organic, shade-grown, fair-trade, and estate coffees can create market share if they are used to:

- Differentiate yourself from the competition.
- Pioneer new coffee markets.
- Address un-met customer concerns and values.
- Increase store recognition and goodwill.

– Continued on page 196

A Quick Guide to Sustainable Coffee

Commercial vs. Specialty

Commercial coffees are distinct from specialty coffees. They are the generic, roasted and ground coffees offered primarily by the three major coffee companies (Phillip Morris/Kraft, Proctor & Gamble and Nestlé). Commercial coffees usually blend beans of both arabica and robusta types. Even if the beans come from only one producing country, the sources or growing attributes of the blended coffees are difficult to trace or identify.

The bulk of coffee sold as specialty coffee is known as conventional coffee. A conventional coffee is not "farm-identified." The designation may describe bean size (e.g. Colombian Supremo) or the altitude at which the bean is grown (e.g. Mexican Altura), but conventional coffees are always processed and purchased in bulk. Suppliers of these coffees, such as processors who mill or export coffee, are hard-pressed to provide specific growing information on the harvesting or labor conditions. Price is the primary variable, although these coffees are priced at a premium compared to commercial coffees.

Farm-identified coffees include single-estate and organic and socially responsible coffees. These come from a specific farm. Elements of the harvest are usually identifiable—for example, the type of arabica cultivar, the shade coverage over the coffee plants, or the farm's ownership structure.

Organic and socially responsible coffees can only come from "farm-identified" sources, because certification provides the only proven means to verify the marketing claims.

Farm-Identified Coffees
Ownership Structures
Estate Coffee

Estate coffees are harvested from a single farm or common soils. The coffee carries the name of the farm or grower. Estate coffees usually exhibit far better quality control and more consistent taste profiles from crop to crop than most conventional, bulk sources.

Cooperative Coffee

A well-organized village grower cooperative can have many of the same attributes as an estate farm. If the coffee is centrally milled, administrative systems are good, and quality control systems are in place, a cupper can identify the coffee as coming from a single group of villagers. For that reason, many cooperatives provide organic, shade-grown or fair-trade coffees. Examples of village cooperatives are the Aztec Harvest cooperatives based in Mexico.

Harvesting Attributes
Organic Coffee

Organic coffee is a coffee production practice. Organic coffee is grown on farms that don't use chemical inputs. To market a coffee as certified organic, a farm must be inspected to receive certification. At each

194

step in the processing chain, inspectors track the coffee beans as they move from source to cup. To protect the integrity of the process, the coffee must be sold through certified importers and roasters. This certification process helps protect consumers as well, guaranteeing the products they buy are genuine. Many states regulate organic products. The USDA is soon expected to regulate organic coffee under the 1990 Organic Food Production Act.

Shade-Grown Coffee

Shade-grown coffee describes a coffee production practice. Shade coffee is grown under native trees and therefore helps protect natural habitats and tropical forests in coffee-producing countries. In shade-grown coffee production, canopies of trees consisting of many species grow over the coffee. The trees provide a habitat for other flora and fauna. Companies that use shade coffee as a marketing claim are making a strong environmental statement to consumers that obviates the need for traceable farm-identified sources to ensure marketing integrity.

Fair-Trade Coffee

Fair-trade coffees refer to the economic system under which coffee is purchased. Roasters must purchase fair-trade coffees from farmer cooperatives, and they must follow established minimum prices. (Conventional coffee, in contrast, is subject to the whims of the New York Coffee Exchange "C" price.)

Fair-trade principles stipulate that farmers are guaranteed a minimum base price when the world coffee "C" market price dips below the cost of production. By buying directly from the worker-owned co-ops, proponents say the money goes directly to those who grow and pick the beans, not the middlemen.

Certification bodies in the U.S. and Europe regulate supplier cooperatives listed on an international register and inspect them annually. Opponents of the concept as it has been established by U.S. certifiers protest that only coffee from farmer cooperatives may be designated as fair trade. Estate coffees are not eligible to participate.

The Value of Certification

The greatest threat facing sustainable organic and shade-grown coffee is the possibility that uncertified product will clutter the market and confuse or willingly mislead consumers. One problem is that many roasters and retailers label their products without obtaining certification themselves. Sadly, whenever people pay premium prices for a particular point of differentiation, free riders will always have an incentive to commit fraud.

Independent certification appears to be the best solution. Certification builds consumer confidence and creates a chain of custody. Furthermore, it helps maintain a price premium for farmers, importers and roasters who abide by the rules. ●

195

Farm-identified coffees share a much more complex and fascinating story with the customer. These coffees have name recognition and a reputation for quality. Their market success is illustrated by the consistently higher prices they fetch. Such coffees include Yauco Selecto in Puerto Rico, Fazenda Monte Allegre in Brazil, and La Minita in Costa Rica.

A drawback of estate coffees is that availability is limited at times. From year to year, the crop can change. Weather problems can destroy the supply. And if the coffee is successful, it usually means prices will rise for the scarce supply in subsequent years.

Sustainable coffees can complement farm-identified coffees because they provide added benefits, such as addressing important environmental, health and social justice needs. They carry special attributes that help roasters enter new markets. And they create a feeling of goodwill for your business among customers.

Keys to Success With Farm-Identified Coffees

1. Learn all you can about the product

Coffee production is among the most exciting aspects of the beverage. It involves many processing steps, a wide range of people, and several different locales. Farmers that sell farm-identified coffees should provide complete information on the product. One tool to accomplish this is a Farm Identification Form. This form lists the relevant conditions surrounding a particular farm, including harvesting and processing conditions. Among the information that might be of interest to the coffee aficionado is farm location, soil composition, climate, harvest conditions, and milling practices.

For example, with full farm information one can explain to customers why a Guatemalan Antigua coffee tastes different than an Indonesian Sumatra. The Farm Identification Form notes the differences in soil composition and the climate between the two origins. It also shows the different arabica cultivars—the types of coffee plants—found on each farm.

The form explains that Guatemalan beans are wet-processed, a method in which the cherry pulp is washed off and parchment is fermented overnight, giving the product more acidity. The form also explains that Indonesian coffee is dry-processed, a method in which the cherry pulp is left on the bean. The bean is then dried on the ground, creating a sweet and more earthy-tasting brew.

Once a roaster has detailed and reliable information, he or she can speak knowledgeably with the most avid customer.

2. Share the story

The hardest part of telling the story of sustainable coffee is obtaining the marketing tools needed to share it with consumers. Visual tools, such as photos and videos, are essential. More and more estate coffee owners understand this need, and are providing posters, photos and written descriptions of their farms.

In the future, coffee roasters and retailers will need more sophisticated point-of-sale information. Consumers will expect brochures, color posters, pictures, and video streamed over the Internet. Site visits to coffee origins will help roasters learn first-hand about their product. Through the development of these promotional materials, companies can encourage the average consumer to explore the fascinating world of coffee.

3. Demand verification of claims

To help maintain premium pricing for everyone in the coffee chain, the industry must substantiate all claims. Sadly, most shade-grown coffee is labeled such without verification or certification. Organic certification is regulated by the USDA, but experts suggest that as many as 70 percent of all coffee roasters are selling "certified organic" coffee to consumers while they themselves remain uncertified.

This is not only dangerous because it breaches consumer trust, but it is counter productive in economic terms. By flooding the market with unsubstantiated product, roasters blur the line between conventional coffees and the higher-priced, identifiable coffees. The media is also quick to ferret out false claims. The best solution is to demand product with valid documentation.

4. Build sales through unique alliances

Issue-oriented marketing should help achieve long-term strategic sales goals. One of the most interesting examples of this in the specialty coffee industry has been the success shade coffee promoters have had in developing new markets. One example is the work of Thanksgiving Coffee Company in Fort Bragg, Calif. Paul Katzeff, Thanksgiving CEO, pioneered selling coffee "That's Good for Birds."

Thanksgiving procured a variety of certified shade-grown coffees from Central and South America and created the "Songbird Coffee" blends. The company then developed a strategic alliance with the nonprofit American Birding Association. Now Thanksgiving sells specialty coffee where it has never been sold before.

The organizations now position colorful coffee displays in bird stores—places where customers typically find only field binoculars and bird feeders. Coffee sales are booming because these customers have a passion for backyard birds, and that gives them more than enough reason to try a new product. Best of all, the quality of Thanksgiving's shade-grown coffee keeps them buying again and again.

5. Pass along the price premium

Not surprisingly, sustainable, organic and socially responsible coffees are slightly more expensive than conventional specialty coffees. Certification is expensive. In addition, each stage of production generally requires more labor, which adds to the overall costs.

But these costs add only a tiny percentage to the price of an individual cup of coffee. This makes it easier to pass the complete story and its cost to the customer. Consumer surveys indicate that coffee drinkers who understand the extra steps involved in producing organic and socially responsible coffees are more than willing to pay a little extra.

6. Commit to an issue, not a specific farm

Issues are powerful. They transcend the boundaries of many countries. But the problem with many cause-related coffee promotions is they focus only on a particular estate.

Unfortunately, any singular relationship has inherent risks. Perhaps a roaster's relationship with the grower will sour. Perhaps the grower will not continue to farm the same way he or she had before. Or maybe your customers will tire of reading about the same place year after year. It is better to promote an issue.

Instead of offering a single-estate organic decaffeinated coffee, for example, focus on the issues behind decaf organics. Make a company-wide commitment to switch all your decaffeinated coffees to certified organic. After all, the customers who buy decaf are primarily concerned with the negative health effects of caffeine. What better way to address those concerns directly than to offer chemical-free certified organic decaf coffees?

Best of all, you'll be able to switch to new certified organic decaf coffees as supply and qualities shift without losing a step in your marketing promotion.

Conclusion

There are many untapped sales opportunities in specialty coffee for those who focus on issues-oriented marketing. Farm-identified marketing goes beyond traditional coffee promotions. It allows you to address tough world issues and not lose customers in the process. It lets you define the kind of company you are and the type of supplier relationships you seek. It motivates employees and may even impress your competitors. Issue-oriented marketing not only brings new customers, but it also helps keep existing ones. ●

Sherri Miller

Sherri Miller, a 23-year veteran of the specialty coffee industry, began her career as a barista in San Francisco in 1976. She is currently developing and implementing a specialty coffee retail concept for Whole Foods Natural Organic Foods and Allegro Coffee Company.

In 1990, Miller joined Starbucks Coffee and for five years held positions as retail manager, district manager, trainer, and coffee specialist. She facilitated the opening of 20 Oregon stores and the company's first drive-thru. At Kittridge and Fredrickson Fine Coffees, she worked as sales and marketing manager and regional trainer for three years.

Prior to joining Starbucks, Miller owned a successful café/restaurant in San Francisco called The Blue Note.

Miller helped open multi-unit American-style espresso bars in Kuala Lumpur, Malaysia, while researching Indonesian coffees. She has visited numerous other coffee-producing countries, including Kenya and Ethiopia at the invitation of their respective coffee authorities, to study growing regions and coffee-processing methods.

Miller is a board member of the Specialty Coffee Association of America and member of the Training Committee, and is an on-screen coffee resource for The Canadian Film Board. She is a frequent lecturer at industry trade shows and writer for industry periodicals. She writes a bi-monthly column on coffee quality for *Fresh Cup Magazine,* and is writing a book on coffee culture while editing another coffee book. She's also compiling a series of her photos called "Faces of Coffee."

199

Chapter 16

101 Guerrilla Marketing Ideas

Your mother was right—nothing is more important than a first impression. This is especially true in your specialty coffee business.

201

Imagine the aroma of freshly ground and brewed coffee—hypnotic and intoxicating, like the sweet scent of jasmine or honeysuckle—wafting into the street, beckoning customers to walk through your door. Small sidewalk café tables are neatly arranged in front of the windows. The tables are in good repair, occupied by sun worshippers sipping tall iced caffé lattés. Napkins, newspapers and cigarette butts are not blowing about the sidewalk by patrons' ankles. Instead, you see flower boxes and a neighborhood newspaper stand. Crossing the threshold, a sensory experience envelops the customer. Colors, textures, sights, sounds, and smells are personal and intimate. Marketing begins with a customer's first impression and ends with a lasting impression.

This chapter is divided into two distinct sections. The first addresses the specialty retail or café environment as an operation. The second addresses it as a guerrilla marketer. A guerrilla marketer can best be defined as a savvy business person who has more creativity and gumption than money to promote his or her business. This is how most of us began—and continue to this day.

The above scenario should provide you with a detail-oriented set of eyes with which to view your business. Open wide and look. Walk through your door. What do you see? Are the tables bussed? Is the condiment bar stocked and clean? Is the service counter tidy, with clean and dusted equipment? Are stray beans collecting under the machinery? What do the rear counters look like? Are dirty bar towels, empty syrup bottles, and half-eaten employee lunches cluttering the area? Look at the espresso prep area. Are the portafilters secure in the group heads and the steam wands wiped of milk buildup? Are the steaming pitchers free of baked-on drips? Are thermometers for steaming pitchers available, ensuring milk is never steamed to a temperature above 160 degrees? Are timers for proper extraction (between 18 to 24 seconds) within view of the espresso machine? Do the airpots have timers ensuring no coffee is served one hour after brewing? This is marketing.

The whole-bean area is next on your tour. Are storage bins and jars free of coffee oil buildup? (Oil can become rancid.) Are containers airtight? Do you see open bags of coffee scattered about? Is ground coffee for brewing in an airtight container or sitting on top of the brewer where heat will cause it to stale even before it gets into the filter basket? Are bin signs dog-eared? Did you spell Colombian correctly? Is all retail merchandise dusted, stocked and priced? Is it displayed logically or stacked haphazardly? Can customers easily access the merchandise? Does your staff know how the items function?

Speaking of staff, they are one of your most valued assets—your front-line people. Next to the quality of your coffee, they can make or break your business. Have they been trained on proper brewing techniques and customer service? Do they know what their job responsibilities are?

Ask your employees the following questions and find out: What is the difference between arabica and robusta coffee? Between light-roast and dark-roast coffee? What does the AA mean after Kenya? Why is the coffee we serve the very best? Can you describe our coffee's features to an inquisitive patron? What does a properly extracted espresso shot look like? Who the heck is Kaldi? And what about those monks?

What do you, as an employer, do to provide a good work environment? This is very important. Ask employees what could be done to create a better workplace, and listen.

Now pretend you've never been to your café before. What are your impressions? Look at the areas I've mentioned. Is there room for improvement? What did I miss? Do you have a competitor nearby? If so, visit his or her shop with the same critical eye. What does your competitor do better? How does he or she do it? What do you do better? What do you want to do better? This isn't rocket science. Define your goals first so you can achieve them later. Selling more beverages in the morning, increasing customer flow and growing your lunch business are all realistic goals. Examine the areas you want to improve and create a simple action plan. If it isn't simple, it probably won't happen. Let's be realistic—all great schemes fall upon deaf ears if they are unreasonable and don't have a plan of attack. Don't use this as an excuse not to do better—find a better way.

Create a retail checklist for you and your employees to use. Define categories within your business. Here are some sample categories: Customer Service, Coffee Quality, Merchandising, Cleanliness, and Pastry/Food. Bullet five or six points that make up the most important part of each category. Place a check box beside each point. If you don't have time to do this, handwrite a simple outline and let Kinko's (or an ambitious employee) do the rest. Use the retail checklist for a quick snapshot of overall café operations to help you and your staff. Don't try using the checklist during the morning rush, however (while also ensuring the rush doesn't become an excuse for poor quality).

I am impressed with the ingenuity of small-time operators everywhere. Their visions of how to be successful could fill an MBA course at Harvard. But don't attempt to introduce all of these ideas at one time—you'll stress yourself out. This chapter is not intended to be a definitive creative marketing guide. Use it as a fluid think tank, a running list generated after too many cups of coffee that will inspire more ideas from you and your staff. Remember, the keys to your marketing plan should be to have fun, make friends, and never, ever forsake quality.

Branding

Branding will plant an image, taste, smell, or moment in your customers' minds. Create a logo that tells a story and gets people involved. The famous mermaid represents the ports of call of countries that ship green coffees. Do you know the company to which I'm referring?

Have a good story, theme or tag line. Who is the person behind the bean? What's the human story?

Once you develop your logo and theme, create:

- Logo aprons (Make sure they're clean and pressed!)
- Logo T-shirts
- Logo hats
- Stationary with logo and theme
- Logo stickers for coffee bags
- Logo to-go cups
- Logos on every car you own

Your Coffee Program

Coffee will first arouse the senses; an educated staff and customer base, however, will set you apart! Keep things simple. Ask your roaster for help if you need it. Coffee is what you do—be the best!

- Conduct fun and informal coffee classes, cuppings and tastings. Advertise the classes on flyers imprinted with your logo, and always invite the media. Here are some sample class topics:
  - Espresso training
  - How to use a French press
  - How to brew great coffee (or espresso) at home
  - A tasting that features your new Holiday Blend, Celebration Caffé, special limited coffee, or an origin coffee
- Start a coffee of the day program to introduce customers to all your origin coffees, blends and roasts. Serve a different house brew daily along with a regular favorite. Try a dark roast and a medium roast, or a blend and an unblended coffee of origin. Place a sign by your cash register advertising this program.
- Display a half pound of prepackaged whole-bean coffee with descriptor signage by your register to stimulate add-on sales.
- Make sure your staff knows coffee. Do they prepare drinks that are good and consistent? Are recipes nearby?
- Sample, sample, sample. On a hot day, brew double-strength coffee in a French press or drip brewer, pour over ice in 4-ounce sample cups, place on a tray, and offer a taste to customers.
- Sample iced vanilla lattés, too. They are always a hit. If you have a new blend, offer samples.
- Create a holiday beverage.
- Hold a contest for customers to name a new coffee blend.
- Use quality equipment to ensure consistency and to *market* your commitment to quality. Customers may not know the function of these tools, but they will know they are used for quality control. Plus they won't necessarily see the tools at your competitors. Use these basic tools:
  - Thermometers on steaming pitchers—to ensure milk is not steamed to a temperature higher than 160 degrees
  - Timers on brewers—to ensure coffee is served no longer than an hour after brewing
  - Timers for espresso extraction—to ensure 18- to 24-second extractions
  - Clear shot glasses—to verify 1.25-ounce espresso shots with crema
- Make sure no grounds are present in cups and no cups have finger prints or drips. Replace lids if they split.
- Do your baristas smile as they hand cups across the bar to the customers? Is the logo side of the cup facing the patron?

203

Merchandising

You can add on sales by offering coffee-related merchandise to your customers. Notice traffic patterns in your location and stack a merchandising rack near the areas of heaviest traffic. Customers can then stand and shop while they wait.

- Sell gift boxes. Offer a travel mug, French press and half pound of coffee in a decorative box or basket. Purchase decorative boxes or bags and fill them with items from your café and then stack them by the register for holiday sales.
- Advertise the availability of corporate gifts. Have a simple order sheet next to the displayed gift to take advance orders.
- Sell logo travel mugs, ceramics and plastic tumblers. Include a free beverage of choice with each purchase (then offer a 10-cent discount for re-use).
- Offer branded merchandise like aprons, T-shirts and hats for sale at cost. Let your customers advertise for you.
- Sell syrups. During holidays these make great hostess gifts as an alternative to alcohol. Wrap the bottles with ribbons.

The Personal Touch

The personal touch is about your people, your coffees and your customers. Share your thoughts, be yourself and get your customers involved.

- Publish a newsletter. Many computer programs have a template available. Ask employees to contribute.
- Submit press releases to trade journals and neighborhood papers often. Again, check your computer for a template. Include a photo. Send to several publications.
- Print articles on coffee-related topics to distribute to clientele.
- Call a local TV station and offer your business as a location for a weather forecast.
- Do a radio broadcast or an on-air interview. Invite the local station down for a remote live broadcast. Use coffee sounds. Treat the radio folks to free on-site espresso drinks.
- Provide coffee service for a movie set. Offer your business as a background, or as a place to shoot a scene.
- Offer customer contact/feedback forms. Also design job applications that have the look and feel of your business. All applicants may not get hired, but they could become customers.
- Distribute brochures. Some ideas:
    - The Story of Good Coffee
    - The Story of Your Café
    - How to Brew the Best Coffee
- Check with the Specialty Coffee Association of America (SCAA) for other printed specialty coffee brochures and resource materials. Join this organization and advertise your membership.
- Give talks at the culinary institute and local high school. Sponsor neighborhood group tastings.

Fun Ideas

Use your imagination and ask employees to get involved. They will feel proud. Also look for ideas in other businesses.

- Offer frequent-customer awards.
- Offer frequent-buyer cards for beverage customers. For example, reward customers who buy 12 espresso beverages with a 13th beverage *free*.
- Design a space on the back of the frequent-buyer card for customers to write their names and addresses. Use them to create a mailing list.

- Customer having a bad day? Give him or her an extra stamp.
- Give customers a free drink on their birthdays.
- Offer coupons or "Bean Bucks" worth 50 cents off any beverage.
- Sell gift certificates.
- If you operate a drive-thru, offer dog biscuits to customers with pets.
- Give lollipops to kids.
- Give away a T-shirt, half pound of coffee or a beverage monthly. Have your customers place their business cards in a bowl to enter. Be sure to log these cards after the drawing and add them to your mailing list. Post the winner's name. Customers will come in to see if they've won.
- Copy names and addresses off checks to add to your mailing list.
- Print business cards for manager, key staff and self.
- Print your mission statement or other pertinent information on the back of your business cards.
- Post customers' vacation postcards. They *will* come in to check.
- Ask a trivia or coffee question each day, allowing customers the chance to win a free drink with a correct answer.
- Host poetry readings, live music and artists' showings.
- Play music for the customer's enjoyment. Set the volume at a comfortable level.
- Host book readings and signings with local authors. Call a local publisher or book store for referrals.
- Hand out recipe cards with instructions for preparing iced coffee drinks or cooking with coffee at home.

Promotions for Local Charities

Plenty of opportunities to do good exist. Sometimes the simplest and least expensive ideas help most. If you do sponsor a promotion, don't forget to send out a press release. Take a snapshot for the newsletter and post it in the store.

- Supply airpots of brewed coffee for a neighborhood cleanup day.
- Cater a symphony fundraising event.
- Send 25 cents of every pound of a particular coffee sold to a charity of choice.
- Donate unused ground coffee to a clinic or safe house.
- Post a small notice identifying the local charity to which you give your coffee.
- Teach a tasting class for a small fee and donate the proceeds to charity.
- Sponsor an event similar to Happy Brew Year! Coffee Kids does this event annually; call the organization for details.
- Sponsor a car wash or dog wash for charity. (I wouldn't recommend a cat wash.)

Signage

Signage must be useful and visible. Can your customers read your hours of operation on the front door, the menu before they actually get to the order station (this saves time, too) and the pastry identifiers? Be creative, and put small logos on the signs.

- Create pastry signage with prices and brief descriptions of products.
- Provide the name and a description of each of your coffees.
- Laminate bin tags or place them in plexi holders to avoid a dog-eared look.
- Spell Colombian correctly; Colombian, not Columbian!
- Use patio umbrellas with your logo, café name or roaster name.
- Design your business cards with an address and map printed on the back.
- Ask your roaster and supplier for his or her point-of-sale materials: posters, coffee-bin labels, hang tags for airpots, table tents, and burlap coffee bags for in-store merchandising.

- Ask your roaster for educational brochures, training and sales support.
- Decorate your walls with travel posters of origin countries or posters with a coffee theme.

Be Green!
Environmental concerns are everywhere. Your business *can* make a difference.

- Recycle green coffee bags for in-store merchandising. Ask your roaster to supply them.
- Offer a 10-cent discount for reusing or bringing in your own cup.
- Offer a 20-cent discount for reusing a coffee bag for whole-bean purchases.
- Donate your used coffee grounds to customers with green thumbs or to community gardens. Supply the grounds in small bags with your signage for customers to take away.
- Suggest customers fill large coffee bags with cedar chips to create their own dog beds, or suggest they use them as holding bags for fishing.

Discounts
Everyone loves a deal. For a small cost you can provide potential customers an opportunity to try your coffees and service.

- Offer discount coupons for businesses that share customers, such as car repair shops, hair salons and veterinary clinics.
- Offer gift certificates.
- Distribute "Bean Bucks" that offer 50 cents off a pound of coffee beans.

206

Not all these ideas will work for you in your business. This chapter, quite simply, has been provided as a tool to generate your own creativity in unique and innovative ways. Positioning your business for competition and differentiating yourself will help you compete with the "Big Boys." I suggest you purchase Jay Levinson's *Guerrilla Marketing Handbook*. It's the best $20 you'll ever spend. And don't forget to save the receipt for your taxes! Now sit down, brew yourself a nice French press of Yemen Mocha and have some fun. ●

section five

YOUR COFFEE BUSINESS

Kent Holloway

Kent Holloway is president of Kent Holloway and Associates Inc., and is a consultant, writer and seminar presenter in the specialty coffee industry. He recently founded and is president of Fox Hollow Coffee Inc.

Holloway's academic background includes an M.A. in administration and formal training in marketing, communications and leadership development. His professional experience includes co-founding Austin Chase Coffee, a Seattle-based coffee roasting company with many retail outlets and worldwide wholesale accounts. He is one of three featured speakers at the Espresso Business Seminar offered nationally four times each year through Coffee Fest—the specialty coffee industry's traveling retail trade show—and is author of the *Espresso Business Seminar Manual* used for the seminar.

Holloway regularly teaches marketing and entrepreneurship courses at a local college using a text he developed. He also serves on the Academic Advisory Committee for Pierce College. Since August of 1994, he has written a monthly column for *Specialty Coffee Retailer* on new business start-ups and retail management. As a consultant to individuals and corporations, he has traveled extensively throughout the U.S. and the world.

Chapter 17

**Financial Considerations:
Understanding Cost of
Goods Sold and Sales Mix**

213

As odd as it may sound, specialty coffee retailers often don't understand how they make money. In fact, you may feel like one retailer I recently spoke with. We were discussing techniques that would help him analyze his cost of goods sold and discover areas in his operations that could be improved. He listened carefully and then stopped me and said, "Kent, I don't really want to know how to analyze my costs. All I know is that at the end of the month, I pay all of my bills and there's money left over ... and that's all I want to know!"

I understand that feeling. When I opened my first espresso bar in 1990, I was somewhat superstitious about our daily sales. I was afraid that if I sat down and analyzed how we were making money, I might somehow jinx our sales. It was evident that we were vastly exceeding our start-up projections. Wasn't that good enough? It seemed simple; if our projections forecasted we would break even after six months and we were already at the break-even point 30 days after opening, why should I care how we were doing it? What if studying our profits by product mix actually ruined our sales? It was a short-lived bliss. Soon I learned that I needed to understand every aspect of my costs, sales, profits, and critical industry ratios. I quickly had to learn how to manage labor, food inventory and variable costs I didn't yet fully understand, such as break-point rent. I realized that my inability to understand and manage my cost of goods sold and my operating costs could easily ruin my ability to do anything more then just move money from my customers through the bank to my employees and vendors.

Sales Mix Analysis

I had to learn how we were making money. I needed to determine which of our products were most profitable—including products of different sizes and options—and their percentage of our total sales. If you set a daily sales goal of $1000, the net profit potential of your specialty coffee retail operation varies greatly. It depends on the dollar amount of each product you sell and its profit margin. This is also known as your "sales mix."

The sales mix analysis adds up the total sales of your products in each category, determines the margin for each product, and compares the results with predetermined profit objectives. Depending upon how detailed you want to get, you'll find slight variations exist in margins even among different sizes of the same product. For example, you may find it's more profitable on a percentage basis to sell a 20-ounce triple-shot latté than it is to sell a single-shot 8-ounce latté. Or you may find a latté made with two percent milk costs you less to produce than a non-fat latté of the same size and retail price.

The first thing you must determine is your "operating" and "capital asset" costs. These are "cost-of-doing-business" expenses you must pay in order to sell your products. They are broken down into two major categories: fixed expenses and variable expenses. Fixed expenses are expenses (such as your base rent) you must pay whether you sell one latté or thousands. Variable expenses are those in which the expense is directly related to your sales volume (labor and taxes are two examples). Capital asset costs are costs associated with your loans, depreciation of property and any leases you may have in the business. You need to identify these expenses to determine what your gross profit must be to create a net profit. Don't get bored yet! Pour yourself a cup of coffee and concentrate because this is important. The more profitable each of your items, the more cash you will have available to pay operating, capital and profit expenses.

There are two low-margin, "cost-of-goods-sold" traps that many specialty coffee entrepreneurs fall into that further complicate their ability to maximize profits. 1) Me Too! traps—"Starbucks carries/sells _____ and so should I." And 2) Impulsive/Reactionary Product Decisions—"Kent, this would be a really great place if you only carried _____ !"

The Me Too! trap goes something like this: Starbucks carries a large inventory of home espresso equipment and resale items for its customers. Therefore, to be respected and competitive, I need to carry the same or similar items for my customers.

214

The danger of this trap lies in your inability to purchase retail items with the same buying power as Starbucks. As I fell into this trap, I found a home espresso machine or coffeemaker often cost me almost as much from my supplier as Starbucks was charging consumers for the same item. Several times I actually bought insulated travel mugs from Costco (our local membership warehouse store) and marked them up because they were less expensive than the same mugs from my wholesale supplier. Unfortunately most of my customers could also buy them at Costco.

Another problem is the "carrying costs" associated with tying up such a large amount of capital. Carrying costs are up-front investments you make in all your retail items and the cost of letting those items sit on the shelf.

Finally, there is the problem of slow inventory "turn rates" (the length of time it takes to sell an item in your inventory). You probably order, sell and reorder coffee every week. Thus all the money you spend on coffee and pastries each week is returned as a profit. We could say our entire coffee inventory turns 52 times per year. With daily pastry delivery, we could turn our inventory (in theory) 365 times per year.

Compare this with the number of turns you typically experience with your resale merchandise. You might turn home espresso or coffee equipment one or two times per year and coffee mugs or clothing three to six times per year. The gross margin (the cost of the ingredients divided by the retail price of the product, expressed as a percentage) for espresso-based drinks is approximately 77 percent. This means that for every $1 in espresso drinks you sell, 77 cents will go toward your operating, capital and profit expenses. Home coffee equipment may have a gross margin of only 30 percent. Because Starbucks is a publicly traded company and has thousands of retail outlets, the company has radically better purchasing power than you will experience even if you grow to 20 or 100 stores.

Impulsive/Reactionary Product Decisions: In this scenario, inexperience, customer pleading, salesperson hype, or poor sales cause the retailer to add products that do not add net profits to the bottom line. "Kent," someone says, "this would be a great place if you only carried a few lunch items and some really cool logo clothing."

It is important to be customer-driven, but it is essential to know who *you* are first. When I opened, I was so focused on the needs and desires of my customers that I was willing to do almost anything for them. (Please don't ask my wife about the time I agreed to watch a customer's Old English Sheepdog for a week.) You must be responsive to your customers, but you can't sell products that don't add profits to your bottom line. Nor can you sell products inconsistent with your concept.

Many times in the early months I was tempted to add a light-lunch program. Soup, salad, sandwiches, and dessert items may seem like profitable additions to your concept when sales are light, such as during the noon hour and evenings. It might seem obvious that an espresso bar with busy sales during the morning could easily evolve into a deli in the afternoon and a dessert destination or wine bar in the evening. The irony is that by adding something for everyone, you may lose your unique (specialty coffee) identity in the minds of the same customers that asked you to add food in the first place. Often an espresso bar/deli wakes up one day and finds that it has become a deli/espresso bar. The owner planned to only add a few deli items for the off hours, but soon found his or her customers loved the deli items (which weren't profitable) and that espresso drinkers were going elsewhere.

When I present seminars on the business of specialty coffee retail, people always ask, "How do you handle the lunch crowd demand?" I have an answer that surprises many: "I starve them out." I've found that I'm a great specialty coffee retailer, but when I wander away from that expertise, I don't do as well financially. I don't bake products efficiently so I don't try. I don't have a passion for deli foods so I don't sell them. I haven't been successful creating an after-dinner dessert location. And I'm too impatient with the carrying cost of equipment to add more than a token amount of retail merchandise.

Many times in the early years when our customers were still sorting out who we were, they would come in and say, "Kent, why don't you add a light-lunch menu? We would love to come in here several times a day." I responded, "When you want a great sandwich go see _____. When you want a great specialty coffee drink come see me!" Another constant customer request was for "a nice place to go after a show for coffee and a fine pastry." I tried to offer products and stay open late to accommodate this request, but our market didn't support the necessary traffic. My espresso bar started to become a hangout for high schoolers and I was taking a lot of expensive leftover cheesecake home to my family.

My ideal concept boils down to expertise and margins. The cost of goods sold on a sandwich or fine dessert is 60 percent (if you're careful), while the cost of goods sold on a latté is only 23 percent. When the majority of my sales are derived from selling espresso/coffee drinks, I simply have to develop high-volume sales of profitable products and manage my costs. If I have a good location, I'm confident that I have the concept (ambiance), customer service skills, product quality, and financial management skills to eventually capture my share of the specialty coffee market. The sales-building phase of new retail operations is sometimes slow and painful. I've learned not to panic.

The following are detailed examples of financials one could expect to achieve in a typical owner-operated specialty coffee retail operation. First, we must establish basic assumptions or an understanding of: costs, sales, yield, margins, shrinkage, and hours of operation. Your operation may vary in your costs related to the assumptions listed below. Don't despair, these costs have many subtle variations. Use the chart on the following page with specific information from your own operation.

215

Assumptions

Daily sales goal:	$1000
Cost of coffee:	$7 per pound
Number of shots of espresso per pound of coffee:	62 (11 cents cost per shot)
Cost of milk:	$3 per gallon (10 oz. per $2.50 drink)
Single shot of espresso:	1.5 oz. of coffee by volume
Ounces of drip coffee per pound of coffee:	360 (23 cent coffee cost per 12 oz. cup)
Food and noncoffee beverage markup:	100% (50% margin)
Food "shrinkage" and supplies:	10%
Hours of operation:	14 (5:30 a.m. - 7:30 p.m.)

Cost of Goods Sold

Figure 1 shows the percentages (by line item) that are common in specialty coffee operations. You will notice immediately the two extremes I have listed as Cost of Goods Sold. Cost of Goods Sold, or COGS, is defined as the operator's cost for the ingredients and products sold, including milk, coffee, condiments, muffins, mugs for resale, and so on. I've presented two extremes to illustrate a point. The lower your COGS number, the higher your gross profit margin. This is critical to understand because it is the gross profit margin (in real dollars) that you use to pay all your other expenses, including your net profit. The two numbers (COGS and gross margin) have a directly inverse relationship.

You are not likely to have a COGS as bad/high as 70 percent. However, figure 5 (page 222) demonstrates that it's difficult to be profitable with a gross profit margin of 54 percent. On the other hand, it is equally unlikely that you will have COGS as low as 23 percent (unless you ask all your customers to bring their own cups from home). The example in figure 4 shows a COGS of 28 percent. The operator could improve upon that number slightly if he or she chose not to sell food or whole-bean coffee. Of course, that might drive key customers to the competition.

I have chosen $1000 per day in sales as an amount for the following scenarios because I find it's a benchmark in our industry. Again, don't confuse sales with profits. As the following examples will point out, an operator may make or lose money at $1000 per day in sales. All things being equal, the product mix plays a critical role in a retailer's ability to be profitable.

There is an additional reason to use $1000 as a sales ideal. In its 1995 research of specialty coffee retail operations for the Specialty Coffee Association of America (SCAA), Business Resource Services discovered that the most successful specialty coffee retailers had annual sales of between $300,000 and $600,000. That equates to daily sales of roughly $825 to $1600. This category also experienced the lowest staff costs, the lowest operating costs, and the lowest capital asset costs.

Business Resource Services concluded from its study that, "as sales volumes increases to $300,000, owners' discretionary profit as a percentage of sales increases. Then as sales increase over $300,000, owners' discretionary profit as a percentage of sales decreases." The average annual sales for the stores ranked in the top 25 percent was $357,000 ($978 per day). This indicates that $1000 per day in sales is almost exactly the ideal number in this industry, not that I would complain about pulling in double that number! One operator at a large metropolitan airport complains if she hasn't hit $3000 by noon.

Remember, these income and expense percentage numbers (figure 1) work at $1000 per day. If you are grossing only $400 per day, your fixed operating expenses will be higher than those shown here (see your accountant if I'm going too fast).

216

Figure 1

Income Statement for a "Typical" Specialty Coffee Retail Establishment

Sales (per day)	100% ($1000)

Cost of Goods Sold

(Depends on Product Mix)	23-70%

Gross Profit

(Depends on Product Mix)	77-30%

Operating Expenses

Labor (Owner/Manager)	11.5%
Labor (Staff: 21 hours per day x $7 per hour not including tips)	15%
Rent	7%
Utilities	2%
Maintenance	1%
Advertising	2%
Insurance	1%
Outside Services	0.5%
Taxes	0.4%
Misc.	4.5%
	45%

Capital Asset Costs

Equipment Leases	0.4%
Depreciation	2.9%
Interest	1.5%
	4.8%

NET PROFIT/(LOSS) (Depends on Product Mix)	**28% (-19%)**

Notice with our two extremes that the operating expenses and the capital costs are the same. It's the radically different costs to produce the products (COGS)—23 percent vs. 77 percent—that translates into a daily net profit of $280 or a daily net loss of $190.

Figure 2 (page 218) demonstrates the distinct difference in gross profit potential of an operation depending upon the mix of products sold. An operator achieves the ideal profit margin when he or she sells only espresso-based drinks. That is why carts, kiosks, mobile operations, and drive-thrus in well-trafficked locations have such an outstanding potential for success. By their very nature, they don't allow the operator to add many low-margin products or to over-staff the location.

Figure 2

Profit Potential of Individual Resale Items (at $1000 per day in sales)

Retail item (cost of goods)	Retail price	Number of transactions needed to achieve goal	Number of pounds of coffee	Gross profit
Double Shot Espresso-Based Drink (19 cents per drink—milk, 9 cents for coffee, 8 cents for condiments & supplies)	$2.50	400	13	23%, $770
12 oz. Cup of Drip Coffee (17 cents per drink—9 cents for coffee, 8 cents for condiments & supplies)	$1.25	800	27	32%, $680
Whole-Bean Coffee (sold by the pound)	$10	100	100	70%, $300
Food Items	Varies	Varies	0	60%, $400
Retail Merchandise	Varies	Varies	0	70%, $300

It is interesting to note that whole-bean coffee sales are not much different from retail merchandise sales on a percentage basis. Remember, however, that there is a vast difference between the two when you focus on inventory turns. Whole-bean coffee turns weekly while most retail merchandise turns quarterly. Food items may turn daily, but have the potential to be financially devastating if you are selling day-old pastries for half price (your cost), feeding your staff free lunch or muffins, or throwing away (donating) unsold items. I try to teach my managers to carefully monitor this category. "I don't want you to have any left over product [shrinkage] and I don't want you to run out of product [lost opportunity cost]," I say. "I want you to try to order the exact right amount of product every day." Think of it as a game and create financial incentives for your managers. (I have a similar lecture on labor scheduling.)

The Espresso Bar

It appears that a drive-thru, kiosk or cart might be the ideal specialty coffee concept because of its potential for high-margin, high-volume sales. Yet not all operators would agree. With a drive-thru, the customer has little opportunity to spend a significant amount of time enjoying the ambiance or company of the owner and staff (many find this a blessing). You certainly won't find many customers scheduling their business meetings there.

Most espresso bar owners simply don't want to spend their working lives "in a box" selling espresso regardless of the profit potential. Carts and kiosks (due to the lack of cars) have the potential to be miniature espresso bars (depending on the location), but usually have less of a sense of place (ambiance). An espresso bar that is well-designed, comfortable, friendly, serves excellent espresso/coffee drinks, and is clean and convenient may well be the most wonderful retail concept ever conceived. The profit potential in a good location is excellent and the quality of life is high.

Figure 3

Espresso Bar Product Mix Strategy (at $1000 in sales per day)

	% of Sales	Sales	Net
Espresso-based drinks	60	$600	$462
Drip coffee	20	$200	$136
Food (and noncoffee beverages)	10	$100	$40
Whole bean	7	$70	$21
Merchandise	3	$30	$9
Sub-Total	100	$1000	$668

Gross Profit Margin: 67% (on sales of $1000 and a gross profit of $668)

Operating Expenses

Labor (owner/manager)	$125
Labor (Staff: 21 hours per day x $7.10 per hour not including tips)	$177
Rent	$70
Utilities	$20
Maintenance	$10
Advertising	$20
Insurance	$10
Outside services	$8
Taxes	$5
Misc.	$7
Total Operating Expenses	**$452**

Capital Asset Costs

Equipment leases	$5
Depreciation	$30
Interest	$15
Total Capital Costs	**$50**

NET PROFIT:	**16.6%, $166**

219

The Espresso Drive-Thru

Although I wouldn't want to work in a drive-thru for more than 37 seconds, they are great to own in a high-traffic, well-educated (espresso not Shakespeare) market. We used to call our drive-thru "a license to print money." I didn't feel sorry for the baristas that worked in them either because they all made more money (including tips) than I did and drove much nicer cars!

Figure 4

Espresso Drive-Thru, Cart or Kiosk Product Mix Strategy (at $1000 per day)

	% of Sales	Sales	Net
Espresso-based drinks	80	$800	$616
Drip coffee	10	$100	$68
Food (and noncoffee beverages)	8	$80	$32
Whole bean	2	$20	$6
Sub-Total	100	$1000	$722

Gross Profit Margin: 72% (on sales of $1000 and a gross profit of $722)

Operating Expenses

Labor (owner/manager)	$125
Labor (Staff: 21 hours per day x $7.10 per hour not including tips)	$177
Rent	$70
Utilities	$20
Maintenance	$10
Advertising	$20
Insurance	$10
Outside services	$8
Taxes	$5
Misc.	$7
Total Operating Expenses	**$452**

Capital Asset Costs

Equipment leases	$5
Depreciation	$30
Interest	$15
Total Capital Costs	**$50**

NET PROFIT:	**22%, $220**

220

The Espresso Café

I am not a big fan of espresso cafés. Not because I don't love to go to them; I certainly do. The problem is I can't manage to make money with one. The following is an (only slightly exaggerated) average day early in our first store's history. It clearly illustrates the miscalculation of thinking I could save money by "scoop and baking" my own cookies instead of buying them from a vendor.

At 10:30 a.m., Lisa prepares a batch of cookies but puts them in the oven before it's fully pre-heated. When she pulls the cookies out after the regular baking time, they're not done. She puts them back in the oven and runs down to the store for ice. (No, we didn't have our own ice machine. Why should we when we could make all of this money with a convection oven, baking our own pastries, in the spot where we would have placed the ice machine?) When Lisa gets back with the bags of ice, she gets a "rush" of espresso customers and the batch burns. "That's OK," Kent says. "It happens."

Martin's shift starts at noon. Lisa tells him about the burnt cookies and asks him to bake a batch as soon as possible. Martin starts a second batch of cookies but doesn't want to burn them, so he takes them out 10 minutes early (cookies only bake for 13 minutes in a convection oven) and runs over to the supermarket next door for more ice. Kent, fearful of salmonella poisoning, throws the batch out when he gets back from making the deposit at the bank. "Don't worry about it," Kent says. "It happens." Martin feels bad, but is too busy to bake another batch during his shift.

Erika comes on at 5 p.m. and will work until close. "Erika, will you please make some cookies first thing?" asks Kent. "We haven't had any all day and the customers have been a little upset about it." "Sure," says Erika, "but first I better run down and get some ice. It looks like we've been busy." Erika makes a great batch of cookies but decides to reduce the price to "day-old" because most of the cookies won't get eaten until tomorrow.

While the oven is still hot, she decides to make a giant birthday cookie for her boyfriend. Kent calls from home to check in at closing and asks how the evening went. Erika assures Kent that it went great, except, "We ran out of ice at eight, and I was too busy with our line of espresso customers and baking to run down and get some. Sorry."

"Hey that's OK," Kent says with a sigh. "It happens."

It should have cost me 25 cents to bake a cookie that sells for $1 (25 percent COGS). I could buy cookies baked by excellent vendors for 50 cents and sell them for $1 (50 percent COGS). But somehow I was managing to bake them myself for $1.25 and sell them for $1 (I was operating a government-like, subsidized "hot cookie" program). Soon I remodeled, the convection oven went out and an ice machine went in.

This anecdote illustrates the challenges facing the owner of an espresso café. This isn't to suggest you shouldn't open one; it just means you have to watch all your costs with an especially critical eye.

So how do you decide whether to open an espresso café?

Here are a few things common to many espresso café owners. Some people consider them pitfalls, but people with the right personalities can harness these qualities in a positive direction.

1) They're all very hard working, often to extremes. No one can make their special "____" as well as they can, so they have to do it themselves.

2) They're all perfectionists and consider their "works of art" (products) a labor of love. They believe they work too hard and too many hours (as do their family and friends), and yet when they do eventually sell their businesses, they usually start other ones just as demanding.

3) They all have very little time for outside pursuits and interests. Their product creations, vendors and customers are their lives.

4) Because they are so good at what they do, everyone is trying to get a piece of them. "Dan, why don't you go into catering?" "Debbie, have you ever thought of doing gift baskets?" "Hey, when are you guys going to open one of these in my neighborhood?" (If you

221

own an espresso café, you're laughing right now because you recognize yourself.) To be successful with a café you must be really good or really rich.

5) If the espresso cafés are not owned and managed on-site by the owner, they are unprofitable (maybe the new Starbucks Café will be the exception).

Figure 5

Espresso Café Product Mix Strategy (at $1000 in sales per day)

	% of Sales	Sales	Net
Food (and noncoffee beverages)	50	$500	$200
Espresso-based drinks	35	$350	$270
Drip coffee	6	$60	$41
Merchandise	5	$50	$15
Whole bean	4	$40	$12
Sub-Total	100	$1000	$538

Gross Profit Margin: 54% (on sales of $1000 and a gross profit of $538)

Operating Expenses

Labor (owner/manager)	$125
Labor (Staff: 30 hours per day x $7.10 per hour not including tips)	$213
Rent	$70
Utilities	$20
Maintenance	$10
Advertising	$20
Insurance	$10
Outside services	$8
Taxes	$5
Misc.	$7
Total Operating Expenses	**$488**

Capital Asset Costs

Equipment leases	$5
Depreciation	$30
Interest	$15
Total Capital Costs	**$50**

NET PROFIT: 0%, $0

In her book *The French Café*, Marie-France Boyer movingly describes why dedicated entrepreneurs and foodservice professionals continue to develop espresso cafés:

"The French do not go into a café only to drink; it may be to make a telephone call, wait for a friend, see and be seen, kill time, work, play, eat, read, shelter from the weather, answer the call of nature, seek out their peers or escape from them. It is one of the few places in our urban civilization where the French can still communicate—or dream of doing so. ... Only cafés are left as places of unique privilege and freedom. They are places open to everyone where anything might happen. For the price of a cup of coffee you can stay as long as you like."

Espresso cafés are wonderful places to visit ... but very difficult to run.

The previous example has a high mix of food simply to illustrate the difficulty of making a profit with products that have a high COGS. You will also notice that labor is slightly higher than in the other coffee concepts, which is typical in foodservice operations. This example is not designed to demonstrate that espresso cafés are unprofitable. They do, however, require more operating skill and expertise. Espresso cafés are very difficult to run for an absentee owner.

This doesn't have to be your espresso café. But owners who go into the business without a firm grasp on their costs are not destined to last long in the realm of espresso cafés. Develop solid operational systems that allow for very little waste.

Cost Controls

It has been said that "high volume sales hide a multitude of sins." If the demand for espresso-based drinks is strong and business is good, even a marginally efficient operation can make a profit. But when strong competition enters a market—as eventually happens everywhere—profits go down and the operator losses money. To experience long-term financial success, specialty coffee retailers must find an excellent location, create an inviting environment, choose and produce quality products, learn and train excellent customer service skills, and continually focus on careful financial management. An operator can do a lot to keep up with his or her profit objectives.

David Pavesic, a long-term professor specializing in hotel and restaurant cost control systems, states the following: "It is not likely that there will be a return to the 'good ole days' where even marginal operations will be able to compete. The successful operations will be run by the seasoned professional who understands the importance of operational efficiency. ... Cost controls are the tools that provide the information used to develop strategies before a problem results in a loss of profit. ... The primary purpose of cost control is to maximize profits, not minimize losses."

Cost control implies advance preparation. You must develop simple and effective cost control systems. One must refine or develop rules, procedures, forms, portion control devices, and eventually a POS system (Point Of Sale—a fancy term for a computerized cash register that tracks sales by programmable categories). You must analyze the data gathered and use it to maximize profits. You must constantly monitor cost controls to determine if the goals set are being achieved.

Many operators don't know where to start. I often hear, "I don't even know what I don't know, so how can I determine where to begin?!"

A great place to start is the aforementioned SCAA/Business Resource Services study. This *Operating & Financial Ratio Study* ("Retailers Ratios" PLU #27) is a critical resource for any operator who desires to review the specialty coffee retail industry's financial benchmarks. This study evaluates the income statements and balance sheets of 46 actual espresso retailers from across the U.S. In short, the average company had one location, occupied approximately 1000 square feet of space, had annual sales of $400,000, had been in operation for three years, was owner-operated, and experienced an "owners discretionary profit" (net profit plus owners salary) of between six and 17 percent.

This resource will help you compare your current COGS with those of the companies surveyed. Further, one can learn the importance of evaluating several key ratios, such as: optimum productivity, profitability, asset efficiency, working capital cycle management, and sales volume analysis. Finally, this study includes a seven-step "action plan for success" to help retailers understand the key financial performance issues of specialty coffee and begin to track and manage them.

If you need a manual to refresh your skills, or, unlike the head-in-the-sand retailer I described earlier, you actually do want to know how you make your money, I would suggest you purchase a copy of *Bean Business Basics* by Ed Arvidson and Bruce Milletto. This is an excellent resource for the start-up retailer and a great source of information on cost controls, profitability, merchandising, customer service, and marketing for those already in the business. ●

224

Sue Gillerlain

Susan J. Gillerlain is editor of *Specialty Coffee Retailer* maga-zine, a monthly business journal targeting the specialty coffee industry. Published by Adams Business Media, which owns over 70 trade publications and has offices in California, Ohio, New York, and Massachusetts, *Specialty Coffee Retailer* pro-vides practical information about the profitable operation of a coffee business. The national trade publication covers such topics as: marketing and promotion, management and finance, business expansion, store design, equipment selec-tion and maintenance, techniques, trends, new products, and more.

Prior to her post at *Specialty Coffee Retailer,* Gillerlain was editor for the Chicago-based Merchandise Mart Properties Inc. and the Appraisal Institute.

227

Chapter 18

Making the Most of Trade Shows—and More!

"With so many day-to-day operational responsibilities and budgetary constraints, I don't have the time or money to attend two- and three-day trade shows." Sound familiar? If so, you're not alone. For many retailers, multiple-day getaways are earmarked for vacations only. But the fact is, when a retailer works a trade show wisely, the long-term benefits can far outweigh any short-term time or monetary discomforts.

Trade Show Basics

Most trade shows feature a concurrent exhibition and conference. Depending on the show, the exhibition may include only a handful of industry vendors or it may feature hundreds, all displaying their latest products and services. This is a retailer's best opportunity to gather and benchmark competitive product/service information—all under one roof and in one stop.

The conference portion of the show typically includes an educational package of seminars, workshops, keynote speakers, and panel and roundtable discussions. This is where you will find the who's who of the industry sharing business successes and failures, presenting techniques and offering insights into the future. Quite often, one of the most valuable segments of the presentation is during the interactive question and answer period at the end. At a seminar I attended during a coffee show on keeping good employees, the audience participation was phenomenal. Every retailer in the room left with at least five proven strategies for keeping good employees and even a few for letting the not-so-good employees go.

While most all shows offer an exhibition and conference, there are a few different *types* of shows available to the specialty coffee retailer. (For a comprehensive list of shows and contact information, see page 234).

- *Specialty coffee shows* are targeted specifically to the owners, managers and staff members of small, medium and large coffeehouse operations, mobile and stationary drive-thrus, carts and kiosks, and teahouses. Educational programs at these shows are geared toward the business of coffee and tea, and usually include brewing and espresso labs, coffee cuppings, business finance classes, management and marketing seminars, customer service workshops, roasting seminars, and more. Vendors participating in specialty coffee shows range from espresso machine manufacturers, syrup companies and roasters to granita machine distributors, confectioners, packaging and label manufacturers, and many more.

- *Gift Shows* not only target gift shop owners, but also coffee and tea retailers that carry gift lines and offer gift baskets or boxes. This is the type of show to attend if you are interested in the latest gift and seasonal trends, retail merchandising ideas or packaging for resale.

  Don't be surprised to find attendees at these shows placing large orders for their shops and not just browsing. Many gift shop owners purchase the majority of their merchandise at these shows. Invariably, a few months after I attend a gift show in Chicago, I see several of the same products decking Pottery Barn's latest catalog or the shelves of my local Pier One outlet. Candleholders, frames, vases, jewelry, holiday decorations, small furnishings, plush toys, silk floral arrangements, wall hangings, pottery, baskets, boxes, bags, bows, and ribbons—even gourmet foods—are all commonplace at a gift show. Educational programs cover such topics as creating gift baskets that sell, effective merchandising, theme merchandising, floral arranging, selling skills, and customer service tips.

- *Gourmet Food Shows* attract a variety of audiences, but mainly specialty food retailers, deli operators, upscale grocery chain owners and managers, and specialty coffee retailers. Coffees, teas, ready-to-drink beverages, pastries, confections, cookies, crackers, jams and jellies, syrups, sauces, breads, meats, cheeses, and oils all line the show floors. Even if you are not currently contemplating the addition of gourmet foods to your retail shelves or menu, it is worth your while to attend a gourmet food show. You'll have a chance to talk to multiple vendors about their products and the potential they bring to your bottom line. Gourmet food shows also provide the perfect opportunity to catch up with other retailers and find out which products are selling and why. Educational seminars typically cover food trends, food merchandising techniques, food safety, and staff training.

Trade Show Planning

Before attending any show, there are a few things you can do to prepare for a hassle-free experience.

Always preregister to take advantage of early-bird admission fees and to avoid waiting in long on-site registration lines. By preregistering, you should receive an attendee packet in the mail that includes your show badge, an exhibitor list, a conference agenda, and discounted lodging and airfare information. Because "show towns" are known to fill fast, it is best to make travel and lodging arrangements as soon as possible. Before you do, however, always ask about show travel discounts, which the show director may or may not promote in your preregistration packet.

Once you have an exhibitor list in hand, review the lineup and place a check next to every "must-see" exhibitor. If time allows, you can always go back to other vendors, but your A-list sets the game plan. (This varies, of course, with the size of the show. Some show floors may take several hours to traverse, others several days.)

Also make an A-list for your conference agenda. Highlight the most beneficial educational seminars, leaving yourself time to walk the show floor and attend social events. Some pre-show attendee packets even include a pre-show planner to help you map out your itinerary.

Prior to the show, read your trade publications. The month prior to a big industry show, many magazines run show previews featuring new product photos and descriptions, educational program information, social event schedules, and even dining and sightseeing information about the host city.

Buy for Customers, Not Yourself

If you are planning to buy products at a show, do your homework on your current inventory before you buy. Analyze your merchandise assortments. Are they broad when they should be deep, or vice versa? What are your current stock levels and your *ideal* stock levels? Identify your key volume items and recognize the trends of your category sales. There is no need to stock up on tea strainers and teapots if several models from last year are collecting dust in your storage room.

Before placing your first order, put together a budget that calculates the totals and breakouts per merchandise category. For example, if you are headed to a gourmet foods show and plan on ordering baked goods, determine your total budget for this category and then break it into subcategories. These subcategories might include holiday baked goods, general baked goods for the retail shelves, grab-and-go impulse items for the checkout counter, baked goods for the pastry case, and baked goods for gift baskets. By breaking your budget into subcategories, it is nearly impossible to come home with 10 cases of holiday shortbread tins but no muffins or mini bundt cakes for the pastry case.

The Master Checklist

Packing for shows is easy with a master checklist. Try this one on for size:
1) Business I.D.: business cards/company stationery/company checks/original sales tax certificate. (Some shows require two business forms of identification and your original sales tax certificate for admission.)
2) Credit reference sheet (if you are planning to place orders). This sheet should include three of your biggest and best-standing vendors' names, addresses and phone numbers. If you are registered with Dunn & Bradstreet, include that as well.
3) Stickers with your store name, address and phone number to place on "sold to" and "ship to" sections of purchase orders (if you are planning to place orders).
4) Credit cards/ATM card.
5) Calling card.
6) Calculator.
7) Sturdy tote bag or briefcase.
8) Pens, pencils, highlighter, and notepad.
9) Blank company expense report.
10) Envelope for expense receipts.
11) Attendee preregistration kit with exhibitor badge, exhibitor list and conference agenda.
12) Airline ticket and lodging confirmations.
13) Color swatches for packaging, display equipment and retail merchandise purchases.
14) Employee phone list for emergency calls.
15) Comfortable shoes. (The dress at most specialty coffee, gourmet food and gift shows is business casual.)

231

Working the Exhibit Floor Wisely

At the door of most shows, you will find bins full of the show management's "official show guide," which details all educational sessions and networking events and lists all exhibitors, their booth numbers and a map where they can be found.

Take time out before entering the show to highlight your "must-see" exhibitors on the show guide map. Then start at one aisle of the show floor and work your way down each aisle until you end up on the opposite side of the floor. If you have time after seeing your

A-list vendors, rework the floor starting from the beginning. By traveling aisle by aisle you don't have to backtrack, saving time and ensuring you don't miss a key vendor.

If you have never attended a trade show before, it can be intimidating to walk up to an exhibit booth. Remember, the trade show is developed specifically for you. Every vendor *wants* to talk to you, so take full advantage of your position.

Before you approach that first booth, load your back pocket with these questions:

1) What trends do you see in this particular category? A confectioner may point out that coffee retailers are buying six times more dark-chocolate-covered graham crackers than milk-chocolate-covered graham crackers.

2) What are your best-selling products for coffeehouse retailers? These are products with proven track records—the winners—and are probably the safest to start with.

3) Can you point out your newest products? These products may signal an emerging trend that your customers will soon enjoy.

4) What is your minimum order?

5) When can I expect delivery?

6) What are your payment terms? Net 30 (paid within 30 days) is typical.

7) Are you offering any show specials? Often times, a vendor will discount products sold at the show or waive the shipping charges.

8) Do you have any special storage requirements for products?

9) What is the shelf life of your product?

10) Do you supply any point-of-sale materials or other marketing support?

11) Do you offer training? Do you offer maintenance? These two questions are especially important when contemplating the purchase of a big ticket item such as a coffee roaster or espresso machine.

12) Are there any merchandising techniques that work particularly well with your product? A vendor may tell you that his or her biscotti sells best in a two-flavor twin pack at the checkout counter.

Collecting Materials

You'll have the opportunity to pick up literally thousands of pages of sell sheets and brochures on the trade show floor. The problem is you have to lug it all home (then read it later). To avoid this hassle, consider these two convenient options:

- Collect brochures, but at the close of the show, bring your materials to a shipping booth on the show floor. Trade shows typically house a booth run by Mail Boxes Etc. or some other shipping service, which you can find on the show guide map.

- If your badge is bar coded, have exhibitors scan it and send catalogs and other promotional materials directly to you. If your badge is not coded, offer your business card in exchange for forwarded materials and be sure to ask exhibitors for their business cards just in case you don't receive their catalogs.

If you attend any of the NASFT Fancy Food Shows, make a point to visit the "Focused Exhibits Showcase," which features new products, a "gift avenue," foodservice products, natural foods, kosher foods, and products that won awards from the show committee. Upon entering the showcase, visitors receive a product information form and are encouraged to check off any and all featured products on the form. Not more than a week after the show, manufacturers start sending out specified product information—and the mailboxes begin to fill!

If a show does have a new-product or award-winning-product exhibit, be sure to stop by. The products in these special exhibits are the ones sparking new trends or are the favored products of industry experts. Take down the booth numbers of any products of interest and pay them a personal visit.

While you need not pick up catalogs at each exhibitor's booth, it is important to pick up business cards from company representatives. It is also wise to write brief notes during your booth visit on the back of business cards (e.g., "Source for coffee-flavored rock candy stir sticks" or "No order minimums"). These reminder notes can save you from making several follow-up phone calls in the future.

Placing Orders and Tracking Expenses

If you are planning on buying at a trade show, the key is to shop prudently; you can always order more later.

For every order you *do* place, make sure you receive a confirmation copy that includes a shipping date and terms of the sale. Most importantly, before leaving the company's booth, read over your confirmation copy for accuracy.

If you are placing orders with multiple vendors, keep track of all your purchases by placing them in *one* folder. You may also want to create a tracking form to list all your orders, costs, payment terms, and dates of delivery to help you organize and anticipate bills and shipments when you return to your shop.

At the end of each night during a show, take the time to go through your collection of expense receipts for lunches, taxis, entertainment, parking, etc., and transfer them onto your expense report. (Expenses must be substantiated as to the amount, time, place, and business purpose.) It is far easier to complete an expense report day-by-day than it is to piece one together a month or two after a show.

Educational/Networking Opportunities

Most educational seminars, workshops and panel and roundtable discussions are run concurrently during a trade show. Because the timing of all these programs does overlap, you may find yourself having to choose between a valuable seminar and an equally valuable roundtable discussion. If you can afford it, consider bringing a manager or staff person with you. Your employee will benefit from the education and exposure to new products and you will cover all your bases at the show. Some retailers even hold sales and customer service contests for staff throughout the year and award the winner an all-expenses-paid trip to an industry trade show. Others simply budget trade shows as an annual training expense for key employees.

At nearly every educational session you attend, you can pick up presentation handouts prior to the start of the program. Pick them up! Many outline the presentation, allowing you to take notes in the margins during the more colorful remarks.

At the end of nearly every educational session, you'll have an opportunity to network with the presenter. Presenters usually linger 15 to 20 minutes following their sessions for individual questions and comments. This presents a golden opportunity for you to introduce yourself and gain a valuable contact for the future. Suppose you are contemplating opening a second café and the presenter from the "Opening Multiple Locations" seminar happens to own five coffeehouses in North Carolina. Perfect! After a brief exchange of words and business cards, you've got an important contact in the bank.

The single best way to meet fellow retailers from across the country and around the world is to RSVP to "Attendee Parties" thrown by trade show management. You should be able to find out the when and where of these special attendee networking events inside your preregistration packet or by calling trade show management prior to the event. Some parties may require pre- or on-site payment, but the price is worth the networking opportunities and fun.

During a show, budget time to visit coffee businesses in the local area. Not only will you meet other retailers, but you may also uncover regional trends, new merchandising ideas, pricing information, and innovative store designs.

Post Show Wrap-Up

Once you return home from a trade show, there are some simple things you can do to organize your product information and impending product shipments.

- If you purchased products at a show, transfer the delivery dates from your confirmation orders onto your shop calendar. You don't want to be surprised (or have your employees be surprised) the day the shipment does arrive.

- After you start receiving product information from exhibitors or the day your shipment of show brochures is delivered, start setting up a filing system. Organize files by product categories (i.e., roasters, roasting equipment, grinders, blended ice drink mixes, paper products, syrups, baked goods, etc.) and slip product catalogs and brochures into their corresponding folders. This system makes life so much easier when you're trying to locate a manufacturer or distributor that sells créme brulée-flavored syrup, single-serve brownies or wild berry granita mix.

Following a show, it is also important to share the information you gathered with your staff. Make copies of the educational handouts, bring back copies of the show guide and talk about the new products you saw, encouraging feedback. Does your barista think ABC company's white chocolate syrup would work for a new signature drink? What does your counter person think about the foiled confections offered by XYZ chocolatier? Would they sell at the counter? Which season would they sell best?

If a staff member accompanied you to the trade show, involve her after the show by asking her to lead the post-show discussion with other staff members.

234

Work on Your Business, Not in It

From a retailer's perspective, the benefits of attending a trade show really boil down to three things: education, exposure to new products/services, and, most importantly, the synergy that comes from gathering an industry. Where else can you work *on* your business alongside industry experts who have walked in your shoes, rather than working isolated *in* the day-to-day operations of your business? The trade show creates this collaborative environment, where a free-flow of ideas is not only encouraged, but expected. And rest assured, the ideas you bring back to your retail operation can only have a positive impact.

Trade Shows

Following is a list of specialty coffee, gift and gourmet food trade shows. For actual show dates, times and locations, call show management at the phone numbers listed below.

Specialty Coffee and Tea Shows

SCAA Annual Conference and Exhibition
Traveling show sponsored by the Specialty Coffee Association of America.
562-624-4100

Coffee Fest
Traveling show held two or three times annually. The largest show is always held in Seattle.
800-232-0083

NASCORE (North American Specialty Coffee and Beverage Retailers' Exposition)
Annual trade show sponsored by *Fresh Cup Magazine*.
800-548-0551

European Coffee Congress
Annual show sponsored by the European Coffee Federation, CECA and EUCA.
+44 (171) 453 2709

Kona Coffee Cultural Festival
Annual festival held in Kauilua-Kona, Hawaii.
808-326-7820

National Coffee Association Annual Convention
212-344-5596

U.S. Tea Association Annual Convention
212-697-8658

National Coffee Service Association's Annual Convention and Trade Show
703-522-9100

Coffee & Tea Exhibition & Symposium
Annual show sponsored by *Tea & Coffee Trade Journal.*
212-827-0945

Canadian Coffee Expo
Annual show sponsored by *Coffee Culture* magazine.
416-703-6099

American Premium Tea Institute's Annual Tea Symposium
562-624-4100

235

Gift Shows
Columbus Gift Show
Columbus Gift Mart
Columbus, Ohio
614-876-2719

Seattle Gift Market
Sponsored by Western Exhibitors
Seattle Gift Center
Seattle, Wash.
800-433-1014

Holiday Jubilee! Gift Basket Show
Annual trade show sponsored by *Gift Basket Review* magazine.
904-634-1902

Atlanta International Gift Market
Americasmart
Atlanta, Ga.
800-ATL-MART

California Gift Show
Los Angeles Convention Center
Los Angeles, Calif.
800-LA-MART-4

Chicago Gifts & Accessories Market
Merchandise Mart
Chicago, Ill.
800-677-6278

San Francisco International Gift Fair
San Francisco Merchandise Mart
San Francisco, Calif.
415-346-6666

New York International Gift Fair
Javits Center
New York, N.Y.
212-685-6377

Washington Gift Show
Capitol Expo Center
Chantilly, Va.
800-272-7469

Dallas National Gift & Home Accessories Market
Dallas Market Center
Dallas, Texas
214-655-6100

Portland Gift Show
Produced by Western Exhibitors
Oregon Convention Center
Portland, Ore.
800-346-1212

CGTA Gift show
Biannual show rotating between the International Center and Toronto
   Congress Center.
Toronto, Ontario
Canada
800-611-6100

Miami Gift Show
Miami Merchandise Mart
Miami, Fla.
305-261-2900

NOWCO Gift Basket Symposium
Traveling symposium sponsored by NOWCO Packaging Co.
800-233-8302

Gourmet Food Shows
Dallas National Gourmet Food Show
Dallas Market Center
Dallas, Texas
214-655-6100

NASFT International Fancy Food & Confection Show
Traveling show held three times per year and sponsored by the National Association
    for the Specialty Food Trade Inc.
212-482-6440

Canadian Fine Foods Show
International Center
Toronto, Ontario
Canada
416-229-2060

National Restaurant Association Show
Annual show sponsored by the National Restaurant Association.
McCormick Place
Chicago, Ill.
312-853-2525

Gourmet Products Show
Traveling show held annually and produced by George Little Management Inc.
800-739-0014

Natural Products Expo
Biannual show sponsored by New Hope Communications.
West Coast Show held in Anaheim, Calif.
East Coast Show held in Baltimore, Md.
303-939-8440

Philadelphia Candy, Gift and Gourmet Show
Biannual show sponsored by the Retail Confectionery Association of Philadelphia.
Valley Forge Convention Center
Philadelphia, Pa.
610-265-4688

237

Terms of the Trade: Shipping and Billing

Advance Dating: Also known as season dating. An agreed upon future date when
  terms are set.

Advertising Allowance: Discount to offset expense of advertising a product line or
  item. Amount varies between two and 10 percent off invoice.

Anticipation: Additional discount from vendors on anticipation that a store's yearly
  purchases will reach a certain dollar amount.

Approval Sale: A sale subject to later approval or selection. Customer has unlimited
  return privileges.

Automatic Cancellation Date: The date specified by buyers on the purchase order as
  the last acceptable shipment date.

Automatic Reorder: The reordering of staple merchandise on the basis of
  predetermined minimum quantities. When minimum is reached, the quantity of the
  initial order is ordered again.

A/O: At Once. Goods are to be received immediately.

A.R.O.: After Receipt of Order.

Backup Order: Additional merchandise reserved by manufacturer at time of initial order so buyer can get fast delivery on subsequent order.

Basic: Inventory needed to cover expected sales demands.

B.C. (or Best Way): Indicates the best way and lowest rates to ship if merchandise can't be shipped UPS.

Bill of Landing: Document that proves a carrier received a shipment, used as a contract between carrier and shipper. In air shipments, an air waybill.

B.O.: Back Order Merchandise. Shipped on a later date or unavailable at time of original shipment.

B.O.M.: Beginning Of the Month.

Cancellation Date: Specifies date beyond which you will not accept the goods. The date refers to the date the goods leave the manufacturer unless otherwise specified.

Charge-Backs: Vendor debits, i.e. billings to vendors for returned or damaged merchandise, cooperative advertising or adjustments.

C.O.D.: Cash On Delivery. UPS drivers will accept checks. UPS adds a COD charge onto the shipping charges.

Close-Out: Offer at reduced price to clear slow-moving stock.

Dating: Refers to manufacturer that allows a buyer to pay bills later than normal terms, possibly 60 to 90 days after shipping to stores. Ask your salesperson if dating can be arranged. Bills are often dated when the order is received early.

Delivery: Time between when the factory receives, processes and ships the order and when the store receives the merchandise.

D.F.I.: Deduct From Invoice.

E.O.M.: End-Of-Month dating.

F.O.B.: Free On Board. Indicates the location from which the merchandise is shipped, i.e. FOB Dallas, FOB Chicago.

Freight Allowance: Discount on freight if store buys a specified amount at a specific time.

Guaranteed Sale: A signed agreement in which a buyer can return unsold goods after they have been offered for sale for a given period.

H.F.C.: Hold For Confirmation. When a buyer asks a rep/manufacturer to hold the order for a few days before placing.

In Store: Date you expect merchandise to arrive at your store. This would be later than your shipping date.

Keystone: When you double the wholesale cost to determine the retail price.

Lead Time: Length of time that elapses until ordered merchandise is available for sale.

Margin/Mark-Up: The amount above the wholesale price you charge for a product. Keystoning a product gives you a 50 percent margin.

Markdown Money: Money a vendor gives you to enable you to reduce the selling price of a slow seller.

Minimum: Minimum dollar quantity per line, minimum pieces per line, minimum units per item.

Net 30: An account that filled out a credit application has been granted 30 days to pay the bill.

New Store Opening: If you are opening a new store, make sure you write "New Store Opening" on all purchase orders. Highlight and request merchandise early. Also make sure to follow up on all deliveries to ensure timely delivery.

O.H.: On Hand.

O.O.: On Order.

O.T.B.: Open To Buy financial plan. Refers to the amount of money a store has available for future purchases ("We have no OTB's right now").

P.O.: Purchase Order. A written order generated by the store that is either executed at time of purchase or mailed subsequently. Usually details specific shipping and invoicing instructions.

Prepay: Buyer pays at time of order. Many manufacturers will pay the freight if order is prepaid. (Be prepared for manufacturer to cash your check immediately even though you specify a future shipping date.)

Pro Forma: Manufacturer bills buyer for the order amount plus shipping charges. Upon receipt of check, manufacturer ships goods. Similar to prepay.

R.O.G.: Receipt Of Goods, e.g., "payment of invoice on or after R.O.G."

R.T.V.: Return To Vendor.

Ship Date: Date you request manufacturer to ship merchandise.

Showroom: A location where a rep or a manufacturer has product on permanent display.

S.K.U.: Stock Keeping Unit. The number of items a manufacturer has in his or her line.

S/M: Side Mark. Instructs shipper to direct the order to a specific person or department. It might involve an individual package or packages wrapped separately and included in one large box, possibly directed to several different people.

Specific Date: Used for future ship dates. Manufacturer will assume this is the date goods leave his or her dock unless you specify the goods to arrive by a different date.

Terms: Pay schedule. Different terms can save you money. Net 30 means the payment is due in full 30 days from the date of invoice. Sometimes discounts can be arranged if paid early.

Turn Rate: How many times inventory turns.

Excerpted from 1998 *New Buyer Handbook* by George Little Management Inc.; 914-421-3200. Reprinted with permission. ●

Eric J. Schiff

Eric J. Schiff is a co-founder of PremiereLink Communications in Eugene, Ore., and has 17 years of experience in design and implementation of technology-integration programs. His experience includes curriculum design, staff development, building/site technology planning, and timeline implementation, as well as technology workshop design and training for the Eugene public school system. He has taught Information Design and Presentation and Multimedia and Online Design and Presentation at the University of Oregon for the past 12 years.

He has served as a consultant, coordinator and instructor/trainer for the Department of Defense Dependents Schools both in the U.S. and in Japan. Other experience includes 10 years as director of the University Of Oregon Summer Computer Camp, an on-campus emerging technology hands-on experience for students.

Schiff holds a B.A. in sociology and an M.A. in curriculum and instruction from the University of Oregon. He currently serves on the board of directors of Maude Kerns Art Center in Eugene.

243

Chapter 19

How Your Business Can Effectively Use the Internet

It's hard for me not to sound like a new media zealot proselytizing about the necessity and benefits of Internet marketing, so be forewarned that I will undoubtedly carry that tenor throughout this chapter.

As with any form of advertising and marketing, it's paramount to use common sense when forming baseline strategies for designing (or redesigning) and implementing a marketing plan. While most people responsible for a company's marketing efforts are familiar with traditional advertising tools, there is a relatively large void when it comes to understanding and integrating Internet marketing opportunities. People's reactions to Internet marketing run the gamut from excitement and blind acceptance to fear and rejection. Time is a great equalizer, and Internet marketing will one day be understood and take its place as an integral component—if not the central focus—of a company's consumer and business-to-business marketing plans.

Compounding the issue of the Internet's relative youth as an advertising tool is the ever-present stigma that Internet marketing and the myriad associated applications and spin-offs are technology-based. Historically, the general public has been slow to embrace technological tools in their daily lives (even while society has seemingly been fascinated by technology).

Up until the last few years, the obvious reasons for this technological paranoia included the high cost of hardware and software, a lack of ready applications, and the fact that many people found computers difficult to use. Less obvious reasons centered around a unique cultural phenomenon driven by individual and collective negative experiences involving technology. These individuals or groups have been unwitting victims of human error, a combination of human and computer error, or just plain computer system failure. Examples include bank record errors, credit reporting errors, unwanted inclusion on mailing list databases, business and personal computer system failures, and hard drive crashes resulting in partial or complete loss of data.

As technology has become smaller, better, faster, cheaper, easier to use, and more pervasive in our daily experience, the "technology bad" phenomenon has diminished some-what—replaced by a "for better or worse, it's here to stay" mentality.

Additionally, many businesses hesitate to invest in Internet marketing because they believe it's expensive and that there is little or no long-term statistical evidence showing profitability and/or other value from the activity. This, too, is diminishing as more and more businesses go online to test the Internet marketing waters. These pioneers are help-ing define and set the standards for these new advertising tools. Momentum to "do busi-ness" on the Internet is growing daily as businesses of all sizes and flavors measure a range of success in their endeavors. Some are merely providing a point-of-business contact with basic information while others are offering full-blown online shopping with complete product and service catalogues and secured e-commerce facilities.

Consumers and businesses are moving from cautious enthusiasm to an active accept-ance of technology in their daily lives for a variety of reasons, including a push by the fed-eral government for technology/computer literacy in public education by the year 2000, rapid development of telecommunication tools, low-cost powerful computers, and easy-to-use productivity and communication software and interface devices. Simply put, con-sumers are now more ready and willing than ever to use technology as a means to obtain greater and varied levels of online information access. This includes purchasing products and services online. And a majority of businesses realize they are already behind and must integrate Internet marketing into their marketing plans immediately.

Getting back to my earlier statement about common sense and business-marketing strategies, today's marketing plan is incomplete without an Internet marketing compo-nent. Internet marketing increases a company's opportunity for profit. The bottom line of any business is profit—it's only common sense!

Put Your Business Online Now!

Do you really have a choice? From a smart marketing standpoint, no! With a little time and effort you can research businesses similar to yours that have an Internet presence, ask questions of professionals experienced in Internet marketing, and carefully plan and assess an effective starting point for your Internet marketing program. There is no excuse to delay putting your business online.

Internet technology stocks are thriving. High-speed Internet connections via faster modems, fiber optic networks, ADSL, and cable networks for businesses and homes are generating new and increased access and activity on the Internet. Affordable, low-cost Internet-ready computers are also helping create a generation of people who understand the information available to them online. With little exception, consumers expect prod-ucts and services of all types to be accessible on the Internet.

People are growing less concerned about purchasing products via the Internet as the ordering and transaction processes on Websites become more refined, seamless and user-friendly. The advent of online shopping carts and inventory databases—including instant order processing and tracking—has made Internet commerce more viable. The fact that more and more businesses are selling their products over the Internet has increased con-sumer confidence and legitimized the activity.

Again, any time society implements a new process—in this case e-commerce—it takes time to fine-tune. Despite the inevitable glitches, the number of businesses and consumers moving towards online transactions continues to grow. Large companies, banks, Internet service providers, and vendors producing e-commerce products are all looking for ways to improve e-commerce hardware and software. Consequently, businesses of all sizes—and certainly consumers—will benefit from these efforts. Without question, consumer and business-to-business marketing on the Internet will become a primary venue for sales transactions.

Increasingly, companies are promoting and announcing their Internet addresses in tra-ditional business advertising mediums—print, radio and television. An Internet address

(URL) in an advertisement is becoming as common and essential as a phone number. I contend that one day knowing a company's Internet address will be just as important as knowing its phone number.

The Experience and the Benefits

When I talk with potential clients about putting their companies online with Website services, they ask questions that range from very basic to specific queries regarding design and functionality. Regardless, the key to getting started in Internet marketing is to take the time up front to hold comprehensive fact-finding sessions. In these sessions, we help our clients define project intent and scope, develop strategies for marketing integration, discuss content structure and design, delegate production roles, create timelines, and develop a system for ongoing management.

Much of my time is spent in initial meetings with clients. Before we discuss the specific needs of their businesses, I give them a general overview of Internet-based information design and presentation and define the benefits of Internet marketing.

The following are some basic tenets and benefits for businesses with an Internet presence:

- Information presentation is interactive and dynamic.
- Design for information presentation is much more flexible than in print media.
- We can easily change and update content.
- Open for business 24 hours a day, seven days a week, promoting products and services at the customer's leisure.
- Expands marketability—no geographic boundaries—increasing exposure, customer base and profits!
- Allows for more complete design and control of information delivery.
- Allows targeted customers customized access. Such a customer can enter private pass-protected areas to learn about product releases, pricing, etc.
- Allows for customer data collection, product and services feedback—market research.
- Affords potential to reduce the amount of printing costs associated with traditional customer information exchange and support.

247

At this point in a client meeting, I am emphatic that creating a business Website—the physical presence of a business on the Internet—will not be effective without developing a plan to integrate Internet marketing.

An effective Internet marketing plan and the steps needed to accomplish it certainly depend on the business type and size, but a company must develop and implement the plan with an eye toward maximizing business and profits. This definitely should be a consideration when choosing who to work with in developing and implementing an Internet presence. Your business could hire a company that offers a complete design, development, marketing, and hosting package. Another option is to balance in-house and outsource services. With informed and careful planning, any number of models featuring a variety of service mixes can be effective. Below are the minimum essential service components necessary for a successful Internet presence:

- Website design is dynamic.
- Information presentation is clear and well-organized.
- Navigation through information is intuitive and easy.
- Functionality pieces are identified, implemented and tested, including integrated contact forms, e-commerce and shopping carts, custom-order forms, database integration, search features, forums, multimedia components, mail lists, reflected e-mail, and Website statistics package.
- Online media planning and placement opportunities are in place.
- Next generation planning and implementation is addressed.
- Integrated marketing strategies are defined.

- Website content management protocol is defined.
- Website hosting services are reliable and in place.

A company must include the following strategies when developing an Internet marketing plan:
- Define clear integration strategies.
- Promote the Website through a variety of Internet avenues, including submitting your site to comprehensive search engines and appropriate directories, reciprocal linking opportunities, listserves, and mail-casting.
- Integrate the Website with all other advertising and promotional material—put your Internet address (URL) on everything!
- Provide incentive for customers to visit your site.
- Offer unique information.
- Update the Website regularly.
- Collect data via interactive forms and usage statistics packages.
- Analyze data and compare results.
- Fine-tune strategies.

Final Steps in The Process

The next step is to identify unique qualities, characteristics and issues that will help present the client's products and/or services on the Internet. At this point, depending on the awareness, knowledge and preparedness of the client, we can generate an outline of the project's scope and general content. This is crucial in determining the extent of work, timelines and initial costs of developing an Internet presence. Although some clients know exactly what they want and have prepared comprehensive outlines before our initial meetings, with the majority of companies we need to schedule additional meetings to gather more information so we can present a comprehensive bid for work.

Along with the bid for the projected scope of the physical Website presence, clients should be prepared to address their Internet marketing plan—how they will develop and integrate it into the overall business marketing plan, what they will include, and who they will involve in its implementation. In some cases clients have already addressed this, but many businesses have yet to broach the subject.

The model for this process depends largely on the internal resources available to the business and the knowledge of the client. Experience has shown that businesses of all sizes new to the Internet—whether or not they employ a marketing director—need consultation to implement a comprehensive Internet marketing plan. It is plain common sense to seek expertise when operating in a new venue.

It should also be noted that many clients complete their Internet marketing in phases. This helps manage the projected costs of a project, gives a business more time to implement its Internet marketing plan, and lets a company gradually test and measure the plan's effectiveness.

Case Studies and Other Scenarios

Turnkey solutions available through online services or Web design firms can range in cost from a few hundred dollars to thousands. Understandably, there are limitations when purchasing complete Website packages. These types of solutions assume that the individual(s) charged with establishing a company's presence on the Internet has certain levels of Internet marketing, design and content-management knowledge. For some companies this approach may work, but they also need to realize that the individual(s) may have a limited range of expertise and will therefore make only a limited impact.

Another approach is to work with Web service/Internet integrators who are versed in designing and implementing a Website as well as building unique and comprehensive Internet marketing integration plans. Both services can range tremendously in scope and

248

price. The key here is that services are scalable, functional and address immediate short-term and long-term needs. Prices can range from a few thousand dollars for an initial Internet presence and marketing guidelines to tens of thousands for a comprehensive Internet presence (including databases, shopping carts/e-commerce, etc.). The latter usually also includes an ongoing content management and marketing integration plan.

All businesses are unique and require careful analysis and assessment of their needs. Again, when integrating Internet marketing in a total business strategy, plan for testing and measuring every phase. A business can certainly design and implement a plan in tiered phases as a means of keeping costs down and allowing time for the necessary assessment studies. The bottom line is that a well-planned, minimal level of Internet marketing, designed for scalabililty, should be a top priority for any business not currently online. Budgeting for Internet marketing is proactive and affordable. I repeat my premise that businesses don't have a choice.

The Coffee Industry and the Internet

Businesses in the coffee industry should definitely market their products and services on the Internet. Opportunities to enhance, expand and tap new markets for their products and services are wide open. As discussed earlier, there are many advantages to integrating or even making the Internet the focal point of a business marketing plan. Businesses that sell coffee products and the myriad related items have huge potential for increased sales, and, ultimately, profits, by using this marketing medium. Any company that is currently realizing sales via traditional marketing means can't afford not to implement Internet marketing strategies. And doesn't everyone drink coffee, tea or cocoa? Don't we all eat chocolate or any of the other delectably delightful goodies that dovetail or handshake the core industry products and services?

My company, PremiereLink Communications Inc.—www.premierelink.com—works with a broad spectrum of businesses that are taking advantage of this next generation advertising tool. We have benefited from watching clients implement Internet marketing plans at a variety of effort and expense levels. Businesses that are successful on the Internet have a concerted, well-designed marketing plan accompanied by a well-planned and designed physical Internet presence (Website).

PremiereLink has been fortunate to work with some of the coffee industry's innovative business leaders—visionaries of sorts—who saw the marketing potential of the Internet when it was still more or less in utero. Maybe we've reached the "terrible twos" as of this writing, having learned to crawl and now stumble—staying upright more often than not—while showing more grace with each step. Some of these companies are selling products and services, some are using the Internet as a means to inform, some use it as a point of contact, and many as a means to reduce other more expensive marketing venues. While some of these businesses integrate and attend to their Internet marketing efforts more than others, without question they are all realizing some measure of success.

Listed below are the coffee industry clients PremiereLink has worked with over the last few years. With the exception of the Bellissimo Coffee InfoGroup Websites, we developed all the other clients' Internet presences via a long-distance relationship. Long-distance clients ship us content by traditional mail, fax, disk, e-mail, and file transfer protocol (FTP). We discuss design and marketing issues via phone conferences, e-mails, faxes, and mailings. Most importantly, we have them view the initial physical Website presence/design online. We continue to proceed online with subsequent Website design, development and implementation. Clients then give feedback and final approval before the site is made "live" to the world. We encourage all our potential clients to look at similar companies' Websites to help them gain a greater understanding of how their company can use Internet marketing.

PremiereLink Coffee Industry Clients:

Bellissimo Coffee InfoGroup	www.espresso101.com
Bellissimo Coffee InfoGroup	www.coffeeuniverse.com
Bellissimo Coffee InfoGroup	www.virtualcoffee.com
Caffé D'arte	www.caffedarte.com
Brenda Jean's Coffee Beans	www.bjbeans.com
Kopi Coffee	www.kopicoffee.com
Java Espresso Concepts	www.javaespressoconcepts.com
Guided Coffee Discoveries	www.coffeediscoveries.com
Caffe Diva	www.caffediva.com
Pony Espresso	www.pony-espresso.com
Grounds For Discussion	www.groundsfordiscussion.com

The Last Word

I highly recommend seeking qualified professional services if you want to develop an Internet presence or analyze and assess an existing Internet marketing effort. Success is measurable in terms of accountability and profits, and while using professional services does not necessarily ensure success, it does improve your chances of realizing a greater return on your investment.

It is extremely disheartening to see businesses of all sizes minimize reasonable and necessary Internet marketing expenses only to diminish their capabilities and effectiveness. I am continually amazed by the attitudes of small business owners, marketing directors and CFOs of large companies in their approaches to Internet marketing. They are willing to compromise the company's marketability by bargain shopping their Internet marketing needs. It's a given to be cost-conscious and responsible in budgeting for this activity, and each step requires justification, but so do all line items in a business marketing budget. Again, my contention is that you must take Internet marketing seriously, plan for it, invest in it, and manage it ... professionally.

One More Word

Behind on deadline and under pressure to complete this chapter, I had no choice but to make final additions on Super Bowl Sunday. I planned to concentrate on the game only when there were big plays and deciding scoring drives. Admittedly, I have a fine-tuned eye and ear for all advertising associated with Internet technologies, and I watch for companies that do or don't prominently display their Internet addresses in their ads. And I am not usually surprised by the unique products and services offered by companies joining the ranks of online businesses, nor their equally unique hooks to get my attention.

I was, however, quite impressed with the bevy of companies—some that only exist in Cyberland—that invested the million and change it takes to air a 30-second commercial during the Super Bowl. Seductive, sexy and in your face, Victoria's Secret announced an all-new fashion show coming soon to you, the viewer ... but only on the Internet at www.victoriassecret.com. Within 20 minutes of airing, 50,000 people took a timeout from the game to visit the site.

Two little-known upstart companies—one of which spent half of last year's earnings for the 30-second commercial—advertised their services to help you find a better job: www.monster.com and www.hotjobs.com. Easily 75 percent of all the other commercials aired during the Super Bowl displayed Internet addresses that were at least as prominent, if not more so, than any other contact information.

Needless to say, I spent way too much time caught in some very clever advertising spins spanning the three-plus hours of the game. Did companies display more Internet addresses because of the hype surrounding this particular marketing venue? No way! They were just that much more identifiable having been done with a larger expense budget.

Take a simple test for yourself. Next time you're watching television, listening to the radio, or reading a weekly publication, track how many advertisers list an Internet address or e-mail contact for their products or services. Rank the businesses on scales of company size, perceived demographics of the targeted consumer groups, and geographic marketing boundaries. You will be impressed by the numbers of businesses—large and small—marketing on the Internet.   ●

Tom Palm

Tom Palm has more than 12 years of experience in the restaurant and foodservice industries. He is a third generation owner of Palm Brothers Restaurant Equipment Company, a family business founded in 1910. Palm Brothers is one of the top 25 independent restaurant equipment dealers in the country.

Palm is the founder of Design & Layout Services, a company specializing in the design of specialty coffee shops. Working with independent operators as well as national chains, he has helped over 200 people open cafés and coffeehouses. His projects have been located throughout the United States, as well as Canada, Japan, Guam, and Saudi Arabia.

Palm is a member of several health department committees that develop policy on the construction of foodservice facilities and is a Certified Food Service Professional (CFSP). He has also written several articles that have been published in industry trade magazines and has presented to audiences at numerous industry trade shows.

Palm works with Brent Miller, who has experience with a small start-up coffee company that grew from three locations to more than 15 in the course of a year. While with the company, Miller gained expertise in all areas of coffee retailing, from barista training to employee management and marketing.

253

Chapter 20

Remodeling and Expanding Your Coffee Business

Prior to opening your first retail coffee location, you spent numerous hours developing your concept, researching your customer base and creating your menu. You designed your store to move customers through your space efficiently while merchandising your products effectively. Since opening, however, you have come to realize that your customers' expectations have changed, and that you will need to modify your concept, menu and traffic flow.

255

Customers are usually not shy about asking for longer operating hours, a children's play area, better cups, a softer chair, or different music. Most of these types of requests are fairly easy to address.

But what happens when your store needs more drastic modifications? Expanding or remodeling after a few years of operation is not uncommon. The experience you have gained in running your café has probably revealed many things you would like to do differently.

Before remodeling or expanding, spend some time analyzing your current operation. What problems do you need to address? Does your store have aesthetic problems? Are operational changes necessary? Does your menu need expanding? Are there problems with customer and employee flow?

This chapter is devoted to common remodeling or expansion issues. Much of the material is applicable to both remodeling an existing store and opening a new store. The last portion of this chapter will focus specifically on expanding to a second location.

Remodeling for Your Menu

Scenario—In discussions with business owners and individuals in your community, you discover the need for a unique lunch spot. Normally, your sales are slow after the morning rush. By adding a light-lunch menu, you may be able to increase your sales between 11 a.m. and 1 p.m. and become an alternative lunch option for your community.

What's involved in adding a light-lunch menu to your daily offerings? Relatively little expense. To add sandwiches, salads and soups to your menu, you need the following pieces of equipment: a refrigerated display case ($3900), a sandwich prep table ($1700), a vegetable prep sink ($400), a panini grill ($1800), and two soup cookers ($300). For a small investment (approximately $8000) plus the cost of plumbing and electrical, you can now service your customers as a neighborhood lunch stop.

Scenario—You would like to offer a selection of fresh muffins each morning for the commuter rush. In addition, your customers would enjoy warm chocolate chip cookies with their lunches.

Adding a bakery to your coffeehouse isn't as difficult or costly as it sounds. On-site baking does not require you to purchase a 30-quart mixer, a proofer or a double-deck convection oven. Partially baked or frozen dough bakery products are available from food-service distributors. Assuming you have enough refrigeration, all you need is a counter-top electric convection oven (approximately $2000).

In addition, it doesn't always require expensive ventilation systems to bake on premise. Many municipalities around the country do not require such systems for baking-only convection ovens. Call the local health and building departments and inquire about the regulations in your area.

An added benefit of doing your own baking is you don't have to worry about meeting your vendor's minimum order and then having to sell what he or she delivers each day.

Scenario—A national chain that offers a large selection of blended drinks and smoothies has moved into your neighborhood. Or, alternately, you want to be the first business in your community that sells a variety of cold-blended drinks.

Depending on the type of drinks you would like to serve, this can require either a little or a lot of effort. To introduce a simple program, select a smoothie mix or concentrate you can add to ice and blend. Many companies offer quality smoothie mixes you can use by themselves or blended with fresh fruit, espresso or nutritional supplements. The only equipment you need is a commercial blender (approximately $400) and a convenient supply of ice.

If your goal is to compete directly with a company like Jamba Juice®, Smoothie King® or a specialty yogurt store, your task will be more difficult. A juice and smoothie addition this size means carefully managing your produce inventory and adding equipment to support these menu items. You could easily spend $15,000 for a walk-in cooler, a juice machine, additional blenders, a refrigerated prep table, and a prep sink to compete at this level.

As you can see, many of these menu solutions require only minimal new equipment and space. Expanding your menu to meet your customer needs and boost your bottom line may be the easiest "remodeling" you can do.

Remodeling for Better Flow

Scenario—New customers are confused about where to order and pick up drinks. A regular waits at your register for three triple mochas—with extra whipped cream—while someone who wants a small drip coffee and a blueberry muffin stands in line exasperated by his or her wait.

Designating a specific area for placing an order and another area for pickup is a constant source of frustration for many operators. Where is your cash register in relation to your espresso machine? Your objective should be to move waiting customers away from the front of the register, leaving that area open to allow the next person in line to place his or her order. Your layout should allow your cashier to pour a drip brew, get a scone, make change, and get that customer out the door in the same amount of time the barista needs to prepare a double mocha and a triple latté with hazelnut. Do you have 12 inches of space further down the counter you can use as a pickup area? If space is cramped, consider installing a small pickup shelf to one side of the espresso machine. Train your barista to pass every drink to the pickup area. Another remedy is adding "order here" and "pick up here" signs. This will not cure the problem, as it is often said customers never read.

Scenario—A customer orders a latté at the espresso machine, walks around another group of waiting customers to look at your bakery case, gets in line to pay, and, after picking up the drink, has to negotiate the line again to make it to the condiment area. Confused? That's how your customer feels!

You can only solve a recurring problem like this by remodeling or reorganizing your counters and equipment. Remember, the front service counter should do more than hold your espresso machine and cash register. A properly designed front counter is a natural traffic management tool, a valuable salesperson, a retail display, and a functional piece of equipment. The front counter is the first thing a customer looks for when entering the store. It should convey the message: "Start Here."

Upon seeing your bakery display case, your prospective customer should wander in that direction. By placing your bakery-display case before the register, the display case is acting as a salesperson, subtly saying, "buy this." You should then move the customer to your cash register to place his or her order. After he or she pays for the order, direct your customer to a pickup area near the espresso machine and then to an area for condiments. Keep your customer flow moving in a single direction, not a random figure-eight pattern.

If your cabinetry needs rebuilding, consider making it more functional by adding a drink pickup shelf, built-in cup dispensers and a knock box. Adding an under-counter ice bin can gain you valuable space on your back counter. A condiment area with recessed holes for sugar, straws and lids keeps things organized. Properly placed, your counters and equipment will make the flow of your business more efficient.

Scenario—During the busiest times of the day, the four employees on duty are constantly bumping into each other. When one employee is busy filling an order for coffee beans, the cashier can't reach the display case. And the barista must reach around the cashier to get milk for the next drink.

Not only is it a headache to work under these conditions, but it may reduce the number of customers you can serve efficiently. You may notice your employees are taking too many steps to accomplish some of the routine tasks of fulfilling a customer's order. Or your barista may constantly bump elbows with the cashier, slowing both the employees' productivity.

The key to a more efficient layout is to break down the activities that take place behind the counter into groups or work triangles. Consider each piece of equipment and each ingredient needed to perform a task. Look at the location of the milk refrigerator in relation to the espresso machine and grinders. Does the barista have everything he or she needs to prepare a drink without taking a step? If you are doing smoothies and iced drinks, is a supply of ice near the blending station?

Another common problem area is the cashier's position. The cashier should be able to do more than greet customers and ring up sales. Organize the space so the cashier can take an order, fill a cup of drip brew, grab a bakery item, and ring up the sale in three steps or less.

Closely related to equipment orientation is counter placement. How much space is there between the front counter and back counter? An aisle less than three-feet wide is not large enough to allow two employees to pass behind the counter. If the space between the counters is more than four feet, it will take additional steps to fill an order. Several extra steps a day, multiplied by a year of busy shifts, means a lot of extra work.

Remodeling to address operational challenges can vastly improve efficiency. It can be as extensive as building new cabinetry and moving equipment, or as simple as properly arranging cup dispensers, bakery bags, the ice bin, and the supply of coffee for the day.

257

Remodeling For More Space

Scenario—Your Saturday morning crowd has grown too large for your seating capacity.

Most successful coffeehouses will experience times when available seating cannot accommodate the number of customers. To add more seating without using much square footage, consider adding bar-height seating along one of the walls or in front of the windows. More and more operators are installing bar seating along the front counter.

Next, look at your tables. Prior to opening, you may have found a good deal on 30" x 30" tables. This size is perfect for groups of four, but inefficient when used by one customer. A 24" x 24" or 24" x 30" table is perfect for two people. You can also slide two together to accommodate a group of four or more. Round tables may look good, but you cannot put them together very easily for a large group.

Scenario—Each time you receive a product or milk delivery, it sits on the floor for an hour while your employee reorganizes the backroom.

The backroom is often the most poorly planned space in a foodservice operation. The first-time operator often builds a backroom around existing interior walls to save money. Usually, the savings are minimal and not worth the ongoing frustration.

If you are ready to remodel your backroom, what can you do? You can create additional storage by adding wall shelving at heights of six and eight feet. If the ceilings are high and the walls are backed by plywood to secure the shelving, this can mean a lot of extra storage space. If your water heater is currently located on the floor in your backroom, consider mounting it on the ceiling. A good place to mount the water heater is above your mop sink. You can use the additional 2 1/2 feet of space for an extra one-door upright refrigerator or ice machine. You may substitute your eight-foot three-compartment sink with a five- or six-foot three-compartment sink. Three extra feet may be enough space to add a vegetable prep sink for your new lunch menu. If you need more refrigeration, you can substitute your four- or five-foot worktable with a two-door work-top refrigerator or freezer.

258

Opening a Second Store

You have found a perfect site for your second location. Your first store is running smoothly and you are ready to take the first step toward becoming a multi-unit chain. If there were no surprises when you designed and opened your first store, your landlord was accommodating, the health inspector was your best friend, the building inspector your uncle, and you had more start-up money than you knew what to do with, this section is for you. The odds are that your second store will pose challenges you did not face before.

The following section will provide a general overview of basic building and health codes and how they may affect your second location. A common mistake made by an operator when opening a second site is assuming that the rules, codes and regulations will be the same as they were for the first site.

For example, on your second store you avoid spending time on a business plan, a loan and a design, only to discover two months later you now need two restrooms, an additional fire exit, four more parking spaces, and a zoning variance. Whenever the particular use of a space changes, the building codes also change. If you are turning a dentist's office into a café, it may require more dedicated parking. Codes differ from business type to business type, and they also tend to become more stringent every year. If the first store you opened nine months ago needed only one restroom, your second shop may now need two handicapped-accessible restrooms due to new plumbing codes and ADA regulations.

The above examples emphasize that it is critical to consult your local health inspector and building inspector. Both individuals will become very involved in your project and will dictate key issues directly affecting how you will build your space, how much it will cost, and how soon you will open.

Before visiting the building inspector and your health department, do your homework. Obtain an outline of your new space from the leasing agent with the square footage, exact address and number of dedicated parking spaces. Next, calculate the approximate number of seats your new space can hold by using this formula: Divide your square footage by two, and then divide the result by 15. This will approximate your number of seats.

For instance, if your location is 1500 square feet, divide 1500 by two. This will give you approximately 750 square feet for the kitchen, service area and restrooms. Then divide the remaining 750 square feet by 15 square feet (recommended square footage per person in a foodservice establishment). The resulting number is 50 seats. The occupancy load will dictate issues such as parking, fire exits and restroom requirements, which are all discussed in greater detail below.

Building Inspector

It's very important to visit the city building inspector for your new location. Explain to the inspector that you are planning to open a coffeehouse. Mention that you have a specific location in mind, but have questions prior to signing a lease. Discuss the following issues with your building inspector:

Zoning—Is your space zoned for your type of occupancy? Your new location may have housed any number of businesses over the years. Whether your new space was once an old hardware store, insurance agency or candy shop, make certain you investigate any possible zoning restrictions.

Parking—How many spaces will be required for your seating capacity? This is a very important question if you are looking at a location in a strip mall or on Main Street. Chances are, plenty of open parking is available at any given time. However, these may not be enough for your operation. You may need to show that a dedicated number of parking stalls are available based on your occupancy load.

259

Fire Exits—How many emergency exits are required for an operation your size? The building inspector may need to review a detailed floor plan to make this determination, but he or she should at least be able to give you some guidelines. You do not want to sign a lease and complete your floor plan only to discover you're required to add another exit right where you were planning to put a fireplace and a couch!

Restrooms—Given the number of seats, how many restrooms are required? The answer may surprise you. In one case, a 300-square-foot drive-thru espresso stand with no seating was required to install two handicapped-accessible restrooms. In another case, a 1200-square-foot space in a historic building only needed one restroom. Each case is different; don't make assumptions without asking the proper questions. Also, if you are serving any alcoholic beverages, your restroom size will be affected.

Septic System—If your space is not connected to city water and sewer, is the septic system adequately sized to handle your new business? Typically, a foodservice establishment will be classified differently than other retail businesses. Find out if you need any upgrades.

Ventilation—Will your café need any special ventilation features? If you are planning to use a small convection oven to bake muffins, cookies and scones, you may need a simple exhaust hood. If you're going to do some light cooking with gas-fueled equipment, your store will require special ductwork and a make-up air system. Some cities require ventilation for panini grills. The issue of ventilation can be complicated and expensive. In addition to your building inspector's requirements, the health department and fire marshal may have additional requirements.

ADA Codes—The Americans with Disabilities Act will govern many aspects of your business. Find out early what's required for compliance—you may save yourself costly delays and headaches. Find out how high your counters need to be. If customers must climb stairs to reach your shop, you may need to install a handicapped ramp. Research the walkway and doorway clearance requirements. Find out what constitutes an ADA accessible restroom in your area.

Historical Buildings—Buildings with historical significance can be great places to open coffeehouses, but be warned that old structures may need costly updating. It is a good idea for a reputable contractor to examine your building before you sign a lease and become legally attached to its problems. The electrical service may be so out of date you are forced to rewire the space. The same may apply to the plumbing.

Architectural Stamp—Find out which construction documents your city requires to obtain building permits. Determine who can prepare your construction plans. Can you or your contractor supply the plans? Or will the city require a licensed architect to supply the pertinent diagrams for plumbing, electrical and construction details?

The primary reason to consult with the building official as soon as possible is to avoid spending a lot of time and money on a location that will be very difficult to conform to current codes. You may decide the location is still worth pursuing, but at least you're familiar with your hurdles ahead of time. In addition, you may be able to negotiate some of the additional costs to upgrade the space into your lease.

The Health Department

In dealing with the health department, try to speak with the inspector that will actually review your plans. Describe your plans and proposed menu. The health department will also provide the necessary forms for the plan review application and food license. Typically, the health department will publish a small booklet outlining the construction guidelines for a foodservice establishment.

In building this second location, you may find your "new" health department is concerned about issues that never came up during your first project. Similar to building codes, health department regulations tend to vary from town to town and inspector to inspector. Here are some areas of concern common to the health department:

Equipment—All food and beverage equipment, new or used, must meet the applicable standards of the National Sanitation Foundation (NSF) or another approved third-party testing lab, such as Edison Testing Laboratories (ETL) or Underwriters Laboratory (UL). These groups ensure that construction materials are nontoxic and easily cleanable and that the equipment will hold temperature under specific conditions.

Walls and Ceilings—The walls and ceilings in food preparation zones, dishwashing areas, storage areas, janitor's rooms, and restrooms must be smooth, nonabsorbent and easily cleanable. Ceramic tile, stainless steel or sheetrock painted with high-gloss enamel meet this requirement. Ceiling tile must also be smooth and easily cleanable. Replace acoustic tile with vinyl tile. The recommended wall surface for splash zones behind sinks and other high moisture areas is fiberglass-reinforced panel (Glasbord®), ceramic tile or an equivalent surface.

Floors—Floor surfaces in the areas listed above must be at least 1/8-inch thick commercial grade vinyl composition tile with a four-inch base coving at the floor to wall seam. Quarry tile is recommended. Generally, you're not allowed to have wood floors in the kitchen or service areas.

Lighting—Lighting in areas where people prepare or serve food or wash utensils should be at least 70 foot candles in power measured 30 inches above the floor. All lighting must be recessed or enclosed to prevent breakage. Shatterproof or coated bulbs are acceptable.

Refrigeration—Size all refrigeration units to support the needs of the operation. Mechanical refrigeration is required to maintain all potentially hazardous foods (meat and dairy products) at 40 degrees F or below. Equipment must meet NSF standards. Each refrigerator and freezer unit must have attached thermometers.

Sinks—The following sinks are usually required: at least one separate hand washing sink easily accessible to all employees in the food preparation area and utensil washing area; a three-compartment sink with attached drainboards for manual dish washing; a separate vegetable or prep sink if food production involves rinsing food and vegetables; and a separate janitorial or mop sink. Some municipalities will not allow you to install food preparation sinks or three-compartment sinks in laminated counters.

Dishwashing Facilities—You must adequately size dishwashing facilities to meet the anticipated demands of the facility. Normally, a three-compartment sink meeting NSF standards will meet the minimum requirement for manual dishwashing. If you install mechanical dishwashers, they must also meet NSF standards. The mechanical dishwasher may use hot water for the sanitizing rinse or a chemical sanitizer in the final rinse cycle. Drying or drainboard space must also be large enough to meet the operational demands of your establishment.

Shelving—Chrome-plated wire shelving that meets NSF standards is acceptable for dry storage. Generally, wood and plastic laminate shelving is not acceptable in food preparation, food storage or dishwashing areas. Chemical storage should be separate from food handling and dry storage.

Ventilation Hoods—All foodservice equipment that generates vapors, condensation, odors, fumes, or excessive heat must be located under a mechanical exhaust ventilation hood and must meet state building code requirements, the Uniform Fire Code and NSF standards. Also note that ventilation hoods for the removal of condensation vapor may be required on mechanical dishwashing facilities.

Service Counters, Bars and Millwork—You must protect all countertop surfaces with stainless steel, plastic laminate or an approved equivalent so that no wood is exposed. The countertop and back-splash juncture should have a curved radius. In all areas where food equipment is exposed to heat or moisture or where food comes in contact with the equipment's surface, code may require a stainless steel or equivalent finish. All counters and cabinetry are required to be on six-inch stainless steel legs or approved four-inch curb.

Food Handling—You must demonstrate an understanding of functional flow processes, indicating how your staff will handle food from the time it enters your establishment until it is served to the customer. The operator should understand the relationships between storage, preparation, handling of soiled equipment and utensils, and the separation of dirty areas from clean areas. Education and proper procedures are critical in the prevention of cross-contamination. A food safety class may be a prerequisite to opening a foodservice establishment in your new location.

261

Prior to construction, the health department will require you to submit the following:
- Plan review application and fee.
- Three complete sets of detailed plans drawn to scale, including plumbing, mechanical and electrical specifications.
- One complete equipment specification book describing the make and model of each piece of equipment. (i.e. sinks, refrigeration, ovens, shelving, etc.)
- One complete set of custom-equipment elevations.
- A room-finish schedule specifying materials to be used for floors, base coving, walls, and ceilings.
- A copy of your menu.
- Seating capacity.

After the health department has reviewed your plans, it will send you a letter indicating any concerns or changes that need to be made. Construction can begin only after the health department approves your plans. The department will also instruct you to contact the health inspector for an on-site inspection prior to receiving any food shipments or opening your establishment. If you pass the inspection, you can then obtain your foodservice license and plan your opening.

This is a sampling of issues most health departments will address. Most construction guides will cover additional areas you should consider as you plan your new space.

If you open a dozen stores each year, much of this may seem obvious. If your last construction project was two years ago, however, or you are moving into a new state, this chapter should serve as a valuable guide.

Conclusion

In summary, any change you want to make in your establishment will result in a chain-reaction of details that require careful planning. A simple decision to bake on-site cannot become a reality until you have considered your budget for buying the oven, the voltage supply it needs, the counterspace it sits on, the need for a ventilation hood above it, the wall surface behind it, and the availability of bakery products, not to mention where to put the freezer for storage and display case for merchandising.

So whether you are remodeling, expanding your menu or adding a new location, don't make any decisions without first involving the city building inspector and your local health department. Consult with professionals, from your contractor, plumber and electrician to your equipment supplier and food vendor. Involving all the necessary people will ensure the smooth implementation of your remodel or expansion.　●

section **six**

RELATED TO COFFEE

Laura Gorman

Laura Gorman is associate editor of *The Gourmet Retailer* magazine, a business-to-business publication focusing on the specialty foods, coffee and tea, and kitchenware industries. Gorman writes on all aspects of the specialty coffee industry, from product knowledge to marketing and merchandising products at the retail level. Prior to this position, Gorman was an adjunct professor of speech communication at Florida International University in Miami, associate editor of *Pet Business Magazine,* and worked in several public relations positions. She holds a bachelor of science in journalism and a master of arts in communication.

267

Chapter 21

Increasing Your Bottom Line With Accessories

The success of the specialty coffee industry is realized in its pervasiveness—in cafés, airports, bookstores, laundromats, and restaurants. It is this pervasiveness, however, that presents a unique challenge for the retailer whose core business is coffee.

269

The specialty coffee retailer focuses on providing quality coffee and consumer education. Where only a few short years ago the mainstream consumer's coffee aptitude was superficial at best—the only distinction was between regular and decaf—now the coffee consumer's vocabulary is a bit more sophisticated, encompassing such words as latté, varietal, Kenya AA, estate, or cinnamon roast. Consumers demand more from their coffee, and, in turn, expect more from a retailer selling specialty coffee.

These success stories have also enticed more businesses to enter the world of specialty coffee. A store that provides customers with a high-quality product and great customer service in a warm, inviting atmosphere must now further compel consumers to visit.

This coincides with another specialty coffee trend—brewing good coffee at home. As more consumers comprehend the effect that origin, processing and roast (among other variables) have on the nuances of the flavor of brewed coffee, their confidence for, and love of, quality coffee has strengthened. Not only must they make frequent visits to their local specialty coffee cafés for their favorite estate coffees to-go, they want to replicate this in the comforts of their own home.

We all know, however, that purchasing quality coffee doesn't necessarily result in quality brewed coffee. Variables such as grind, water quality and brewing temperature can drastically alter the final taste of your coffee. Hopefully you've established customer confidence through your knowledge of, and enthusiasm for, the coffee you purchase for sale. But are you a total resource for your customers? Do you offer the means and the methods to prepare quality coffee? Take the opportunity to educate customers on the entire process, from selecting quality beans to proper brewing techniques. You may bolster the confidence the customer has in you as a credible source of information by adding accessories to your product line. You will better your bottom line as well.

Challenges of Accessories

In the specialty coffee industry today, you make the greatest retail margins on consumable beverages. A retailer quickly earns back the pennies per cup cost when he or she charges $1.25 for a 14-ounce cup of coffee or $2.50 for a cappuccino. Another profitable segment is in take-home beans, where retail prices for a pound of specialty coffee range from $7 for an estate blend to $50 for a limited quantity origin bean.

Bringing up the rear in store profits are coffee-related accessories. These potentially profitable products are compromised by the large number of outlets selling mugs, brewers, grinders, and the like. It's a competitive retail environment, especially as single entity shops, department stores, upscale kitchenware shops, and mass merchants compete for their share of the accessories market.

Single entity retailers simply do not have the purchasing power of chains, department stores, or mass merchandisers, who all reap the benefits of quantity discounts. As a result, specialty coffee retailers usually end up selling the same product at a considerably higher price than the big boys in order to make a profit. The result? Slow inventory turns that force retailers to discount these previously unsellable accessories.

Why get into the coffee accessories business if all it promises are headaches and excess inventory? It's as simple as this: If you're in the coffee business and your customers look to you as a credible source of information, you need to carry all the tools necessary for brewing and consuming coffee and espresso beverages. More importantly, accessories can make you a nice profit—if you market them properly.

What's Selling?

Sources indicate that coffee-related accessories are in demand. According to the 1997 Annual Coffee Survey, presented by *The Gourmet Retailer* magazine and the Specialty Coffee Association of America (SCAA), the average annual gross sales of accessories at coffee and tea retail stores—represented by retailers whose majority of sales is not from coffee beverages—reached $168,732. Products accounted for in these sales include: drip coffeemakers, thermal carafes, mugs, espresso/cappuccino makers, stovetop espresso makers, teakettles, grinders, permanent filters, teapots, French press brewers, paper filters, and flavoring syrups.

The two categories carried by most coffee and tea retail stores were mugs (64.8 percent) and teapots (60.6 percent). Other popular coffee accessories carried by these stores included paper filters (52.1 percent), grinders (50.7 percent), flavoring syrups (49.3 percent), and French presses (43.7 percent). While electric brewers—such as drip coffeemakers and espresso/cappuccino makers—were not carried by the majority of coffee and tea retail stores, they did bring in average gross sales of $20,989 and $21,895 respectively.

Any business venture is a risk and success comes from risk-taking—stepping forward into unknown territory. If you're not already offering your customers the accessories to complement coffee, take the risk. Many sales opportunities arise when customers who visit your store for beverages are confronted with an exciting array of accessories, all related to coffee preparation and enjoyment. Every beverage customer is a potential accessory-buying customer. And building the sale is key to the success of your business.

Choosing What to Carry

Remember back to when you started the business. You probably had a business plan that provided direction as you embarked on this new retail adventure. The business plan encompassed a basketful of ideas, from financial projections to location to product selection. Because it is a tool to evaluate your business, now is the ideal opportunity to revisit that business plan to ascertain how accessories fit within your original proposal. You should only alter your product mix as part of a well-planned process in which you sit down and analyze your business philosophy, including reviewing your mission statement, your target customer and your current product offerings.

Integral to your business plan is your store philosophy, which you should explain in your mission statement. The mission statement is the core of your business plan; it describes the who's and what's of your business. Who runs the business? Who is the customer? What products will I carry? What distinguishes me from my competition?

The most basic mission statement may say something like: "I will provide customers with quality product and great customer service in a warm, inviting atmosphere."

A more encompassing business plan will include any potential products and financial projections. It will touch on the start-up business, then outline a growth plan that will serve as a tool to guide your business growth within certain parameters—something you will turn to time and time again.

Of course a business plan should leave room to grow. Perhaps coffee accessories didn't fit with your mental picture of the business when you first opened. Now that you're established, they may seem a natural addition.

When you revisit this business plan, reassess your target customer. Since your store opened, the retail landscape in your neighborhood has probably filled out, offering consumers a multitude of shops to visit, each with a growing repertoire of products. Is your store one that stands out among the crowd?

Ask yourself, who are your customers? Are they college-aged students, young professionals or retired folks? Do they like to travel, exercise or entertain at home? Assess not only the demographics of your customers, but investigate their psychographics and lifestyle information. Do they visit the store on a weekly basis? Is a customer alone or with friends? Does a particular group of friends gather afterwards for a quick bite to eat and drink? If an office complex is across the street, do its inhabitants have a penchant for coffee and espresso? If so, are they in a hurry when they seek out their coffee? Is there any business on the weekend?

Ascertain their buying patterns. When you're finished evaluating your customer's needs, desires and demographics, you'll have a physical and social description of your customers that will help you decide which accessories to sell.

271

In your business plan, you outlined the details of the goods and services you will offer. But how do you put that plan into action? How do you come up with a desirable product mix that is priced right, doesn't clash and is ultimately poised for optimum financial success? Essential to this re-evaluation of your business plan is to venture out into your business neighborhood and beyond to see what your competition is offering *and* selling.

In a perfect retail world, products chosen for sale will catch the customers' attention, fill their needs, be priced appropriately, *and* bring you retail margins worth bragging about. But back in reality, you must use some forethought. Be honest with yourself when choosing which accessories to sell. Use the same tactics you use when choosing coffee. You've diligently sought quality coffee from a reliable source whom you trust to deliver the quality or service level you expect. Do the same when seeking vendors for accessories. The quality of your product will reflect on your business.

Next, step back from your own likes and dislikes and determine what your customers will like. Too often a retailer makes product decisions based on his or her own likes and dislikes. Make your purchasing decisions based on your customers' tastes. Don't second guess them. Simply ask them what they want if you don't know.

Use your competition and other local businesses as case studies. Their product mix will give you clues to their target market and help you choose a good combination of accessories. For instance, the upscale dress shop located across the street may cater to a mature female clientele with considerable disposable income. Expensive French presses and glitzy home espresso machines might make a perfect match.

Also make note of how much product these businesses are stocking. If a store stocks one item particularly heavily, it's probably very popular. Visit these stores frequently to see how the product moves off the shelf.

What and How Much

A product assortment should complement your business. It may sound elementary, but how many times have you walked into a retail shop only to be confronted by a melange of products that made you scratch your head and say, "Why is this sold here?" Customers expect to go to a coffee shop to buy a coffee grinder, not a waffle iron. If your products reflect your business, your customers will know what to expect from you when faced with a shopping quandary.

Make a mission statement for your accessory department. Should you offer an eclectic selection of product that can't be found anywhere else? Or should your store develop a mix of mainstream coffee equipment that identifies you as a major player in the house-wares game?

Another important question is, how much space should you allocate to coffee-related accessories? The customer who religiously visits your store every day to enjoy a beverage in your environs must still feel comfortable in your store once you add a line of accessories. The space dedicated to showcase your products shouldn't squeeze out seating, cause commotion or interrupt a café customer who's escaping from the stress of his or her day. Nor should the addition of accessories slow down your beverage service.

This relates directly to staffing issues. You must have sufficient staff on hand to prepare beverages on-site. But what about the customer who desires a pound of ground coffee or has a few questions about which espresso machine he or she should purchase? Will your current staff allocation allow an employee to provide quality service to this customer? Budget your staff time accordingly.

Many retailers make the mistake of confusing the customer by making too much product available in too many places. An easily accessible product showcased at point of sale, for example, will certainly help with add-on sales. But a line of mugs crowding the edges of the condiment station may be more distracting then suggestive.

Be careful not to make the customer numb to these products by displaying them everywhere. Draw customers to the product without slapping them in the face. Small shelves and displays throughout the store can entice customers, but it's generally wise to keep accessories together so the customers see your dedicated presence in the category. They'll make a visual connection the next time they're thinking of buying a home espresso machine.

Buying Well

The delicate balancing act of keeping retail prices down while maintaining profitable margins finds its genesis in good buying. When first ordering accessories, make broad enough selections to give the customers plenty of choices. Their purchasing patterns will help you pare down your product choices later. Buy enough of a product to create exciting displays, but don't buy too much of one product until you see how well it performs. This wait-and-see mentality will allow you to tweak your product mix to find which products sell best.

During the initial stages, ask your customers to respond to your product choices. As a specialty retailer, your ability to discover and fill your customers' needs will determine your store's success.

Your choice of accessories will also be determined by your customers' finances. An espresso/cappuccino maker retailing for $400 or more may be a bit out of the spending range of your college-age customers, whereas a stovetop moka pot or a French press might fit right in. Offer a balance of products that meet the price range and desires of your average customer, in addition to people who just wander into your store. Knowledge of your clientele will guide you when fixing prices for accessories.

Start by taking the wholesale price you paid for a product, then figure out the per unit cost. Know your competitor's prices for the same items, then carefully decide how you will position your pricing in comparison. Be competitive in your pricing strategy, even if you don't carry identical brands. As competition increases, consumers become more price sensitive. While you may be able to beat the competition on some items, others may be impossible to beat. Let personal service to the customer, a thorough knowledge of your products, and attention to customer needs be the added benefits that will justify your higher price.

Merchandising and Selling

If you can't offer certain products exclusively, you must find another way to draw customers to your store, whether it be ambiance or the personal attention your staff gives to customers. People don't need to buy coffee in a specialty store, and the same holds true for coffee accessories—coffeemakers, mugs, thermal carafes, filters, and so on. To make your store a destination for coffee products, create an environment that will draw the customer to your store time and time again. Successful merchandising can make your products jump off the shelf.

Your environment should encompass more than the look of your café; it should also include the feel, the amount of consumer education you offer, and the product sold. The relationship you built with your customers through coffee education must continue once you add accessories. Here, the role of the employee becomes ever more important.

The same intensity you put into employee customer service training and education for coffee must be given to the accessory business. Whether it's a $400 espresso machine or a $5.50 mug, each sale adds up. That mug customer may eventually become an espresso machine customer. Don't assume the customer whom you've nurtured to understand specialty coffee will understand how to properly prepare it at home, let alone choose the proper brewer to meet his or her needs. Customers may be able to tell the difference between a coffee and an espresso, but when they stand at the counter looking for an espresso machine, they are often intimidated by the price, if not the machinery.

Nine times out of 10, a bad coffee or espresso beverage is the result of improper brewing and not bad coffee. This holds true both at the store level and at home, where untrained consumers unhappy with their beverages blame it on the equipment. Quality equipment and quality coffee does not assure a quality beverage.

Educating the customer about mugs, filters, grinders, and other accessories can take several forms. Utilize all training tools available to the specialty coffee industry, from books to videos to seminars, and teach employees to understand not only the methods of brewing coffee and espresso, but the "why" behind the processes. Most importantly, the impression an employee leaves with the consumer will make or break a sale.

Aside from arming employees with knowledge on preparation, you should train them to suggestively sell all products in the store. Teach employees to recommend the coffeemaker to all customers, even those who come in for a to-go beverage. They may not buy today, but when they're in the market for a coffeemaker, they'll know where to go. Similarly, when a customer purchases a pound of coffee, ask if he or she needs filters for brewing, making them easy add-on sales.

In addition to creating an inviting atmosphere through a well-trained and informative staff, proper merchandising can add to your desired ambiance. The proper color scheme, for instance, will help create an ambiance in your store. You can follow those same color tenets when merchandising coffee accessories. Create a color scheme backdrop that reflects the products in general. You can choose dark shades to reflect the coffee's color, or you can create a contrast by choosing bright colors to help products leap forward from the display. Use accessories as props in displays that can change their look and feel with a few minor alterations.

Make your presentation tell a story. The customer recognizes this as a formal display and probably won't pick product off the display for purchase. The grouping of products by color, theme or product category in this formal manner will allow the customer to view products in a somewhat natural environment. Be sure, however, to have product

273

readily accessible for the consumer to purchase. If he or she has to ask an employee where a product is located in the display, he or she might not even bother.

A less formal method of presentation is to merchandise the accessories within product groups. This method makes sense for customers looking for a product within a specific category—a coffee grinder for example. In this display, present the customers with all your coffee grinder options, from low-end blade grinders to more expensive burr grinders. Showcase grinders with an array of kitchen-matching colors as well. With product categories grouped together, consumers can view all their options so they can comparison shop before making their purchasing decisions. It's important that no matter what type of display you create—formal, informal, or anywhere in between—that the products function well together.

Store design includes an architectural element as well as marketing and merchandising elements. When working in the confines of your space or budget, you can still make dramatic changes. A new coat of paint or carpeting can do wonders; paint graphics on the wall and use them to educate the customers. Merchandise the entire store, paying special attention to product labels, the color of your accessories and even how you place them on the shelves. Coordinate your merchandise with your store's personality. Nothing is worse than sending mixed messages to your customers by mismatching your design and your product mix.

Finally, keep your department clean and organized. Dust is a nuisance that you must deal with on a weekly or twice weekly basis. You can't ignore the dust blanket that inevitably settles on your shelves, packages of coffee beans, nooks and crannies of coffeemakers, or mugs waiting to be filled with tasty cappuccinos. If your business is not clean and the shelves are not re-stocked and organized, all the efforts and capital you have invested in adding accessories may be in vain. The environment tells the customer a lot about a business, and a dirty one won't welcome the customer back for future purchases.

274

A Smattering of Accessories

Training the staff to suggestively sell accessories to every customer is imperative. Don't just stop at the bean sale. Your customers may be heading home to make coffee. What else might they need to make their experience special? Following are a few of the coffee accessory essentials that can help you increase your bottom line.

Drip coffeemakers come with a wide range of options, from the basic drip maker to a machine with built-in grinders, brew timers and thermal carafes. Make a statement with drip coffeemakers, but don't make the mistake of offering every machine available. Carefully choose the range you will sell, and be ready to explain to the customer why you carry the machines that you do.

The variety of *espresso/cappuccino machines* is nearly as extensive as coffeemakers. From the low-priced steam machines to the expensive combination coffeemaker, grinder and semi-automatic pump espresso machine, the customer has many choices. You can't carry them all, so decide what your customer will be inclined to purchase.

Mugs are an integral part of the accessory business. The coffee craze has certainly led to a boom in upscale hand-painted stoneware. Whether it be mugs or related items such as creamers and sugar bowls, the retailer has a choice among numerous patterns and looks. These may prove to be easy add-on sales because they are relatively inexpensive and their beautiful styles are enticing to customers. You have to market these well, however. A wall of mugs shouldn't be unattractive and unexciting. Don't we all have enough mugs already filling our kitchen cupboards? Create interesting displays and constantly rearrange them to make the merchandise look new and exciting. Most importantly, the price—as well as the product—must be easily accessible to the consumer.

Morning noon and night, when coffee drinkers want their coffee, they'll do what it takes to get it. *Travel mugs* offer that customer a low-priced item they can use daily, and, of course, they can fill it up daily at your store.

The *French press* is the coffee accessory that has proven its success in the retail world of late, but only through proper demonstration. Once consumers realize how easy it is to prepare, how delicious the brew is, and how inexpensive the press is, sales should soar. Don't just let the press sit on the shelf and expect curiosity and good looks to make the big sale. Bring it down to where the customer can see it and observe it in use. Brew sample coffees for your customers.

They come to you for their coffee, so why should they visit the grocery for their *filters*? Carry an ample stock of paper filters for easy add-on sales. And don't hesitate to ask what type of filters your customers are using. If they're using paper, explain why they might like gold filters.

The proper grind is an essential component of a deliciously brewed coffee. Be sure your staff is aware of all the types of *grinders* you sell—blade or burr—and help the consumer meet their individual needs. This will also be the perfect time to impress upon your customers the importance of the different grinds needed for drip, press and espresso coffees.

Tea-related items do have their place in a coffee café. These items add color and variety to your product mix, and teapots, kettles, cups, infusers, or full-service sets are also great gift items.

While this list is incomplete, it should give you a start on the most popular coffee-related accessories now sold in retail outlets. Pick and choose accessories according to your business plan, taking into account what type of products your customers will be most inclined to purchase.

Become a source for all coffee-related items, from beans to brewers, from filters to French presses. Stocking a unique range of coffee-related accessories will help round out your collection of quality coffees, making your retail establishment the store of choice for consumers. With an increasingly competitive specialty coffee retail environment, you must distinguish yourself as superior. If you offer all the essentials to brew and enjoy a perfect cup of coffee or espresso at home, you'll have a definite competitive edge. When done properly, the advantage gained from the addition of accessories will manifest itself in an increasing bottom line.

275

Wendy Rasmussen

Wendy Rasmussen has worked in the specialty coffee and tea industries for 10 years as an author, freelance journalist, public relations consultant, trade organization director, and marketing consultant. As a partner in R2 Consultants, she assists clients in all areas from staff training to product development.

Rasmussen is co-author of *Tea Basics*, a primer on premium tea, published by John Wiley & Sons in the fall of 1998. She is a frequent contributing editor to industry trade publications dealing with specialty coffee and tea, and is a regular speaker and moderator at industry functions. She is currently executive director of the American Premium Tea Institute and serves on the Conference Committee of the Specialty Coffee Association of America.

277

Chapter 22

Marketing Tea to New Heights in Your Operation

Why are you bothering to learn about tea? Why spend the time and effort to market it? Because tea is a product that demands education and effort. Unlike a bar of chocolate you can place on the counter, tea is not an impulse item. It doesn't sell itself. A successful program requires time, creativity and a certain amount of fanaticism.

279

But don't despair, now is the time for all good tea drinkers, well, maybe not to come to the aid of their country, but at least to come to a beverage that is well-prepared and thoughtfully presented. Interest in tea is at an all-time high due to a number of diverse reasons.

Which brings us back to why you are bothering with a tea program in the first place. Because tea is hot! The tea market is growing. Offering a quality tea program prevents your specialty coffee business from missing important opportunities and attracts and maintains customers.

I. Where to Start?
Educate Yourself
Tea is a lifetime journey. To successfully market premium tea you must understand the product—its history and cultivation, how to discern qualitative differences, and how to correctly handle it.

Where do you acquire this much-needed information? There are many great resources available to the earnest student of tea. Aside from the American Premium Tea Institute (APTI), there are numerous books, organizations, magazine articles, available mentors, and interest groups. The high-tech world of computer communications has also given us a fabulous tool. The number of websites about tea on the Internet is constantly growing and the quality of information continues to improve. There are also a growing number of enthusiastic vendors who are willing to lend their expertise and experience to up-and-coming tea purveyors.

The greatest thing about learning is that it is always a self-directed journey. You can pick and choose how you wish to pursue tea knowledge. Head for the highlands of India and help in a harvest, attend a protocol school and learn to put the cream on your scone before the preserves, or spend hours tasting tea and discover parts of your palate never before exercised. Each of these methods brings its own rewards for your business.

The Tea Menu

Now that you have gained all this tea knowledge, it's time to put it to good use. You know your business and your philosophy, now you need to choose the tea program that works within these parameters. Deciding what to sell starts with tasting tea. Dip your spoon into as many different teas from as many different vendors as you can. Taste thoughtfully, then consistently record your impressions.

While it is true that there is a certain cachet to single-origin estate teas—and while I admit that I love drinking them—be realistic with your own program. Single-estate and origin teas are not the entire premium tea market. Know *your* market. If your customers love flavored products, then by all means offer them flavored teas. If you serve everything on ice, look for the best quality iced tea you can find. If you are serving a health-conscious community, focus on green tea and herbal infusions. It doesn't make any sense—and it certainly won't make much of a profit—to offer teas that don't appeal to your existing customer base.

Whichever menu you pursue, maintain a consistent image. If you are offering Victorian-style service, create a compatible ambiance and offer teas that work well with the necessary accouterments and foodstuffs. This is not the arena for Fanciest Formosa Oolongs, but you will probably go through a lot of English Breakfast and Earl Grey. If you own a coffee store and sell whole-bean origin coffees, sell loose-leaf origin teas. If most of your business is "to-go," find a teabag selection or a service methodology that takes this into account.

Do not accept that there is only one correct model for a premium tea program. Premium tea encompasses loose-leaf teas, but there is also room in the marketplace for teabags, ready-to-drink teas, herbal infusions, and flavored teas. There is enough in the world of tea to support your wildest ideas; you simply need to keep quality at the forefront of your expectations.

Service Options

The methods of steeping and serving tea are almost as varied as the styles, colors, flavors, and aromas of tea itself. You must choose a service option or options that not only deliver great cups of tea, but take into account the nature and style of your business.

The most traditional Western method of serving tea is quite simple. You need boiling water, a vessel to hold the leaves and hot water, a device for straining the leaves, and a serving vessel. The problems for many foodservice outlets are also quite simple. There is no means for delivering freshly boiled water, no space to store teapots and strainers, no dearth of staff and customers to break (or outright steal) items, and a complete lack of comprehension on the part of staff and customers as to how long to let tea steep, when to strain the leaves, etc. This doesn't make traditional service impossible, just challenging. And all this may be outweighed by the absolutely fabulous benefits of this method— namely the huge array of serving vessels in existence. Whimsical, elegant, inspiring, modern, homey, or sophisticated, you can develop a tea service that matches your business.

What about the other common option—the poor, maligned teabag? Teabags are certainly easier on staff, and most customers are already comfortable with them. But if you are using a string, tag and bag from a commercial vendor, the quality of your product is not discernably better than the product of a local diner. Should you bag the idea of teabags? I believe it's hard to establish a program without them, but with the proper effort you can stake out and defend a level of quality that the "me-too" teabag product line can't touch.

Some teabag manufacturers care more about quality than others. Look for quality purveyors, or, if your size permits, think about private labeling or packaging your own.

There are also myriad products and methods for bringing your loose-leaf offerings to the customer by the cup, negating the need for pre-packaged teabags. These mainly let you create your own personalized teabag, often in larger formats to allow more expansion of the leaf. This category can also include tea balls, tea "spoon" mechanisms, and a variety of ingenious—but unfortunately not very effective—gizmos.

There is also an emerging interest in more ethnic methods of brewing tea. The *Gong Fu* style, which uses beautiful Yixing pottery and involves multiple infusions, is entrancing and offers the additional benefit of offering more "bang for the buck." The traditional Chinese brewing vessel—a simple cup with a lid/saucer—is another romantic way to serve tea. Both of these methods also come with cultural hurdles: Westerners don't like to pick tea leaves out of their teeth.

II. Marketing Your Program
Your Very First "Customers"
Okay, the first step you took was educating yourself. Just as your program can't work without a solid foundation of tea knowledge, your marketing can't work unless your staff is also knowledgeable. The most important thing employees should know is what your tea tastes like. So taste the tea! You don't have to perform tasting in the classical cupping format, but you should conduct regular samplings of your teas and encourage your staff to describe their taste sensations and choose their own favorite teas. It is often good to bolster this program with basic training about where tea comes from, how it is processed, and what makes your product special. One of the most critical parts of this basic training is teaching employees how to brew tea using your chosen service-delivery method.

As you go about the business of staff training, holding regular samplings, inviting vendors in to discuss product, and conducting your own tea university program, it should become fairly easy to identify those members of your staff who have a natural interest in, or affinity for, the product. One of the best marketing moves you can make is to encourage and cultivate these budding tea experts. These staff members are the single most important weapon in your marketing arsenal.

Reward the enthusiasm of these staff members in numerous ways, from simply adding "tea expert" to their name tags to increasing their wages and responsibility. Use the flavor profiles these staff members propose in your literature, listen to their comments and critiques on purchasing decisions, and encourage them in their pursuit of tea knowledge.

Beyond identifying those who already have a predisposed tea nature, look for potential converts. The convert is often more enthusiastic than the "born" tea lover. One of the best ideas is to find a staff member who enjoys the experience of tasting anything and everything. This is the person who samples balsamic vinegars and goat cheeses and delights in subtle variation. Tea is designed for the lover of subtlety. Use all of the rewards and incentives you can think of to motivate these "first customers" and you will see their enthusiasm spread.

Don't stop here. Don't conduct great training exercises for the first two weeks of your program and assume the excitement will continue forever. Make training a regular and integral part of your interaction with your staff. Always continue to reward the pursuit of tea knowledge and experience.

Finding New Customers
Finding new tea customers is largely about education. In fact, APTI is based on the belief that by educating people in the industry about tea, the industry will continue to grow and prosper. With tea, however, education is a little different. To me, it follows the old adage, "You can lead a horse to Harvard, but you can't make him think." What I mean is that your educational efforts must be easily accessible without being aggressive.

Customer education can take many forms. The most important I have already covered: maintaining a knowledgeable and excited staff to answer questions and convey enthusiasm. It is also important to create educational materials the potential tea customer can see and touch. Brochures on tea issues, seminars on tea topics, a regular newsletter that features or focuses on your tea program, selling tea books, merchandising tea accouterments—all play vital roles in educating your customers and creating a new audience for your tea program. But nothing is so powerful as "the sip." In other words, taste the tea! (Are you beginning to get my point?)

Respect the customers' level of desire and make sure all the right tools are available to aid them on their journey to discover tea. It makes your customers part of the marketing process. As much as you need to be prepared to teach about tea, you also need to be prepared to learn. Learning is best accomplished by listening. Solicit customer response to your tea program. Hand out evaluation forms for special tea events, open the newsletter to customer editorial, and make sure that question and answer is a large part of any of your efforts.

Keeping Current Customers Satisfied

Remember the business of business—attracting and maintaining customers. Use education and enthusiasm to attract customers, but use consistently excellent products and services, combined with programs that reward loyalty, to maintain them. Frequent-buyer cards are a common but effective approach to rewarding customer loyalty. You can also create additional, unique methods such as a customer-of-the-month program. Create and support a local tea lovers club and offer your store for its regular meetings. Devise as many schemes as is practical to recognize and reward your loyal customers.

Also be sure to retain the interest of your true "regulars" with new offerings—in teas, in accouterment, in programs—regularly and frequently. Don't let your menu become the same old thing. Solicit customer and vendor input, talk to people in the tea trade, and use your imagination. Retain the best parts of your tea program and change or upgrade the parts that don't work. Don't be afraid to try new teas, especially in small quantity, and offer them for what they are—"special offerings." Perhaps when the first-flush season arrives, select five or six estate teas and purchase a small quantity of each instead of committing to one garden. Give your loyal customers advance notice of these "limited edition" or "special offering" teas, and maybe give them special pricing.

Finally, widen the horizons of your most loyal tea customers. Be comfortable with the fact that you know and they know you are not the only tea resource in town. Let them know about upcoming tea events from trade associations like APTI, special teas offered through charitable groups, book signings by tea authors at bookstores, and organized trips to places of interest for tea lovers. Rather than taking business away, this knowledge sharing serves to legitimize your role as tea expert.

III. Guerrilla Marketing Tips
Making Tea Work on a Tight Budget

These tips were compiled by Tomislav Podreka of Serendipitea in Ridgefield, Conn.

- Advertise the arrival of new teas with prominent signage.
- Approach an historical society and ask to cater its next event with an emphasis on the historically, or near historically, correct tea.
- Approach the local library. It would probably be very interested in conducting tea-related events and exhibits.
- Arrange safe space for the display of your customers' tea collections and feature a new one on a regular basis (offer tea in exchange for the privilege of displaying it).
- Barter with tea-loving customers who are artists and arrange for original tea art.
- Bring in a "special" tea of a select amount and have a tea auction, complete with cupping and viewing.

- Bring Your Own Cup program, and offer one set price regardless of cup size (maybe 10 to 15 cents less than standard cup price).
- Collect anecdotes from your customers about growing up with tea, then serve their second cup gratis.
- Collect songs that mention tea, offering free cups of tea to any customers who add to your collection.
- Conduct mini-lectures for parent/teacher or student nights at your local schools giving educational tea-focused presentations. Highlight wares from your store.
- Display paintings, ceramics and other works from artists who feature tea in their work, then have a "gallery" opening.
- Sponsor a Favorite Teacup Day then make customers pay for only the first cup, giving them bottomless refills from that point on. Get a social thing happening. Encourage customers to talk to each other about the history and origins of their favorite cups. Encourage them to bring other cups from their collections the following week.
- Feature a set tea-time menu once a month. Encourage customers to bring recipes.
- Feature weekly "Tea & Food" suggestions, describing which foods best accompany the featured tea of the week. Print and distribute a list.
- Give away a free (personalized with your logo) tea scoop with loose-leaf tea purchases.
- Give away free filters or a strainer with loose-leaf tea purchases.
- Create a monthly in-house blend for a Guess the Blend contest. Ask customers to try to identify all the ingredients in the blend to win a complimentary cup.
- Hold a beau-tea-ful promotion with tea-related beauty and bath products.
- Devote a regular newsletter solely to your teas.
- Pick a weekly "historical" quote and ask customers to guess the famous, if sometimes esoteric, historical figure attached to the quote. Offer a prize.
- Offer different food items for purchase or to give away with featured tea(s).
- Offer family specials that encourage customers to introduce their families to the establishment and enjoy a tea—or tea with treats—at a special rate.
- Publish suggested "Blending" lists. Encourage customers to select complimentary teas to blend themselves for their own signature blends.
- Get involved with the Historical Society, Civic Centers, Local Schools, and Adult Ed programs by running "Tea" programs and giving attendees a special "I attended the [blank] event and now get a discounted or free-cuppa card."
- Host a Boston Tea Party celebration.
- Host a first-flush Darjeeling party similar to the Beaujolais nouveau wine celebrations.
- Host a Teddy Bear Tea for customers' kids.
- If you offer seating, host a weekly "Tea & Eats" program.
- Invite tea authors for a book signing and tea tasting.
- Keep a kid-friendly (sweet, cool and caffeine-free) tea on hand and sample it.
- Keep a tea quote on the menu board at all times. People will start to look forward to your next posting.
- Make one day a week your official "Tea Day" and offer incentives for buying tea.
- Most Americans focus on Western tea customs and ambiance, so try to introduce Eastern tea customs, then alternate between the two. When focusing on Eastern customs and rituals, seek knowledgeable locals to speak and demonstrate.
- Bring someone in during slow times to circulate the shop/café and "read" customers' tea leaves. The news is sure to spread and it could become a popular attraction.
- Offer a free tea tin (with your logo) for customers who purchase large quantities of loose tea.
- Offer a separate and distinct tea menu, frequent-buyer cards, and packaging.

- Offer refills at a discount (encourage diversity).
- Offer Senior Citizen discounts during slow parts of the day.
- Offer Tea Talks with a focus on culture: Display tea and accouterments (provided by your shop and clearly marked as such) accompanied by a variety of appropriate cultural books (perhaps a series of books that focus on a different country each week).
- Offer Tea Talks with a focus on tea: Display tea and accouterments (provided by your shop and clearly marked as such) with a variety of appropriate tea books.
- Offer your tea expertise at local schools, charities and churches for fundraising tea events.
- Put the word "tea" in as many words as you can until it threatens your sanitea.
- Print and laminate tea-related information on tea-themed paper/stationery and display it throughout the store.
- Hand out recipes and specify the teas they accompany.
- Promote an origin country—use textiles, music and handicrafts in your efforts.
- Sample your teas for customers religiously.
- Set up a book-of-the-month club where you read excerpts from books and authors that mention tea.
- Every few months (not too frequently) offer a Show & Tell time where customers can gather and bring in a special tea they purchased on an exotic trip. Offer the tea in informal tea tastings, encouraging your customers to share experiences and information (this could be very educational for the shop owner as well).
- Start a tea lovers club and give special offers/discounts to members.
- Take tea seriously.
- Hang a "Tea Quotes Board" where customers can jot down their musings on tea. Select quotes should make it into the newsletter (if one exists). If a newsletter does not exist, perhaps you should hold a weekly/monthly reading of the quotes complete with a vote. The winner gets a few ounces of tea as a prize.
- Post a weekly tea trivia question (fairly difficult), and give a small prize to the winner.
- Offer tea gift baskets for Valentine's Day, Mother's Day, Secretary's Day, etc.
- Stock tea mugs with your logo on the side.
- Install tea-related knobs and handles on your cabinets.
- Ask your staff to wear tea-related jewelry. Wear it yourself. Sell it.
- Volunteer to conduct a tea education session/series or lead a tea discussion for the library's adult daytime program (provide all the tea yourself and say so in the promotions).

Ed Arvidson

Ed Arvidson is director of operations for Bella Italian Foods, a restaurant corporation operating in the U.S. Virgin Islands. He is the former vice president of Bellissimo Inc., a U.S.-based company specializing in consulting services and the creation and distribution of high-quality educational tools for the specialty coffee industry.

Arvidson accumulated over 20 years experience in the food-service industry while working for national and regional restaurant corporations. He has also owned his own successful restaurant. During his career, he has held positions at a variety of operations as: corporate food and beverage director, corporate management trainer and owner/general manager. He has managed high-volume units with annual sales approaching $3 million and has supervised staffs in excess of 100. He is an expert in all aspects of restaurant operations and menu research and development. His experience, creativity, people skills, and problem-solving ability qualify him as an authority. Arvidson has written for several coffee industry periodicals and has appeared as a frequent seminar speaker at industry trade shows on product preparation and business operations.

287

Chapter 23

Adding Food to Your Specialty Coffee Operation

To serve food or not to serve food ...

289

W hen I worked as a consultant to the specialty coffee industry, the one statement I heard from perspective entrepreneurs time and time again was, "We don't want to serve any food!"

For many who enter the specialty coffee business, much of the attraction is that a retail location is a fairly simple beverage operation that does not encompass the complexities and vulnerabilities associated with the typical foodservice establishment.

So why do so many coffee bar owners add food to their menus when they were so adamant about not doing so at the start? Why might you want or need to add food to your operation? There are several good reasons for considering this option.

Economic Factors

Numerous specialty coffee operators offer a diversified menu of food items for the same good reason—a positive impact on their bottom line. Many who have gone into the coffee business with the intention of serving only beverages have discovered they cannot generate enough revenue through beverage sales alone. Serving food has become necessary to realize a profit.

Typically, high rents and loan repayments can be the "straws that break the camel's back."

I have often said that small is beautiful when considering a specialty coffee concept. To be profitable, you need to generate revenues that total approximately 10 times your combined monthly rent and loan payments. This means if you are paying $2000 a month in rent and another $1500 a month in loan payments, you will need to generate $35,000 in sales ($2000 + $1500 = $3500 x 10). The truth is, very few coffee operations generate this level of sales with coffee beverages alone.

This explains why many times a cart, kiosk or drive-thru operation may generate more net profit than a beautiful sit-down coffee bar. Typically, these types of operations will cost far less to open, and the monthly rent will be much lower. If the loan payment on a cart operation is $500 per month and the rent is $300, then sales of only $8000 per month should realize a profit ($500 + $300 = $800 x 10). With a decent location, you should achieve this level of sales with beverages alone.

Now don't panic! I'm not suggesting you sell your coffee bar and buy a cart. I'm simply explaining why the increased overhead usually associated with an in-line coffee operation will often motivate a retailer to add food items.

The other economic factor that may have an impact is competition. Perhaps there are four other coffee bars located within three blocks of your operation. Or maybe a national chain is coming to your neighborhood. By offering a menu of food items unique to your establishment, you can create a competitive advantage.

In Italy, there are at least 10 times more coffee bars than in the U.S., all concentrated into an area the size of California. Competition is extremely fierce. Many Italian coffee bars have added specialty pastries, paninis (sandwiches) and gelato to create a broader appeal.

The Coffee Cultures of Italy and the U.S.

There are over 200,000 coffee bars in Italy and virtually no carts, kiosks or drive-thrus. How do they all survive economically?

It's difficult to compare coffee operations in Italy and the U.S. because the two cultures consume coffee in such vastly different ways.

In Italy, most people drink straight shots of espresso, with maybe a cappuccino in the morning. Cappuccinos in Italy are never larger than six ounces, and are served at approximately 140 degrees F so people can consume them immediately.

Brewed coffee and large volume lattés are nonexistent. Most Italians enjoy their beverages in less than five minutes while standing at the bar. Customer seating is limited or absent in most cases. If one chooses to sit, the bar usually adds a handsome service charge.

Bars in Italy offer not only espresso, but also liquor. Espresso sales supply the principal revenue in the morning and afternoon, while liquor sales round out business for the day by attracting the after-work crowd for a "quick one." Like espresso, customers usually consume this after-work libation within a short period of time, typically while standing at the bar.

The successful Italian bar is much more than just a beverage stop, however. It is also an important social gathering place where one may establish long-term relationships with the baristas and other patrons. One may enjoy their first cup of the day, coffee breaks, lunch, and an after-work refreshment all in the same bar while visiting with the same familiar faces.

It is this "multiple quick visit" mentality of the Italian coffee consumer, combined with strong patron loyalty, that makes it possible to achieve an impressive volume of beverage sales while operating out of minimal square footage. Many of the Italian bars I visited were less than 500 square feet. In contrast, most coffee bars in the U.S. tend to be much larger in size, adding to an operation's financial challenges.

Even though U.S. consumers order a substantial percentage of their beverages to-go, consumers who want to enjoy their beverages in-store typically desire seating. Also, because the majority of coffee consumed in the U.S. is brewed (served at 180 to 200 degrees F), and 12- and 16-ounce beverages are common, a consumer usually spends 15 to 20 minutes drinking it. This means you must dedicate a significant area to seating, usually at a premium price per square foot.

American coffee bars typically sell a variety of products to help offset the increased rent. These products are seldom seen in Italian bars, and include such items as bulk coffee beans, brewing devices, cups, books, and T-shirts. While some Italian bars serve only coffee, most offer an array of pre-prepared food items to create greater appeal and increased revenue. Serving food has also become a necessity for most American coffee bars. Competition may not be as fierce in the U.S., but for most owners the additional revenue is still necessary to help offset the excessive fixed expenses. Food has become the obvious way to create this revenue.

Should I Add Food?

Before you develop a menu, bring in food products, hire a cook, and attempt to create additional revenue by selling food, answer these questions.

Do you really need to add food to your present operation? The best way to answer that question is to look at your ledger. Do you need to generate greater sales to become profitable? Do your combined lease and loan payments in an average month represent more than 10 percent of your average monthly sales? In other words, if your combined lease and loan payments consume more than 10 percent of your monthly gross income, it may prove difficult to achieve profitability with your present sales. If the payments consume 20 percent, 30 percent or more, it may prove impossible. Using the ratio of rent/loan payments to sales, you should be able to determine if your ailing profitability is a result of insufficient sales volume.

If your combined lease/loan payments represent significantly more than 10 percent of your gross sales, then you will need to increase sales. Assuming you have marketed your business and determined that your beverage sales have reached their full potential, food may prove a smart way to increase revenues.

If your combined lease/loan payments represent 10 percent of your gross sales or less, you should be profitable or close to it. In this case, serving food may not be necessary. The reason you may not be making a profit could be improper menu pricing, poor operational controls, improper budgeting, or a combination of these variables. I will not discuss cost controls and budgets in this chapter. If you are looking for a good source of information on these subjects, however, the coffee business manual *Bean Business Basics*, available from Bellissimo Inc., discusses them in detail.

Do you need to differentiate yourself from your competition? If increasing competition has you concerned, or if you hear the "big green mermaid" is moving to your neighborhood, creating a menu of unique, high-quality food items can be an effective way to develop and maintain a competitive advantage.

291

Labor and Equipment Considerations

After you have analyzed the economic factors and determined whether adding food will help you achieve your desired profit, you'll need to make some important decisions about the items you'll serve.

Will you add some simple pastries and baked goods to accompany and complement your coffee beverages, or will you offer a more extensive menu that includes desserts, salads, sandwiches, and soups?

Once again, base this decision on the additional revenue necessary to position your business "in the black." In other words, if you only need to increase your sales by a nominal amount—let's say $1000 per month—then it may be sufficient to add some simple pastries to complement your coffee beverages. But if your monthly sales are $10,000 short of the necessary level, then you'll need to consider adding more than muffins and scones.

Other important factors to consider are the expenses associated with producing those sales. Let's say you add muffins to your operation. You pay 50 cents for a ready-to-serve muffin and sell it for $1. There is a 50 percent cost associated with the sale of that muffin. This means that if you sell $1000 worth of muffins in a month, your net profit will only be $500 (at best). If you need to add an additional $1000 to your bottom line each month, $1000 in muffin sales will only move you halfway toward your goal.

You might also have additional labor and equipment expenses. Try to avoid menu items that require significant amounts of additional labor to produce or a substantial investment in equipment.

It will probably be wiser to buy items that are pre-prepared and resell them than to produce these items from scratch, even if the food cost associated with selling pre-prepared items is higher. Using the muffin analogy again, let's say you could bake your own muffins from scratch at a cost of 25 cents each instead of the 50 cents you pay for ready-to-sell muffins. This may seem an appealing option. After all, if you sell both muffins for $1, haven't you increased your profit margin from 50 to 75 cents?

You need to remember, however, that someone must make that muffin and that there is a cost associated with that effort. Let's say you pay your bakers $8 per hour and it takes them one hour to create the muffin batters, bake 40 muffins and clean up their work area and tools. If this is an accurate assumption, there will be a 20 cent per muffin cost associated with creating each muffin. Your 75 cent profit margin has now been reduced to a 55 cent margin. In addition, if you had to spend $3500 to buy a convection oven, mixing bowls, whips, spoons, muffin pans, and oven mitts, it may take you years to recoup your investment by tallying the additional five cent per muffin advantage you now have over ready-to-serve muffins. Furthermore, what are the energy costs of operating your convection oven? What happens if your baker burns an occasional pan of muffins? What happens if your baker gets sick for a week—will you have to assume his or her job function? Remember, there are costs associated with the production and sale of every item. You must analyze all your options carefully.

Obviously, some equipment expenses are unavoidable, and if you project that adding these food items will cure your economic woes, then by all means you should probably make the investment. If you want to sell pastries, for example, then you may need to invest in a pastry display case. If you plan to make panini sandwiches, then you will certainly need to buy a panini grill. Perhaps you'll need an extra refrigerator and/or freezer to store certain food ingredients. You may even need a deli slicer, prep table and prep sink.

Unless you have excess cash (and I'll assume you do not, which is why you're reading this chapter), avoid entertaining thoughts of creating a full kitchen. When you start adding items such as griddles, broilers and deep fat fryers, you will be required to install a stainless steel hood with an exhaust fan, a fire suppression system and a return-air unit. This will certainly run into the thousands, if not tens of thousands, of dollars.

If you want to do some simple baking—such as proof-and-bake or brown-and-serve items—you may want to think about buying an electric convection oven. In many areas you can use this piece of equipment without an exhaust system, but check with your local bureaucracies first to verify that this is the case.

Regardless of the food items you are considering, run your proposed menu by your local health department, building department and fire marshal first to ensure there will be no unforeseen restrictions or costly requirements.

Understanding Your Market

Before you start creating your food menu, consider the following important factors:

1. Who is your target market? Who are your customers? You'll probably offer a different menu if your operation is located across the street from a high school as opposed to in a hospital.

Remember, just because you like prosciutto and herb brie paninis doesn't mean your customers will. Be sure you understand the taste preferences of your customers.

2. Be sure to take regional or ethnic preferences into consideration. Grits may be popular in Alabama and Mississippi, but they probably won't sell in Idaho.

I had a consulting client in San Antonio, Texas, who offered a large selection of Mexican-style pastries and candies. Because the community had a large Hispanic population, these items were a must and sold extremely well.

3. Regardless of the food items you decide to serve, select quality products. Remember, you are a specialty coffee operation, not a convenience store. The quality of your food

292

items should match the quality of your coffee beverages. If you are charging your customers $2.95 for a superior cappuccino, don't serve a Danish that looks and tastes like it came out of a package from the local supermarket.

Remember, most independents don't have the marketing punch and financial resources of the large coffee chains. Quality is generally the one area where you can differentiate yourself from the big boys.

Selecting Menu Items

Now that we have addressed many of the important aspects of planning a food menu, let's discuss some specific items you may wish to consider.

Morning offerings:

Because most coffee drinkers start their day with a cup of brew, it only makes sense to develop a menu of items to accompany their morning beverages. Some of the more common morning items include muffins, bagels, scones, cinnamon rolls, Danishes, croissants, and toasted bread. Oatmeal (cooked in a microwave), cold cereals and juices are also viable products. You may even consider selling waffles, because a waffle iron will not usually require an exhaust system. Most institutional purveyors sell waffle batter mixes that require water only. The same syrups you use to flavor coffee beverages and Italian sodas will also work well over waffles, giving you a multitude of flavor options. Try raspberry, strawberry, blackberry, coconut, banana, papaya, mango, almond, hazelnut, macadamia nut, or caramel.

Because items such as eggs, hash browns and pancakes require larger kitchen equipment, most coffee bars do not serve them.

As I mentioned earlier, you must carefully evaluate whether to bake from scratch or purchase finished baked goods from a quality bakery. It is perfectly acceptable to run a food cost as high as 50 percent on finished items because they save on labor and do not require a significant equipment investment. Because the majority of consumers buy baked goods in addition to their normal coffee beverages, the less generous profit margins of pre-baked goods still represent valuable additions to your cash register.

Snacks and desserts:

Outside of breakfast, lunch and dinner times, consumers will still come into your establishment seeking a coffee fix. Here again, offering a bite to eat with their beverages can enhance your profit potential. In the evening, customers may visit you primarily for your quality desserts and snacks, viewing beverages as an accompaniment.

Items that might prove viable at these times are biscotti, cookies, brownies, dessert bars, bite-size pastries (such as rugulach or Stroopwaffles), desserts, cakes, and candies. Many high-quality desserts and dessert bars are available in frozen form. When thawed, they are ready to serve and prove difficult to discern from high-quality homemade desserts. The only factor to consider with frozen products is your available freezer space.

Two frozen-dessert companies with impressive product quality are Sweet Street and Bindi. Talk to your local institutional food purveyors to see if they stock these lines.

Lunches:

Lunches present more of a challenge. You need to draw consumers away from more traditional places of dining. Sandwiches, salads and soups are good options for the average coffee bar. To avoid the additional labor cost of a dedicated sandwich maker, consider offering a variety of panini sandwiches.

Paninis (pronounced pa-nee-nees) are pre-made sandwiches that are usually displayed in a refrigerated pastry case and grilled to order in a panini press (an appliance similar to a waffle iron). Panini presses are available from most espresso and restaurant equipment companies.

293

Because cafés serve these sandwiches hot, lettuce is not found on paninis. And although you can make paninis on a variety of breads, typically focaccia, French rolls and pitas work best. Paninis are not piled high with ingredients like the average submarine sandwich. Instead, a thin layer of quality ingredients is dispersed evenly over the bread. The bread is usually brushed with olive oil on the inside to enhance flavor and moistness.

It usually takes about three minutes to grill the sandwich, and the heating of the ingredients in the press promotes the migration of flavors into the bread. This explains why seemingly meager ingredients can result in an unbelievably delicious finished sandwich. The limited ingredients also makes these sandwiches very cost-friendly. The sandwiches will flatten somewhat in the panini press when grilled, which is perfectly acceptable.

Paninis can incorporate nouveau ingredients or traditional favorites. Many of the following ingredients are available for a reasonable price at Costco, including sliced meats and cheeses. Here are some panini ideas to try:

Nouveau:
- mesquite-broiled chicken breast, chévre cheese, roasted red bell peppers, fresh rosemary
- prosciutto ham, brie cheese
- Italian salami, provolone or mozzarella cheese, leaf oregano
- fresh tomato slices, mozzarella cheese, fresh basil
- sliced artichoke hearts, sun-dried tomatoes, kalamata olives, feta cheese
- sliced roasted eggplant, roasted red bell peppers, feta cheese

Traditional:
- ham, Swiss cheese, sliced dill pickles, horseradish/mayo/brown mustard (Guldens brand) spread
- turkey breast, cranberry, cream cheese
- turkey breast, sliced roasted ortega chilis, cheddar cheese
- roast beef, grilled onions, cheddar cheese, mayo/horseradish spread

Breakfast:
Breakfast paninis are a viable gourmet alternative to a fast food chain's egg and muffin sandwich.

You can scramble and cook eggs with the steam wand of your espresso machine in a steaming pitcher. You can cook bacon between sheets of paper towels in your microwave oven. Try the following:
- scrambled eggs, bacon, cheddar cheese
- scrambled eggs, prosciutto or copa, mozzarella cheese, fresh basil
- scrambled eggs, chunky salsa, cheddar cheese

The true beauty of paninis is they taste wonderful, are cost-friendly, are unique (most people have never heard of them), and can be made in advance. One employee can prep enough paninis for the day within one or two hours. Your cashier or barista can pop a panini in the press, and within three minutes your customer has a gourmet sandwich. Because paninis are premade, your customers must "have them your way," but the savings you will realize by not paying a full-time sandwich maker will make up for any hassle you'll have with a picky customer.

Salads & soups:
Salads and soups are two other quick-serve lunch alternatives you should consider. You can create your own fresh salad mix on a daily basis or purchase high-quality, ready-to-use bagged mixes.

There are a variety of salad dressings on the market in single-portion packets that customers can pour over their salads. You can also spoon dressings from a bulk container over the greens in a small bowl. Don't dress salads in advance because the greens will become soggy.

Salad varieties are only limited by your imagination. If you are already stocking turkey, ham and cheese for paninis, creating a chef's salad becomes a fairly simple proposition. You can buy frozen, pre-broiled chicken breasts or grill raw breasts in your panini press to offer a Caesar with chicken. Dice the chicken and mix it with minced celery and mayo, thereby adding a chicken salad to your menu. For a real treat, try tossing a variety of gourmet greens with a raspberry vinaigrette (made with red wine vinegar and raspberry syrup) and top it with walnut pieces and crumbled goat cheese.

Regardless of the salads you decide to serve, make sure all ingredients are prepped and portioned in advance. It shouldn't take longer than a minute to create a finished product.

Don't forget high-quality premade pasta and potato salads. You can serve a generous portion on a bed of leaf lettuce as a stand-alone meal, or offer a small scoop as an add-on to a panini sandwich.

Soups are another viable lunch item you can serve in an instant. Ask your institutional food purveyor about high-quality frozen or canned soups. Soups can be heated in a countertop electric soup cooking/holding unit.

A slice of French bread or a good roll brushed with a garlic or herb butter and then grilled in the panini press will make the perfect accompaniment to any salad or soup.

Some final thoughts on selecting items for your food menu:

1. Check with your food purveyors to make sure ingredients for your food items are available in your market.

2. Make sure that the ingredients are available year-round, and ask if they're vulnerable to seasonal quality and price fluctuations.

3. Plan your menu so that you can use ingredients in more than one recipe. In other words, try to avoid bringing in an ingredient for just one menu item, especially if it is highly perishable!

Menu Presentation and Pricing

Once you have selected your menu items and created delicious recipes, you will need to produce your physical menu and determine how much you will charge for each item.

Assuming your coffee operation employs counter service, you will need a menu board for your food, which should be located next to your beverage menu board so customers have no trouble seeing it. It should also be attractive and easy to read. I strongly recommend commissioning a professional sign maker to make your menu board.

In a similar manner, display point-of-sales signs for your pastry case, countertop and shelf items. You can produce these with your computer. Print or photocopy them onto attractive paper or card stock, and laminate them so you can clean them easily while retaining their attractive appearance.

Be sure to include at least a brief description of each item to minimize any uncertainties your customers may have about the product. For example, calling a sandwich "The Southwest Panini" will not tell your customers the contents of the sandwich and may make them hesitant to order. However, if the description reads, "The Southwest Panini— a mesquite-broiled chicken breast covered with mild green chilies and Monterey jack cheese grilled on a French roll," little doubt will exist in the minds of customers as to what they will receive. People want to know what they are buying.

When pricing menu items I recommend the following:

1. If you buy ready-to-serve items (such as muffins, bagels or frozen desserts), doubling your cost is usually sufficient.

2. If you or your staff must prepare the item, multiply the cost of the ingredients by three or four (depending upon what your competition charges for similar items).

It is acceptable in certain instances to bear a cost higher than the above parameters if an analysis of gross profit dollars shows an advantage.

295

Gross profit dollars are the profits you put in your cash register every time you sell an item. This is a confusing concept to understand. Let me give you an example: If you sell a Crab Louis salad for $9.95 and it cost you $4.95 to produce, your cost of making that salad is just under 50 percent. If you make a Caesar salad for $1 and sell it for $4, your cost of making the Caesar salad is 25 percent. So what do you want to sell, Crab Louis or Caesar? While Caesar offers you a more efficient margin, Crab Louis nets you more money. Let me explain it to you this way: If every time a customer orders a Crab Louis you put $5 of net profit into your cash register, and every time a customer orders a Caesar you put $3 of net profit into your cash register, which would you rather sell?

If you wanted to run a 25 percent food cost on a Crab Louis salad, you would need to charge almost $20. Unfortunately, you would probably never sell any at that price. However, upon evaluating the gross profit dollars gained by selling it at $9.95, it is still advantageous to offer this item. So be aware of the gross profit dollar potential of an item as well as its cost as a percentage of its sales price.

Make it Good!

In closing, let me emphasize once again that if you intend to add food to your operation, you must be committed to serving quality products. Plan thoroughly. Explain to your food purveyors what you're trying to accomplish. Listen to their ideas and have them bring you lots of products to sample. Check out your competition. Investigate all the options.

As an owner or manager, you must actively supervise the purchasing, production, portioning, storage, rotation, preparation, and presentation of all your food products on a daily basis.

Over time, you will be able to evaluate which items are a hit and which haven't gained customer acceptance. Make adjustments as necessary and always keep innovating. ●

Books  by Bellissimo

Bean Business Basics
$199.95
Bean Business Basics is a 670-page start-up/operational manual that serves as a definitive guide for those starting a retail coffee business and those who have already opened their doors. *Bean Business Basics* was written by professionals who have consulted and trained thousands of gourmet coffee bar employees across the country and around the world. Buying this book is like purchasing tens of thousands of dollars of consulting services.

Some of the book's 40 chapters:
- Coffee Trends
- Proper Brewing Principles
- Basic Espresso Bar Beverages
- Selecting the Right Coffee & Roaster
- Ordering, Handling & Storing Coffee
- Your Financial Resources
- Finding a Great Location
- Codes, Permits & Red Tape
- Negotiating a Lease
- Design & Construction of Your Coffee Bar
- Planning Your Menu
- Choosing & Buying Equipment
- Operational Systems
- Hiring & Managing Employees
- Marketing Your Business
- Record Keeping
- Budget & Cost Controls
- How to Achieve Profitability

Videos  by Bellissimo

"Espresso 101"
$89.95
"Espresso 101" is the award-winning professional video training tool for you and your employees. This tape will cut the normal 20-hour employee-training cycle down to three or four hours. This tool pays for itself with the first employee trained. Each "Espresso 101" package includes a study guide, multiple-choice test with answer key, barista diploma, and durable library case. "Espresso 101 Basic Training" is also available in Spanish.

"Espresso 101" covers:
- A Brief History of Coffee
- Coffee Bean Roasting and Blending

lissimo Coffee InfoGroup

- Espresso Equipment
- Extracting Perfect Espresso
- The Art of Steaming and Foaming Milk
- How to Prepare Espresso Bar Drinks
- Fundamentals of Brewed Coffee Preparation
- Cleaning, Safety and Maintenance

"Espresso 501"
$69.95

"Espresso 501" is a 75-minute advanced course in coffee and espresso for the specialty coffee industry professional. The perfect companion piece to the award-winning "Espresso 101" video, this tape provides a detailed understanding of the variables essential to create a superior espresso beverage experience. Respected industry professionals share their knowledge and opinions concerning:

- Important factors related to espresso equipment performance
- Attributes of excellent espresso coffees
- Understanding the chemistry and nuances of proper espresso preparation
- Beverage presentation/ fancy pours
- Principles of superior customer service

"An Evening with the Experts"
$99.95

A two-video set that includes four hours of interviews with five of the specialty coffee industry's most highly respected professionals. This video explores in detail factors related to green coffee production, roasting and blending, beverage preparation, and the industry's future. Spend an evening learning from Dr. Ernesto Illy, Mauro Cipolla, Kenneth Davids, Ted R. Lingle, and Don Holly.

"Spilling the Beans"
$39.95

"Spilling the Beans" is a complete video overview of the specialty coffee business. Spend 40 minutes with the experts learning about investment, profit potential, cost factors, location considerations, and much more.

"The Art of Coffee"
$24.95 (Retail)
This video teaches the home consumer proper handling and preparation of coffee using a wide variety of techniques. Educate your customers about the exciting world of coffee from seed to cup. Wholesale prices available for retailers. Call for pricing details.

Clip Art by Bellissimo ───────────────────

Sip Art: The Original Coffee Clip Art
Volumes 1-3 and Countries of Origin
Each volume: $49.95
Any two volumes: $79.95
All three volumes: $119.95
Countries of Origin: $79.95.

Sip Art Volumes 1, 2 and 3 on diskette each contain 100 coffee-related images for the PC or Macintosh. Sip Art Countries of Origin contains 50 images associated with coffee-producing countries. Use these creative images for menus, flyers, advertising, point-of-purchase sales, Web design and labels. Also available on CD-ROM for PC.

Bellissimo Coffee InfoGroup carries a wide range of other books and videos. Call or write for your free catalog.

800-655-3955
Bellissimo Coffee InfoGroup
260 East 15th Avenue, Suite D
Eugene, OR 97401
Fax: 541-683-1010
E-mail: ciao2000@teleport.com